Grow Your Own Cigars:

growing, curing and finishing tobacco at home

by

Robert C.A. Goff

Dreamsplice
Christiansburg, Virginia

Grow Your Own Cigars: growing, curing and finishing tobacco at home

Dreamsplice
3462 Dairy Road
Christiansburg, VA 24073

www.dreamsplice.com/books

Cover design by Robert C.A. Goff, Copyright © 2020 by Dreamsplice

ISBN: 978-1-7333979-5-7
Library of Congress Control Number: 2019917726

First Edition: January 2020

The cigar on the front cover (behind the author's name) is wrapped in his own, home-grown Florida Sumatra leaf.

Contents

Other Books by the Author

Non-fiction by Robert C.A. Goff

> **Blend Your Own Pipe Tobacco: 52 recipes with 52 color labels**
> **How to Read a US Roadmap**
> **Climbing Out: Grand Canyon Hikes 1997-2006**
> **Just Walking Home: Appalachian Trail Hikes 1996-2013**
> **In the Ozone: collected essays, poems and non-fiction**

Fantasy-fiction by Robert C.A. Goff

> **Ternaria: Legacy of a Careless Age**

Science-Fiction by Robert C.A. Goff

> **Impact Mitigation and other Science-Fiction Short Stories**

Fantasy-fiction by Robert C.A. Goff and Micah M.A. Goff

> The Counterspell Chronicle
> **Counterspell: Guardian of the Ruins**
> **Counterspell: The Second Law**
> **Counterspell: Age of Fools** [upcoming]

Foreword

This is a book for ordinary folks who may have an interest in growing tobacco at home. The idea for it has percolated in my head for nearly a decade. But it remained mostly a slowly lengthening outline, with a few snippets of actual text. With so many other priorities, it just never happened until now. Like the foreword of most books, this foreword was written after the rest of the book was finally completed.

I had initially assumed that such a book would require full color photographs to be useful. But that route would have raised the cover price of a book this size into the stratosphere. It finally dawned on me that color is critical only for *illustrating* cigar wrapper colors, and is sometimes useful in diagnosing certain microbial diseases of tobacco. Once I was willing to forgo those few color illustrations, the book began to gleefully write itself. I trust that the 200 black and white illustrations are nonetheless helpful to the reader. YouTube will have to provide videos for rolling a cigar. IPM Images (see appendix 7) can provide the color, diagnostic photos—of even the most obscure tobacco maladies.

Needless to say, I have had to leave out far more content on tobacco than I was able to include. An encyclopedic coverage would require thousands of pages. So my primary criterion in culling content was to focus on material that might be helpful to those ordinary folks, home-growers. I've tried to clear the fog created by marketeers and magazine "experts", and present down-in-the-dirt, useful information.

A book like this could not have been as complete or as informative without the experience and contributions to our home tobacco growing knowledge provided over the years by the members of the Fair Trade Tobacco Forum. One person's lifetime cannot possibly encompass so broad a swath of experimentation and discoveries as have been presented and discussed on the forum. Thanks to all of you.

Larry Butcher, a forum member and a commercial tobacco grower from Kentucky, has contributed a number of informative and sometimes entertaining vignettes, which I've sprinkled here and there in the book. Thank you to Larry.

A special thank you is offered to Don Carey, who founded, and has footed the expense of the Fair Trade Tobacco Forum, as well as endured the exasperation of maintaining it, while fighting off the trolls and bots.

Bob *[deluxestogie]*

Long Red

The author, holding a tied hand of his Long Red.

Introduction

Modernity funnels us into becoming consumers, dependent on others to create and supply all of our needs and desires. The act of growing tobacco allows us to regain a modicum of control over this one small aspect of our lives. We become artisans of tobacco. It is that sense of control—of power over our own lives—that is so seductive. Because growing tobacco is dirty, gooey, buggy, exhausting work under a hot sun, there must be more to its attraction than just the having of the final product.

Many home tobacco growers have stated that growing tobacco is more addictive than smoking it. While that may or may not be true, this book is my attempt to explain the details of small-scale tobacco growing, so that an inexperienced grower can successfully grow tobacco, and carry that process through curing and finishing, to produce high quality leaf.

Each year, at my home in the Blue Ridge Mountains of Virginia, I plant, grow and harvest 100 to 200 tobacco plants in under 1000 square feet of hand-tilled garden beds. My goal in growing is to provide high quality, finished leaf of the different tobacco varieties that I use to roll my own cigars and blend my own pipe tobacco. I will cover what I have learned through trial and error, extensive reading and experimentation, and the wide-ranging knowledge of other tobacco uses from home-growers across the world who have participated in posting and discussing these on the fairtradetobacco.com forum.

The available literature on tobacco growing is vast, and much of it is freely available. The problem for the home-grower in attempting to use these resources (much of it generated by the Agricultural Extension Services of several tobacco producing states in the US) is its focus on large-scale, commercial production, with its dependence on specialized machinery, agri-chemicals and dedicated farm buildings. The home-grower is unlikely to have access to most of these, and may wish to avoid the use of agri-chemicals.

An alternative set of resources in the literature is a number of classic books on the subject, written in the late nineteenth century—before the availability or use of modern machines and chemicals. Some of these are listed in Appendix 7. They do describe essentially pre-industrial tobacco growing, but often lack sufficient detail for the modern grower. Also, many were written before Gregor Mendel discovered the laws of genetics.

One additional source of literature consists of scholarly articles published in scientific journals. Many of these from the past three or more decades are available only for a substantial fee. Another drawback for some new growers is that these articles often assume that the reader is well versed in college-level biology, genetics, chemistry and botany, and can be a challenge for that reason.

New growers should begin by reading The Short Course (Chapter 1) in this book, which touches on all the essentials.

One of my goals in exploring home tobacco growing was to find the simplest, bare minimum of techniques and equipment needed to accomplish a satisfactory result. That is also my goal in presenting this book. There are more expensive and complicated and highly technical approaches than those that I present, and you are invited to explore them. But by understanding the basic requirements of a particular process, you gain the foundation of knowledge upon which the more sophisticated (industrial) approaches are based.

As an example, modern flue-curing of tobacco (primarily used for cigarettes, though also a key ingredient in many pipe tobacco blends) is performed in cabin-sized chambers, equipped with electrically controlled blowers and dampers, and gas heaters. I was nagged by the thought that flue-curing was invented and regularly performed in the mid-nineteenth century in log tobacco curing sheds, heated by hand-fed wood placed into brick stoves that simply passed their hot flue pipe through the barn. Initially, and for the decades that followed, many of these flue-cure barns may not have been equipped with even a simple thermometer— never mind a hygrometer with which to measure humidity. If flue-curing could be successful in a primitive, fire-heated barn, then all the modern equipment was ascribable to market pressures and labor costs. I found a simple way to flue-cure tobacco in a galvanized, 32 gallon trash can, heated with a Crockpot. How that is done, and many other simple approaches to tobacco curing and finishing are presented in the chapters that follow.

Cajun Muse*: a pipe blend created at home from whole leaf. Latakia 37.5%; Flue-cured Virginia Red 25%; Flue-cured Virginia Bright 12.5%; Basma 12.5%; Perique 12.5%. It rests in a large, clear, polystyrene jar, with a custom-printed, full-color label temporarily taped to the lid.*

Vuelta Abajo

A 5-foot by 12-foot bed of 16 Vuelta Abajo plants, about 5 weeks after transplant. Notice that at least two of them had failed, and were replaced. Starting extra transplants for each variety makes it possible to easily address the inevitable transplant mortality. I regularly start 25% more of a variety than I expect to plant (with a minimum of 4 extras per variety).

The unused extras should be heartlessly destroyed, once the tobacco is well established. Attempting to squeeze in more plants than you have decided to grow usually results in crowding and poor quality tobacco.

1. Growing Tobacco: the short course

If you need to convert the units of measure presented here, try www.onlineconversion.com.

An overview of growing tobacco.

Tobacco is grown from seed, usually indoors, then transplanted to the growing bed when they reach about 6 inches tall. The mature size of a tobacco plant ranges from 3 to 8 feet, with most being about 4 to 6 feet tall. The flower head is often removed prior to maturing, in order to produce larger, richer leaf. Tobacco is harvested either by priming (one leaf at a time), or by the whole stalk. It must be hung and allowed to wilt and die slowly, in relatively humid conditions, so that all of the green chlorophyll is broken down, and the leaf turns yellow or directly to brown. This requires weeks to months. Following this stage, the dead leaf must be aged, enabling its natural enzymes to render it smokable. Aging requires months to years. The aging process can be shortened to about a month or two using controlled heat and humidity (a kiln). Expect 100 to 200 cigarettes per plant; 6 to 12 corona-size cigars per plant; 2 to 5 ounces of pipe tobacco per plant. As you progress from leaves lower on the plant to higher, the flavor and nicotine strength increase.

1. Is it legal to grow your own tobacco?

Within the US, there are (at the time of this writing—2019) no federal restrictions on growing your own tobacco. You should check your local laws.

2. Where will tobacco grow?

Tobacco will grow from the tropics to as far north as Scandinavia. It grows in lowlands, in mountains and places in between. As for maximum altitude, there is commercial tobacco production in Nepal. The important factor is that you have at least 90 frost-free days.

3. What varieties of tobacco are there?

There are over 70 species of *Nicotiana*, the genus which includes smoking tobacco and all its plant relatives. *Nicotiana tabacum*, the tobacco of commerce, comes in nearly 3000 named varieties. There are also dozens of named varieties of *Nicotiana rustica*, originally cultivated by the natives of North America. *N. rustica* is usually much more potent than *N. tabacum*. In the discussions in this book, all reference is to *N. tabacum*, unless otherwise indicated.

4. What tobacco varieties should I grow?

Any variety of tobacco can be used for any purpose. The US Department of Agriculture (USDA) classed tobacco into commercial classes, based on their common use in the late nineteenth and early twentieth century.

Burley
This is a group of traditionally air-cured, flavorful tobaccos with relatively high nicotine. They tend to be fairly easy to air-cure. A common major ingredient in cigarettes, though it makes wonderful cigars and pipe tobacco, as well as smokeless products.

Flue-cured
These varieties, often just called, "Virginias," grow well in sandy-loam, and are traditionally cured with heat. Used as a major ingredient in cigarettes and pipe blends. They can be successfully air-cured.

Dark air-cured
Producing large, dark green somewhat sticky leaves, these varieties are commonly used in making chew and snuff.

Dark fire-cured

Fire-cured varieties tend to produce dark, heavy, sometimes sticky leaves that are usually subjected to a multi-week exposure to both the heat *and the smoke* of open curing fires. The resulting leaf is tough, darkened, and gives off a distinct smoky aroma and taste. Traditionally used for chew, snuff, cigarette blending, and is blended in some Appalachian-style cigars and stogies. Sometimes used in pipe blending. It can be air-cured.

Maryland

These tobaccos resemble the large, seedleaf varieties, from which they are derived, with mild aroma, and moderate nicotine. They are traditionally stalk-harvested and air cured, and often used to adjust the nicotine content of a blend. Used for pipe blending and cigarette blending. Can be used as cigar wrapper / binder / filler. They absorb sauces and flavorings well, and can also be used to make Cavendish pipe tobacco.

Cigar Filler

Since most tobaccos can be used as cigar filler, this formal class includes only those that found a major market as filler with cigar manufacturers, either in the U.S., or in its primary growing regions. Varieties that regularly produce leaves which are thick or corrugated or intensely rippled are unsuitable for use as wrapper or binder, since they can not be easily flattened. Some of these varieties are nearly identical to varieties classified as Cigar Binder. The cigar terms, "volado," "seco," "viso" and "ligero," refer to leaves from the lower to higher stalk positions on the plant, respectively.

Cigar Binder

Binder is a diverse class of tobacco varieties that tend to produce a leaf with sufficient elasticity to withstand the stress of compressing a bunch of cigar filler. Some of these varieties are nearly identical to varieties classified as

Cigar Filler. Their flavors, aromas and burn qualities are not a consideration in classification. Often, they may also be used effectively as wrapper.

Cigar Wrapper

Wrappers for cigars require a leaf (or portion of a leaf) that is without flaws, both for reasons of air flow as well as aesthetics. While some are preferred to be thin, such as Connecticut Shade leaf and Indonesian Besuki, others are noticeably thicker, such as Florida Sumatra, Connecticut Broadleaf, and most wrapper leaf that is grown in full sun. Some traditionally shade-grown wrapper varieties can be successfully grown without shade.

Oriental

Also called "Turkish" tobacco, since many of its traditional growing areas were part of the former Ottoman Empire. Today, these are frequently grown in Albania, North Macedonia, Greece, Bulgaria, Turkey, Cyprus and the Republic of Georgia. Oriental tobaccos have a reputation for being small-leafed, delicate, aromatic and low in nicotine. This is true of some, though not all. Oriental tobaccos are traditionally sun-cured, though they are successfully cured by any of the available curing methods. [Latakia, grown in Syria and Cyprus, is an indeterminate Basma-like variety that is intensely fire-cured.] Uses: Cigarette blending, pipe blending. The larger leaf Oriental varieties can be used as cigar wrapper / binder / filler.

Hungarian

This wide-ranging collection of tobaccos has its origins in the tobaccos grown within the various Eastern European member states of the former Austro-Hungarian Empire. There is no distinctive characteristic of the class, though some grow blossom heads that are mostly nested within the upper leaf crown. Some are notoriously strong; others are mild.

Primitive

These are varieties that are clearly *Nicotiana tabacum*, but have been subjected to little or no agricultural improvement effort, in comparison to the "wild" types. Their splayed venation patterns may make it difficult to utilize as cigar wrapper or binder. Some have distinctive, sometimes odd, aromas and flavors. Some make excellent and rich cigar filler and cigarette blending leaf.

5. How many plants should I grow?

Depending on the variety, you can expect 100 to 200 cigarettes per plant; 6 to 12 corona-size cigars per plant; 2 to 5 ounces of pipe tobacco per plant. Most full-size tobacco requires about 3.75 sq. ft. in dug bed. In traditional row planting, it is spaced 3 feet within the row, with 4 feet between rows. Small Oriental varieties may be densely planted, with spacing as close as 5" to 9". The curing space required is about 0.5 to 1 sq. ft. per plant, hung in a single tier. (see "Air Curing" below)

6. Can I grow tobacco in pots?

Tobacco will grow in a pot, so long as it has adequate drainage, and the sun exposure is sufficient. A minimum 5 gallon container is suggested. Potted tobacco seldom grows as large as that grown in the ground.

7. Can I grow tobacco indoors?

Yes, with expensive lighting or good sun exposure. But indoor growing tends to produce mild, bland tobacco that may not be worth the effort and expense. It is possible, though, to produce seed from indoor plants, even in small (3-1/2") pots.

8. Where can I acquire dependable tobacco seed?

The most reliable (for both seed purity and disease-free certification) and comprehensive (for choice of varieties) source of tobacco seed is

www.northwoodseeds.com/Seed%20List2.htm
[Washington state—ships worldwide.]

Seed may also be purchased from the following sites:

www.jlhudsonseeds.net/SeedlistN.htm#Tobacco
[California]

www.nativeseeds.org/collections/tobacco
[Arizona]

www.seedman.com/Tobacco.htm
[Mississippi—vague varietal identifications]

www.tabakanbau.de/de/sitemap.php
[German Language. "samen"= seed]

www.b-and-t-world-seeds.com
[France, but multilingual]

www.coffinails.com/order.html
[UK]

www.victoryseeds.com/tobacco.html
[Oregon]

www.sustainableseedco.com/collections/tobacco
[California—ships worldwide]

www.onlinetobaccoseedstore.com
[UK]

9. When do I start my tobacco seed?

Seed should be started 6 to 8 weeks before your last frost date.

10. How should I start my tobacco seed?

Tobacco seed is quite tiny (~1/2 mm). A typical packet of seed will contain 50 to 200 seeds. Using a standard "seed starting" soil mixture in a small container, moisten the soil (not soggy) and lightly sprinkle seed uniformly over the surface. Seal the container with a lid or plastic wrap, then minimize direct exposure to sunlight, making sure the temperature is between 70°F and 85°F. After four to six days, the tiny, coffee-colored seed should reveal a white radicle sprouting from one end. (Some seed may require several weeks to germinate.) At this stage, the seed has swollen, and can be easily picked up with a toothpick. Transfer one sprouted seed each to seedling cells (36 to 72 cell tray) or to individual 3" pots, and place them in partially shaded sunlight. Any seedlings remaining in the initial starting container should be left uncovered, and kept moist. In order to keep different varieties separate, *use a separate container for each variety*, and sprinkle the seed at a safe distance from the containers for other varieties. Even a slight electrostatic charge can cause the tiny tobacco seeds to jump several inches from their intended target.

11. How do I prepare tobacco transplants?

Seedlings should grow to transplant size (6" tall or more) in about 6 to 8 weeks. They should be kept watered, and allowed good drainage. They will need to be gradually introduced to full sunlight exposure. Starting 4 days before you intend to transplant them, stop watering. The day prior to transplant, water them thoroughly. You should produce about 25% more transplants than you require, in order to replace any field mortality. When the seedlings grow enough to begin shading one another, the individual leaves (not the growth tip of the stalk) can be safely clipped with a pair of scissors, removing up to 2/3 of their length. Clipping can be repeated as necessary, until you are able to transplant to the field.

12. Where can I buy ready tobacco transplants?

If you wish to avoid the production of ready transplants, you may be able to purchase them for shipment to you. They travel well, and can be immediately planted in your garden. They should be ordered during the winter, for shipment in late spring. Inquire with any local growers.

Check www.fairtradetobacco.com forum for members offering transplants for shipment.

www.newhopeseed.com offers transplants for shipment.

13. When do I transplant to the field?

A newly planted tobacco transplant is delicate, and is unlikely to survive a hard frost. The safest date is 1 to 2 weeks after your average last date of frost. Many home-growers transplant with success earlier than that.

14. Where should I place the transplants?

Tobacco should be planted in soil that is not prone to flooding or prolonged standing water. While the plants require a lot of water, the soil must drain well. Full sun is ideal. Second best is at least half-day sun plus reflection from a light colored wall. If grown in partial shade, tobacco will be taller, thinner and milder. Soil should be tilled at least 12" deep, and kept weed-free. Plant the tobacco at the same depth as it has been growing, or slightly deeper. If planting deeper, remove the lowest 1 to 3 leaves with your fingernail or scissors. Water immediately after planting with 2 cups of water per plant. Water the new transplants whenever the soil dries, or if the plants appear droopy. (See "How often should I water the growing plants?" below.)

15. What fertilizer should I use?

If you plant in newly broken lawn, then no fertilizer may be necessary. You can fertilize prior to transplanting with aged or composted manure. Raw manure should only be used if it will have at least a few months to rest in the soil before transplanting. With one notable precaution, common tomato fertilizer (10:10:10) may be used according to tomato instructions. High chloride in the soil will cause the finished leaf to burn poorly. So avoid fertilizers which are made with chlorides (which can also be called muriate of potash or muriatic acid). Discontinue fertilizer before the flower head is in button stage.

16. How often should I water the growing plants?

Most varieties of tobacco will droop during the heat of the day. If the leaves do not assume a "praying hands" position over night, water them the next morning. Over watering is a very common mistake made by home-growers. You may never need to water.

17. What about topping?

For highest leaf yield and strength, the bud head should be removed just before the blossoms open. Tobacco is commercially topped when 10% to 50% of the plants show at least a single flower in bloom. Weaker plants can be topped to fewer total leaves, in order to improve production. If you wish to save seed, you must not top the plant. *Most Oriental varieties are not topped*, in order to retain their mild, aromatic character.

18. Do I have to remove the suckers?

Small buds will form at each leaf axil (where each leaf stem meets the stalk), and sometimes at the base of the stalk. If these are not removed, they will grow into branches, decreasing total yield. Suckers are stimulated when the plant is topped. A sucker up to 3 inches long can be snapped cleanly from the plant with your fingers. In general, suckers do not cure as easily as main leaf, and will seldom equal it in quality. Suckers can also serve as a nursery for aphid infestation.

19. How and when do I harvest my tobacco?

Individual leaf priming follows the maturation process of the plant, moving from the bottom to the top of the plant. You can prime leaves whenever the leaf tip begins to yellow and curl. For cigar leaf, wait until the leaf shows increased thickness and some bumpy puckering of the surface. This is the mature stage. The stem of a mature leaf will snap cleanly from the stalk with a sideways turn of the wrist. Primed leaf can be strung on a wire or sturdy cord for hanging. An entire stalk can be hung by driving a nail diagonally into the base of the stalk, or with any other clever device that can support a 10 pound plant. Lighter Orientals can be stalk-harvested and hung by improvising a wire hook twisted about the base of the stalk.

For stalk-harvested burleys and Virginias, you may find that they color cure most easily if they are allowed to yellow fully or at least partially, while still standing. The woody stalk is cut just above the ground. The whole plant may be allowed to wilt a few minutes to hours in the shade (while kept out of the rain), then hung entire in the curing area. Garden loppers are the easiest and safest way to cut the stalk.

20. How does the green leaf turn into usable tobacco?

Color-curing takes advantage of metabolic processes within the living leaf to consume carbohydrates and proteins, and break down the green of chlorophyll. If the leaf is allowed to fully dry (thus die) green, it will remain green. So it should not be allowed to dry crispy until after the green color is gone or mostly gone. Once yellowed, the leaf may be allowed to fully brown (to die) by drying. Following color-curing, the leaf should be allowed to age. The aging process utilizes oxidizing enzymes within the dead leaf to break down the albuminous proteins, and release the resulting ammonia. Other unpleasant aroma compounds slowly dissipate.

21. How can I color-cure my tobacco?

There are four common methods of promoting color-curing.

Air-curing

Leaf or entire plants are hung in the shade or in a shed, and allowed to slowly die. This requires typically two weeks to two months. Fan circulation is helpful in preventing local pockets of very high humidity to cause rot. Once the leaf is brown, higher humidity is likely to cause mold. At this point, the leaf can be dried down and stored, or left hanging to age. Curing space may be an issue. In a single tier, estimate 1 sq. ft. / plant for primed leaf; ~1/2 sq. ft. / plant for stalk cured (with at least an 8' roof). [Remember that, once wilted, the upper leaf of a stalk-harvested plant will hang straight down, adding to the plant's total length.] Watch the weight. An entire tobacco plant may weigh over 10 lbs. A 10' x 10' shed hung with whole plants at 0.5 sq. ft. / plant (200 plants) adds over 1 ton of weight to the structure. Primed green leaf at 1 sq. ft. per plant weighs only 8% of that. Dried leaf alone will weigh only 3% of the weight of the whole green plant on which it grew.

Sun-curing

The leaf is fully wilted in the shade, then allowed to hang in direct sunlight until cured. If strung closely together or hung close to the moist ground, green mottling will be kept to a minimum. The process is usually complete in about three weeks. The process requires bringing the leaf indoors if rain threatens.

Flue-curing

Most home-growers may not have the necessary equipment to flue-cure tobacco, though there are plans for two different flue-curing chambers discussed in the chapters of this book. The process requires slowly raising the temperature over 5 days to 165°F, while simultaneously lowering the moisture content. When finished, the tobacco retains its light color, and is immediately ready to smoke without further processing.

This is the commercial method used for much of cigarette tobacco production and the "Virginia" of pipe tobaccos.

Fire-curing

This can be accomplished in a home smoker (as used with meat smoking). The leaf is heated to moderate temperatures (below 140°F), while being exposed to the smoke of a fire. This requires 1 to 4 weeks, minimum. Latakia production is similar, using specific Mediterranean woods and herbs, and continuing for 6 to 12 weeks.

22. How do I finish my tobacco?

Immediately after color curing, tobacco can be smoked, but it will be harsh, and have a "raw," ammonia-like odor. It also tends to burn poorly at this point. If the leaf can be left hanging in an area that exposes it to rising and falling humidity, in temperatures that go above 60°F, it will mellow over 6 to 12 months, and develop a typical tobacco aroma. This aging process can be shortened to about one or two months with the use of a kiln, which can be built for about $100. Many creative, alternate methods exist.

During this period, the humidity should not be allowed to remain above ~80% RH for more than a two or three days, in order to prevent mold.

23. How can I handle dry tobacco without breaking it?

You can't. If it is hanging tobacco, just wait for a couple of rainy days. Stored tobacco can be re-humidified with a mist of water. When in a proper state for handling, it should not be noisy like dry leaves, but rather have a softer rustling sound, like stiff vinyl. The texture will be supple like calf skin.

24. Is there an easy way to stem tobacco?

While the stem will burn fairly well, and is smokable, it gets in the way of cigar rolling, and can be a road hazard for most tobacco shredding devices. It should be removed.

Bring up the moisture content of dry leaf until the noise of touching it quiets. Hold a leaf with the base of the stem away from you, and the underside (ribs are most prominent) facing up. Starting near the tip, split one side away from the central vein and gently drag toward the base of the stem. Go slowly at first. When done correctly, little or no leaf will remain on the stem, and each half-leaf strip will be intact. With time and practice, stemming one leaf should take about 10 to 20 seconds, faster if you plan to shred it. Another common method of stemming a leaf is to fold it at the stem, and strip the stem away from both leaf halves simultaneously. Carefully stemming one side at a time is the safest way to handle leaf intended for cigar wrapper or binder, until you gain more experience.

25. How do I shred tobacco?

Dedicated tobacco shredders are now available on the market, in both power and manual models. These are worth their cost if you desire larger quantities of finely shredded leaf. Home-growers have used blenders, meat grinders, pasta cutters, paper cutters, paper shredders, knives, chavetas (curved, hand-held cigar blades), scissors and other tools, with varying results.

26. What's the story on blending tobacco?

It is a rare tobacco that reaches its full potential alone. Most varieties, in most uses, are improved by blending with one or more other varieties. A typical American cigarette blend may be 60% Virginia, 30% burley, 10% Oriental. Cigar fillers typically blend milder leaf (seco) with various proportions of stronger leaf (viso or ligero). English-style pipe blends may mix Virginias, Oriental, Perique, burley or dark-air and Latakia. Flavored pipe tobacco may consist of burley, Maryland and Virginia, plus one or more flavoring agents.

27. How do I store my finished tobacco?

Tobacco can be stored completely dry in any container. If kept with more moisture, the RH should be 75% or lower to prevent mold. Tobacco can be re-humidified for smoking with a light mist of water, some steam from a kettle, or simple exposure to the humidity on a rainy day. Properly stored tobacco will continue to age and mellow for years.

28. How can I make my favorite Marlboro cigarette or Punch Cigar etc.?

You're on your own here. You will most likely, with time, find many unique blends using your own tobacco. The blending possibilities are infinite, but in the absence of the chemicals added to many commercial tobacco products, you may become one of the many home-growers who don't just "get by" with home-grown blends, but actually prefer them to what is available to purchase. "Premium" cigars utilize well-guarded blending recipes.

29. How can I save my tobacco seed?

If more than one variety of tobacco is grown within a range of 1/2 mile, the varieties may cross-pollinate. This usually occurs from insect borne pollen. Wind pollination seems to be minimal. Happily, tobacco is self-fertile (an isolated blossom can fertilize itself). In order to save seed of a pure strain, for yourself or for sharing with others, you should bag the bud head before the first blossom opens. An ideal fabric for a bag is a thin, spun fabric, such as Agribon AG-15. Some use organza or "wedding veil," while others have found commercially available "paint strainer" bags to be adequate. You can sew your own bags, or purchase them ready-made. Some varieties of tobacco will produce a bud head that more than fills and stretches a 24"w x 30"h bag, though some bud heads are much smaller. Ideally the bud head is left on the plant until most or all of the 1/2" to 1" seed pods (there may be over 100 on a single plant) have yellowed or browned.

This may require 4 or more weeks beyond harvest time. The bagged head can then be hung inverted to dry completely (away from rodents!). It requires ~1 sq. ft to hang 1 full seed head. A single pod may contain no seeds, or up to 10,000 seeds. (Very few of the 1/4 million seeds will fall out on their own.) Once dried, the seed pods are crushed to release the tiny seeds. Dry, clean seed, in a tight container kept in a dry, cool, dark place, will remain viable for 10 or more years.

30. As a total novice, what can I really expect?

Growing tobacco is not complicated. Growing tobacco is sometimes dirty, sticky, tedious work. By just following this basic set of instructions, you will produce smokable tobacco that you will be proud of.

During your first year, you will make mistakes, and acquire an enormous amount of experience with the process. Your second year will be noticeably better, as you cruise along your way to becoming expert. By your third or fourth year of growing, you will be producing leaf comparable to that from commercial growers.

In addition to the growing and harvesting process, which any grower of tomatoes can relate to, you will also be learning how to cure and finish your tobacco in ways suitable to your desired uses, while gaining the skills needed to produce your final product. This is way beyond what most folks employed in the tobacco industry learn, working in their cleanly segmented roles. In contrast to the magazine article "experts", you will know all the *real steps* along the way from, for example, seed to lit cigar, or seed to a perfect pipe blend. Myths and mystique will fade away.

One seedling per 1020 tray cell, with a wood label (Popsicle stick marked with a Sharpie) for each pack of cells. In this 48-cell tray insert, every 4 cells (a 4-pack) can be separated from the others. The nested 1020 trays rest on a wire shelf, in an enclosed back porch. They are exposed to direct sun for about half of each day.

2. How to Grow Tobacco

Why Grow Your Own Tobacco?

Home tobacco growers on the fairtradetobacco.com forum have expressed a number of reasons why they started growing.

- to save money
- to legally avoid the taxes levied on commercial tobacco products
- to acquire a survivalist skill that might be valuable to them, should things become chaotic
- to impress friends or relatives
- to challenge the mystique of premium tobacco production
- to avoid the chemicals and pesticides present in commercial tobacco
- to explore a new hobby

While the most commonly cited reason for starting seems to be the first in the above list, I began for the final reason: I wanted to see if I could produce a small amount of tobacco that could be used for pipe blending. Though a cigar smoker for decades, I had read and believed the marketeering hype about how difficult and specialized the crafting of "premium" cigar leaf is to master—not to mention the daunting skill level that was supposedly required for rolling a cigar. I had no thought of growing cigar leaf. In fact, I had carefully reasoned that it would be foolish to even try. My first year, I obtained seed exclusively for varieties suitable for pipe blending, and ultimately grew 16 beautiful tobacco plants. (At the time, 16 plants seemed like a nicely sized grow.)

When one of my brothers (Ron) asked if I was planning to roll some cigars from my leaf, I patiently explained why that would not be possible in the absence of a substantial industrial infrastructure. But the notion stuck. The following year, I was up to 80 plants, including varieties for cigar wrapper, binder and filler. I was now determined to discover if I could grow my own cigars.

From that first crop of cigar leaf, I quickly learned to roll some quite smokable stogies, even if they didn't win a beauty contest. I had proven to myself that it could be done, and that I could eventually solve every piece of the puzzle. After all, if ordinary country folk 200 years ago could manage to do it on their own, it couldn't be as complicated as the Aficionado crowd makes it out to be.

And I was correct in that assumption. Over a span of a few years, I conquered the challenges of each category of finished tobacco in a home-grower setting, and in some of the simplest possible ways. I can now produce entirely at home (from seed to the finished, smokable result) flue-cured leaf ("Virginia"), cigar wrappers, binders and fillers—in a vast array of varieties, Oriental sun-cured leaf ("Turkish"), black Cavendish, fire-cured leaf, Latakia (of a sort), Perique and dark-air cured leaf. I now enjoy cigar blending, pipe blending, and experimenting with uncommon combinations.

While, at the time of this writing, I have rolled well over 10,000 cigars, that is a mere drop in the bucket, when compared to the labor of a cigar factory worker. Yet my cigars are every bit as enjoyable to me as nearly any "premium" cigar on the market.

Now that my concern about the unknown challenges have dissipated, I grow my own tobacco for the joy of doing it, and the satisfaction of smoking the results. Growing tobacco from seed varieties collected by the USDA Agricultural Explorers 80 years ago, from locations as wide ranging as Machu Picchu in Peru to Timor and Java in Indonesia, gives me a sense of historical connectedness. I have grown varieties of Turkish tobacco that are no longer grown in the industry-centric tobacco fields of Turkey today. (One Turkish botany scholar requested that I send him seed for Mutki, a curious, large-leaf Turkish varietal no longer available there.)

Why do other home-growers continue to plant tobacco year after year? Their reasons certainly contain a mix of their original motivations (the list above), but also for many, the same, newly discovered pleasures that I have found.

Recommendations for which varieties you should grow for a specific use are highly subjective. The suggestions in this section are a reasonable place to start. After all, there are nearly 3000 named tobacco varieties of *Nicotiana tabacum*. Each region of the world, each country, and each cultural group may have their own unique preferences. I have personally grown over 100, and handled and sampled between 150 and 200 varieties.

A more expansive list, still much abbreviated, is contained in Chapter 5: Tobacco Varieties.

Growing for Cigars

From the standpoint of many taxing agencies, a cigar is simply any tobacco wrapped in either tobacco leaf or reconstituted tobacco sheet. But tobacco varieties that are classed as one of the cigar categories (wrapper, binder, filler) has the ability to age (or ferment) into a state that produces a more typical cigar aroma. Non-cigar classes can be aged (or fermented) as much as you like, but do not take on attributes recognizable as "cigar." The differences seem to be in the sugars, proteins and final pH (acidity) of the finished leaf. So, cigar leaf is different by its very nature. It is true that you can roll a cigar from any tobacco, and even enjoy it, but a smoker of traditional cigars will really want to grow tobacco varieties that are specifically cigar leaf.

Any cigar variety, whether wrapper, binder or filler, can be recruited to fill any of those uses. But a wrapper variety, by virtue of its leaf size and shape, its vein angle and its tensile strength will provide a higher percentage of desirable wrappers than cigar leaf of other classes. For a home-grower who is not interested in constructing a shade cloth canopy, an excellent choice for sun-grown wrapper is Florida Sumatra, seed for which is widely available. Another that produces quality wrapper when sun-grown is Machu Picchu Havana. Connecticut Broadleaf seed is easy to find, but I have always had difficulty getting a uniformly color-cured leaf with that specific variety *in my location.*

Binder varieties tend to grow large leaves with an advantageous vein angle, as well as good tensile strength. Their excellent burn characteristics are helpful for a steady cigar burn. But their taste and cosmetic quality may make them less desirable for use as wrapper. That being said, some binder varieties, such as Comstock Spanish, can make superb wrapper. (Glessnor, a filler variety, also makes excellent binder and wrapper.) Keep in mind that the "classes" were assigned by the US Department of Agriculture (USDA) over a span of over a century, and based on typical use of specific varieties by the tobacco industry at the time of their classification. So the class may or may not be meaningful for your own use.

What about filler? It just needs to be a cigar variety. That's about it. Leaf from lower stalk positions burns particularly well, but tends to lack flavor, aroma and body. Leaf nearer the top of the plant typically does not burn as well, but is loaded with flavor, nicotine, body and rich aromas. Most of the filler of a commercial cigar is made up of leaf from between those extremes, with bottom leaf added for combustion, and top leaf added for potency. And all of this can be had from a single plant.

Most cigar filler varieties will produce a more enjoyable cigar if the qualities of two or more varieties are blended. Sometimes magic happens when several varieties are brought together. For rich, American traditional cigars, Little Dutch and Pennsylvania Red are hard to beat as fillers. Swarr-Hibshman and Lancaster Seedleaf, which produce large quantities of huge leaves, would be other candidates. For more of a Caribbean-style cigar, Vuelta Abajo, Olor, Piloto Cubano, Criollo 98 and Corojo 99 are a good place to start. To add a Brazilian flair, Bahia (the source variety of Mata Fina cigar tobacco) can be added to a blend.

Growing for Pipe Blending

You may find any variety of tobacco enjoyable in a pipe. That, of course, depends on your preferences. Some pipe smokers may not like a "cigar" taste. Others may want food flavorings in their pipe tobacco. Still others prefer "English" style blends, which predominantly use Virginia types, Orientals, unflavored Cavendish, Latakia and perhaps Perique, burley and Dark Air-cured. Then there are those who enjoy a straight burley or straight Oriental.

If your intent is to flavor your tobacco with flavoring concentrates, then any mildly flavored tobacco will do, such as Maryland varieties or even some of the mild Havana varieties.

For "English" style blending, and good choice would be Virginia Bright Leaf (which you may or may not decide to flue-cure), an aromatic Oriental, such as Xanthi Yaka or Prilep (though the much more readily available Izmir varieties—sometimes called "Smyrna"—can work as well), and just about any other varieties to be made into black Cavendish, Latakia or perique.

Black Cavendish is simply steamed tobacco. The basic technique is detailed in Chapter 3. Once made, it tends to have a soft, smooth, slightly sweet taste, with its strength entirely dependent on the leaf you start with. After it is finished and dried, flavors can be misted onto it, if that's what you would like.

Latakia can be made in a smoker, probably from any variety of leaf, though small Orientals are typical of the Latakia from Syria and Cyprus. The 6 to 12-week process is explained in chapter 3.

Perique is made by placing moist leaf under enough pressure to disrupt the laminar cells of the leaf, and spill out their enzymes. Again, it can be made from any variety (though the Perique variety is used in St. James Parish Perique manufacture), and a simple, inexpensive press is shown in Chapter 3. While perique can be enjoyed on its own, its relatively high pH (less acidic) allows its nicotine load to be more readily absorbed. So it is usually smoked in a blend. For pipe tobacco, perique is particularly useful for eliminating the tongue bite of flue-cured (Virginia) tobacco, which produces acidic smoke.

Smoking a straight variety of tobacco in a pipe is an excellent way to explore the characteristics of specific varieties. If you grow your own tobacco, you will discover that even a single plant will produce pipe tobacco that ranges from mild and bland to dark and strong—progressing from lower on the stalk to higher, respectively. In addition, a single plant will produce generally milder, more aromatic leaf if it is not topped (removal of the blossom head). Not topping the plants is a common practice in traditional growing of Orientals. When topped, the leaves become larger, thicker and more nicotine laden. The degree of leaf maturity when it is primed (harvested by individual leaves) also affects the strength and aroma of the final tobacco. All this can be a source of experimentation, without the need to perform any special curing techniques.

Burley varieties are available in scores of choices. For a mild and smooth burley, Harrow Velvet—a Canadian-developed variety—and Golden Burley are a good choices. TN89 and TN90 (commercial varieties) will produce stronger, larger leaf. Kelly Burley is stronger than the mildest burleys, but not as intense as some of the present commercial varieties.

As with burley, there are numerous varieties of Virginia. Virginia Bright Leaf is an example of one for which seed is readily available, and which can make a good, straight pipe tobacco, either air-cured or flue-cured. Virginia tobaccos are generally recognized to be varieties derived from the Orinoco variety adopted in colonial Virginia (after the failure of native *N. rustica* tobacco to find an eager market in Europe).

The several dozen varieties of Orientals are interesting to explore as a straight pipe tobacco. Some, like Shirazi, Samsun, Trabzon and Yayladag are rather rich and strong, while Samsun-Maden,

Bafra, Xanthi varieties and Prilep tend to be mild and aromatic. Izmir (Smyrna) and many others are in between.

Growing for Cigarettes

Some popular brands of Canadian and British cigarettes are made of straight Virginia (of which there are abundant varieties, and variants of stalk position). Popular American cigarette blends tend to be a blend of a Virginia, a burley (sometimes toasted), and Oriental leaf—not to mention the hundreds of flavorants used in well hidden proportions. By weight, a "typical" American cigarette blend might be 60% Virginia, 30% burley and 10% Oriental. The beauty of growing your own cigarette blends is that you can adjust the proportions and the specific varietals to your liking.

Virginia tobacco that is used in commercial cigarettes is flue-cured. A method for flue-curing your own tobacco is described in Chapter 3. Virginia Bright Leaf seed is widely available, and is a reasonable starting point for exploring flue-cure varieties.

You may be relieved to discover that many home tobacco growers enjoy Virginia type tobaccos that are simply air-cured. Which Virginia variety can be used as a stand-alone, unblended cigarette filler, when the leaf is only air-cured? Well, that is a deeply subjective choice. You can start by choosing from Virginia Bright Leaf, Hickory Pryor, Frog Eye Orinoco, or Costello Negro for air-curing. Reams 158 can be sun-cured to a fairly bright leaf. There are so many flue-cure (Virginia) varieties to investigate, that you could spend years trying them, and not taste them all.

Growing for Smokeless

Smokeless tobacco can be categorized loosely into dry snuff, moist snuff (snus), and chewing tobacco. Your choices of tobacco varieties for any of these is wider than for any other tobacco use.

Both dry and moist snuff are begun by grinding very dry tobacco leaf (and sometimes leaf stems) into a fine powder. It can be a single variety or a blend. Some home-growers have made

Swedish snus entirely from *Nicotiana rustica*, as opposed to common smoking tobacco, *Nicotiana tabacum*. After grinding, the recipes for dry and moist snuff are different, as explained in Chapter 10.

Chewing tobacco can be as simple as chewing on a piece of tobacco leaf that has sun-cured itself out in the field. Most folks will want to air-cure, then age or kiln the leaf prior to use. And, of course, there are many recipes, using various kinds of flavorings, to alter the taste and consistency of chewing tobacco, which may be cut into a broad shred, or into small pieces. I can offer no specific guidelines on which tobacco variety you may prefer. It can be burley, a Virginia, any of the cigar varieties, or any of the other tobacco classes. Maryland and burley varieties are particularly efficient at absorbing flavor casings.

How Much to Grow

Your Needs

Some first-time growers appreciate guidance on how much tobacco to grow, based on their current tobacco use. As a general formula, expect 100 to 200 cigarettes per plant; 6 to 12 corona-size cigars per plant; 2 to 5 ounces of pipe tobacco per plant. These wide variances naturally raise the question of whether to aim for the bottom or the top of a range. Your first grow will clarify this a bit.

If you harvest and cure the trashier leaf at the bottom of each stalk, remove suckers diligently, and top (cut off the flowering head) high, then careful harvesting and curing will approach the higher limits of production. Expect a yield somewhere in the middle. Experience will serve as a more reliable guide for subsequent years.

One reasonable approach is to undertake a relatively small grow for the first year. A small grow will lower the risk of failure, and give you a better notion of the time and labor commitment that will be required for a larger grow.

If, instead, you chose to jump right in, be sure to consider the limitations of your curing space.

Your Curing Capacity

Tobacco requires a covered (perhaps fully enclosed) space in which to air-cure. This is where the tender green leaf will transition to yellow, then to brown—a process that will require 2 to 6 weeks or longer to accomplish, depending on the variety and environmental conditions. The most important requirement is to shield the curing leaf from rain. This is true of both air-curing as well as sun-curing. Air-cured tobacco is also shielded from direct sunlight.

A secondary function of your curing space is control of temperature and humidity. This aspect is less important for sun-curing. Curing space for air-curing is usually a shed of some sort, and requires some method of ventilation. Depending on your climate, you may need to regulate the ambient humidity and ambient temperature. The most basic curing shed is simply four walls and a roof, with some means of circulating or blocking off the outdoor humidity and temperature—a wooden shed with a window fan. Sometimes, this is a garage space or a barn. In low wind situations, with favorable outdoor conditions, a roof overhang on a house may suffice, but more commonly, you will need an enclosed space.

The required amount curing space depends on several factors. Primed (individually harvested) leaf that is hung on string or wire takes up more square footage in a single tier than does stalk harvested tobacco, while stalk harvested tobacco requires considerably more height.

In a single tier, estimate 1 sq. ft. per plant for primed leaf, and about 1/2 sq. ft. per plant for stalk cured (with at least an 8' roof). Once wilted, the upper leaf of a stalk-harvested plant will hang straight down, adding to the plant's total length, but also allowing the stalks to be moved closer together.

The total weight of green tobacco is also an important consideration. An entire, single tobacco plant may weigh over 10 pounds when first harvested. A 10' x 10' shed hung with whole plants at 0.5 sq. ft. per plant (200 plants) adds over 1 ton of weight to the structure. Primed green leaf at 1 sq. ft. per plant weighs only 8% of that. Once dry, the leaf itself will weigh only 3% of the weight of the whole green plant on which it grew.

So, as a rough guide, a shed that is 10' x 10' will accommodate about 200 stalk-harvested plants all at once, assuming the structure can support the added weight. With primed leaf, which comes into the shed in stages, removal of color-cured leaf—as it is cured—will allow the same 10' x 10' shed to handle strings of leaf from 200 plants. Different stringing methods can change these figures.

By contrast, if you are growing tobacco that will be flue-cured, you don't have to worry about shed space. Instead, you will need to construct a flue-curing chamber large enough to hold at least 3 or 4 leaves from each plant. A flue-curing run lasts from 5 to 7 days, which is happily how often you will need to prime 3 or 4 mature leaves from each of the plants. So you will either need to build a flue-cure chamber to accommodate your desired number of flue-cured plants, or you will need to limit your flue-cure grow to what will fit the chamber size you have or plan to construct. Flue-cure chambers perform poorly when overfilled.

Your Work Capacity

If you are young, healthy and available for full-time labor, you can probably manage up to one acre of tobacco without human or mechanized assistance. That was the general rule of thumb for freeholders or sharecroppers since colonial times. If your (presumably large) family will join in the labor, then perhaps 3 acres can be achieved. Community leaders in those times were responsible for maintaining the quality of the tobacco produced in their jurisdictions, and often enforced the above guidelines to prevent the production of inferior quality leaf. In the same spirit, they frequently banned the growing of sucker crops, and might destroy sucker crops when discovered.

Keep in mind that there are several phases to the labor of tobacco growing, curing and finishing:
- soil preparation
- seed germination and production of seedlings
- transplanting
- weeding, suckering and pest management
- harvesting and hanging
- various curing methods aside from air-curing
- providing long-term storage

Soil preparation is the most arduous labor. Harvesting and hanging is a close second. Weeding, suckering and pest management is tedious and repetitive, but far less physically intense. My grow of 200-300 plants was reached after several years of gradually expanding the tilled area from a start of only 60 square feet in the first season, to about 1000 square feet. Each year, I broke new ground, until I reached (actually exceeded by a bit) my curing shed capacity. I now grow 100-200 plants.

Typical home-growers (as opposed to commercial growers) plant between 50 and 500 plants per year.

Since the quality of leaf that you produce is likely to improve significantly from your first year of growing to your second, there is no shame in starting small. If you dig by hand, then the labor of soil prep can be a guide to how much to grow. If, instead, you have access to a mechanized tiller, and feel yourself physically up to the task of a big grow, then your curing space capacity—either existing or what you are willing to construct before harvest—should serve as your limit to the size of the grow.

Starting Tobacco Seeds
You should acquire your tobacco seed during the autumn prior to planting them. Seed should be started indoors 6 to 8 weeks before your last frost date. For my area, the last frost date is mid

May, so I start my tobacco seeds in late February or early March. *Plan ahead.*

Soils for Seed Starting and Seedlings

Many home and garden stores sell soil of various kinds, as well as soil amendments. For germination and early seedling care, a "germination mix" will likely offer a finer texture and fewer sticks and twigs. The quality of "germination mix" and "potting soil" differs significantly between manufacturers. Some are finer than others, and some contain fertilizers suitable for germination and early seedling growth.

Commercial tobacco seedling production in float trays utilizes a "soilless" mixture that is capable of wicking water from below, while avoiding saturation. A "soilless" mix can be easily prepared in a 5 gallon bucket, from 3 ingredients:
 • 4 parts peat
 • 1 part vermiculite
 • 1 part Pearlite

My preference is to use Miracle-Gro sphagnum moss (peat), which has slow release fertilizer included. (In side-by-side comparison with "organic" coconut coir that had no fertilizer, seedlings in the Miracle-Gro increased in height, leaf size and stalk diameter noticeably faster than those in the coconut coir.) A batch that fills a 5 gallon bucket about 2/3 of the way—leaving enough room to mix it thoroughly with a long kitchen spoon—is sufficient to fill the cells of two 1020 trays.

Some home-growers have seen excellent results using Bacto brand potting soil. If your selection of soil products is limited locally, then experimentation and comparison may be necessary.

Although many home-growers have recommended adding additional fertilizer or magnesium sulfate (Epsom salts) to their starting mix, my experience has been that the initial fertilizer in the Miracle-Gro peat was sufficient for the duration of growth from germination through transplant time.

Purchasing Tobacco Seed

Tobacco seed from companies that primarily sell to commercial growers is usually offered in minimum quantities that are too large for the needs of a home-grower, and their selection of varieties is quite narrow. In addition, many commercial varieties are under current patent, which disallows the grower from harvesting seed. Another caveat to keep in mind about commercial tobacco seed is that some varieties are F1 hybrids (seed won't breed true) or sterile.

The websites listed in Chapter 1 offer numerous heirloom varieties, which can be used to start your own seed collection, and are worth exploring.

Within chapter 1, a list of on-line seed vendors which were active at the time of this writing can be found.

A typical "packet" of tobacco seed for home-growers contains over 100 seeds. Those from Northwood Seeds are closer to 300 seeds per packet. Unless you know that you will be planting a huge number of a particular variety, 100 seeds are more than enough for each variety. If you harvest all the seed produced from a single plant, you may easily end up with a quarter million seeds for future planting, and if properly stored, they can remain viable for 10 years or more.

Germination

If you are planning to grow more than one variety, then use a separate germination container for each variety, to avoid seed mixing. (The tiny seeds of tobacco, about 500 microns each, are notorious for jumping several inches, as a result of a minimal electrostatic charge.)

Your germination container can be a small paper or plastic cup, or a shallow glass jar. The chosen container does not require drainage holes. Provide at least 2" of germination soil mix, and add enough water to thoroughly wet the soil. It should not be waterlogged. Lightly sprinkle seed over the surface. Keep in mind that you will likely end up depositing two or three times as many seeds as you believe you are sprinkling. The seed should remain on the surface of the soil. For cups, tightly cover each with plastic wrap. For jars, close with the lid. Germination containers should then be placed either in a relatively warm spot, or under grow lights. [If you use grow lights, they should be on a timer synchronized with the current daylight period.] If ambient temperatures are below 70°F, a seedling heat mat beneath the germination containers may accelerate germination. Soil temp should be kept below 85°F.

Eight ounce plastic germination jars rest on a cookie sheet atop a seedling heat mat. About 1/4 cup of water is added initially, and the lids are closed until germination.

Without additional effort or attention, the seed will germinate after 4 to 10 days, though it may take up to 3 weeks for some varieties. If there is no germination after 10 days, seed another jar (not the same one) of that variety. On germination, a white root radicle and two tiny, green seed leaves (cotyledons) will emerge, signaling the time to transplant single seedlings into separate containers. If you wait too long to do this, the seedling roots may form a dense mat, and be difficult to separate.

There are many ways to transfer a single seedling into a tray cell or small pot. It's possible with the tip of a wooden toothpick. If you have a pair of forceps (tweezers), the you can use them to grasp the soil just beneath a seedling, but be careful not to grasp the seedling itself, since that would likely cause fatal damage.

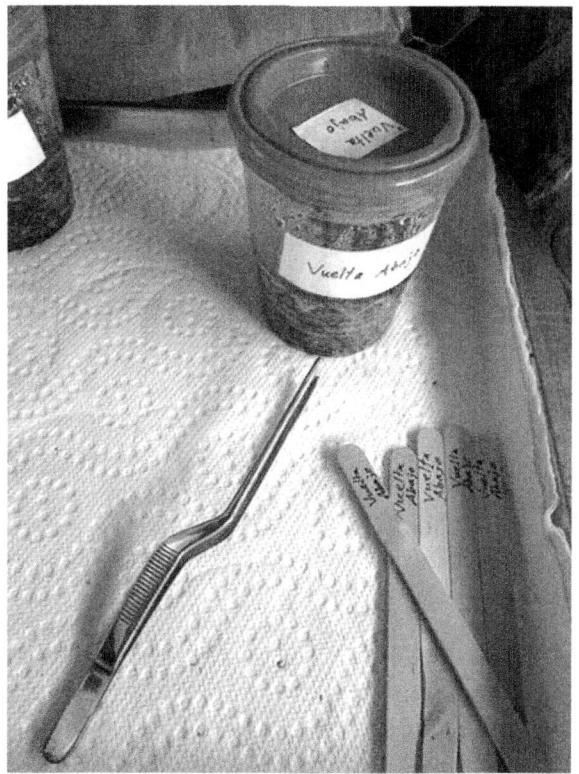

Seedling Trays

Seedling propagation trays come in over a dozen cell patterns and depths. The 1020 tray, named for its general dimension of 10 by 20 inches, is fairly common in garden stores and big box stores in the U.S. Consider how much space you have for your required number of transplants. As for the required number, you are likely to require extras of each variety, in order to replace field mortality. Commercial growers may create as many as 50% more seedlings than they expect to use.

My general practice (which usually works out) is to start 25% more seedlings of each variety than I expect to plant outdoors, but a minimum of 4 extras of each variety. So if I expect to plant

32 of a particular variety, I will create 40 seedlings. If I expect to plant only 4 of a variety (a small test grow, for example), then I create 8 seedlings.

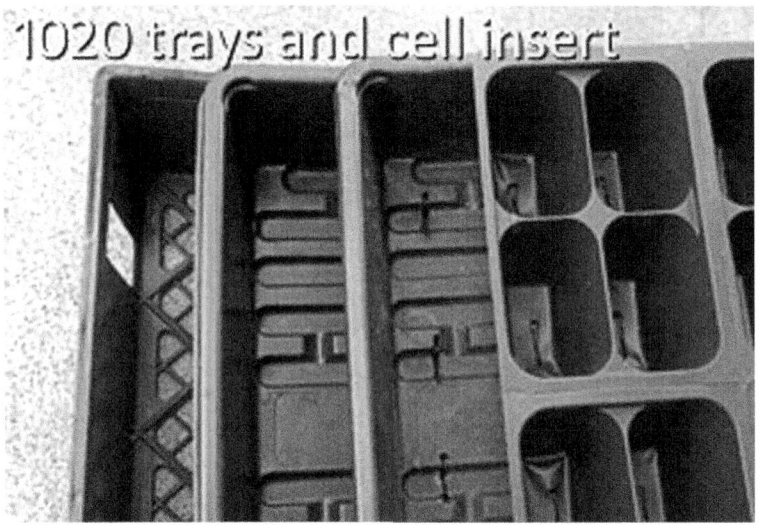

From left to right, lattice, without holes, with holes, insert.

After counting the number of seedlings that you need to start, look at how much space you have for the 1020 trays to occupy for 8 weeks. If you have room for 4 trays, then divide the number of seedling starts by 4. This is the minimum number of cells that need to be squeezed into each 1020 tray. Cell inserts are available for 24, 36, 48, 72, 96, 100, 144 and 288. The higher density inserts are a pretty tight squeeze, and will allow only the tiniest amount of seedling mix (or soil) per plant. My choice for quite a few years has been to use 48-cell inserts in my 1020 trays. If you can't find inserts of the desired density locally, there are a number of on-line grower and garden stores that offer a wide selection.

In addition to the insert, the trays come in three basic basic forms: a lattice tray, a tray with drain holes, and a tray without drain holes. Since I often need to lift and move my trays, I use one of each for every insert. A 1020 lattice tray goes on the bottom for support. Into that, I nest a 1020 tray without holes (since my propagation is done in an enclosed back porch, rather than in a greenhouse). My third layer is a 1020 tray with holes, which allows excess water to drain into the tray beneath it. And into this third layer, I drop the 1020 cell insert.

I use new 1020 cell inserts each season, but reuse all of the other trays, after a thorough washing with a hose, a spraying with a mild Clorox solution, then a rinse. The cleaning minimizes transmission of disease from one season to the next.

I mix my own seedling start mix, which is the same that I use for seed germination. I purchase Miracle-Gro peat, any brand of Pearlite and any brand of vermiculite. I mix them in a 5 gallon bucket. The rough proportion is 2/3 peat, 1/6 Pearlite and 1/6 vermiculite. This mix is also great for a general potting soil.

When it is time to transfer tiny seedlings into a tray with my starting mix in the cells, I add 1-1/2 quarts of water to the tray with holes an hour or two ahead of time. For each seedling, I make a shallow dimple into the center of the mix within a cell (to make it easier to deposit the seedling), then place a single seedling onto the surface of that dimple. After every 4 or 8 cells have a new seedling, I mist the surface with non-chlorinated water, to settle the seedlings in place, and improve wicking of the water beneath the cell into the seedling mix.

Every separate section of the tray insert (every 4 cells, in my 48-cell inserts) requires a means of identifying the tobacco variety (unless you are planting only one variety for the season). For that, I purchase a box of 500 Popsicle sticks (called craft sticks) from the arts and crafts section of a big box store. In advance, I label each stick that will be required with the name of the variety. I do this with a fine-point Sharpie marker. After seedlings are transferred to the cell insert, I insert the stick into one of its cells.

Mix-ups, confusion, dropped trays and other accidents are an all too common problem for beginning growers. Without adequate labels, it will be difficult or impossible to tell which variety is which, should they become "rearranged". The other most common problem for beginning growers is over watering, which often leads to mold, damping-off and feeble seedling growth.

For the first few days to a week, I keep the trays covered with a 1020 clear plastic dome, to keep in the moisture, and if it is mostly sunny, add a single sheet of Agribon AG-15 over the top of it for a 15% shade. If the domes are left in place too long, it increases the risk of mold.

For watering, I remove a single section of the insert (in my case of 48-cell inserts, that is a 4-pack of cells), then pour in a quart and a half of water into the tray with holes. Frequency of watering depends on the temperature, humidity and sun exposure, but averages every 3 to 5 days. *The wood stick will show the moisture, by wicking it visibly up the surface.*

If you continue to maintain your seed germination jars for the first two or three weeks after all the transferring of seedlings is complete, then you will have a reserve of healthy seedlings, should one or more in the 1020 tray fail. If one of the seedlings in the tray dies, just replace it.

Clipping

About 2/3 of each leaf can be clipped. Avoid clipping the stalk's growth tip.

When the seedlings have grown sufficiently that their leaves begin to shade their neighbors (around 4 weeks), then it is time to clip the leaves. This sounds harsh, but in commercial tobacco nurseries, a lawnmower on tracks running just above the seedling float trays uses the vacuum created by its sharp, whirling blade to suck the seedling leaves upward, and lop them. You will be using individual judgment on each leaf, and clipping with a pair of clean, sharp scissors.

The benefits of clipping the leaves can easily be seen, if you do a side-by side comparison of a tray clipped and a tray not clipped. The clipped seedlings allow their neighbors to compete, assuring a larger number of usable transplants. The stalks of the clipped seedlings will grow thicker. And, unseen, the roots will grow more robustly, and produce nicotine earlier, which reduces insect nibbling at the time of transplant.

These "damaged" leaves would have become nothing but trash at the bottom of the stalk anyway, so don't mourn them. Simply put, clipping the leaves (not the growth tip of the stalk) gives you healthier transplants. But be sure to remove the clippings.

Once you begin to clip, you will likely have to repeat clipping every 5 to 7 days during that final month before the plants go into the ground.

Soil, Water and Fertility: your garden

Soil Considerations

Home tobacco growers often have little choice as to where their tobacco will be located. If possible, the tobacco bed(s) should be located well away from the canopy line of neighboring trees, and exposed to direct sun for most of the day during the summer. The bed should have ready access to water, and possess a structure and composition that is rich in nutrients, yet drains well. A long enough garden hose will save lugging a bucket.

Tree roots pose a problem for growing tobacco. The intrusion of tree roots into the tobacco bed will stunt the growth of tobacco plants. Roots of large deciduous trees as well as those of large conifers may extend a distance of 10 to 20% farther than their canopy radius. Tobacco planted in a marginal zone of tree roots typically exhibits progressively decreasing plant size nearer the tree trunk.

On sloping ground, a southern exposure provides a more advantageous sun angle, but for gradual slopes with no shading, that doesn't matter much, unless you are in the far North. A partial day of direct sun may be sufficient if the bed is close to a light-colored, sun-reflecting wall, which could amplify the available exposure of the plants. Sloping ground improves drainage, but if too steep, increases the risk of significant soil erosion and fertilizer leaching during rain storms.

Although tobacco is a sub-tropical plant that can easily utilize a lot of water, it's roots must have adequate aeration. If a tobacco bed becomes flooded with standing water that does not drain away with a span of 12 hours, the leaves may begin to yellow, and the stalk may flop over. Tobacco beds that must be located on relatively flat ground that does not naturally drain well may benefit from mounding the soil, or creating raised rows into which the seedlings are transplanted. This practice provides an additional 6 to 12" of clearance from standing water.

The drainage qualities of the soil itself can be directly altered by the addition of compost, but a relatively impenetrable layer of sub-soil or hardpan may require more active measures, such as the installation of drainage "tiles" beneath the bed. An easier and less expensive alternative would be to simply construct raised beds for the tobacco.

A traditional raised bed begins with double-digging (down to about 24") an area that is 5' wide, and however long you desire. The "raising" is created by both the loosening of the soil from the digging, as well as the addition of compost. It's sides are sloped down to the surrounding ground. In the 5' width, transplants are placed in 4 staggered rows, which accommodate 16 full-size tobacco plants for every 12' of length. For small Orientals, such a 12' bed could hold 100 plants.

A fancier raised bed can, of course, be created with framed sides of whatever height is desired. But the cost goes up significantly. This is the approach required if the level ground is frequently water saturated, or if it is nearly barren. Whatever size you choose, you will have to obtain (likely purchase) all the soil needed to fill it.

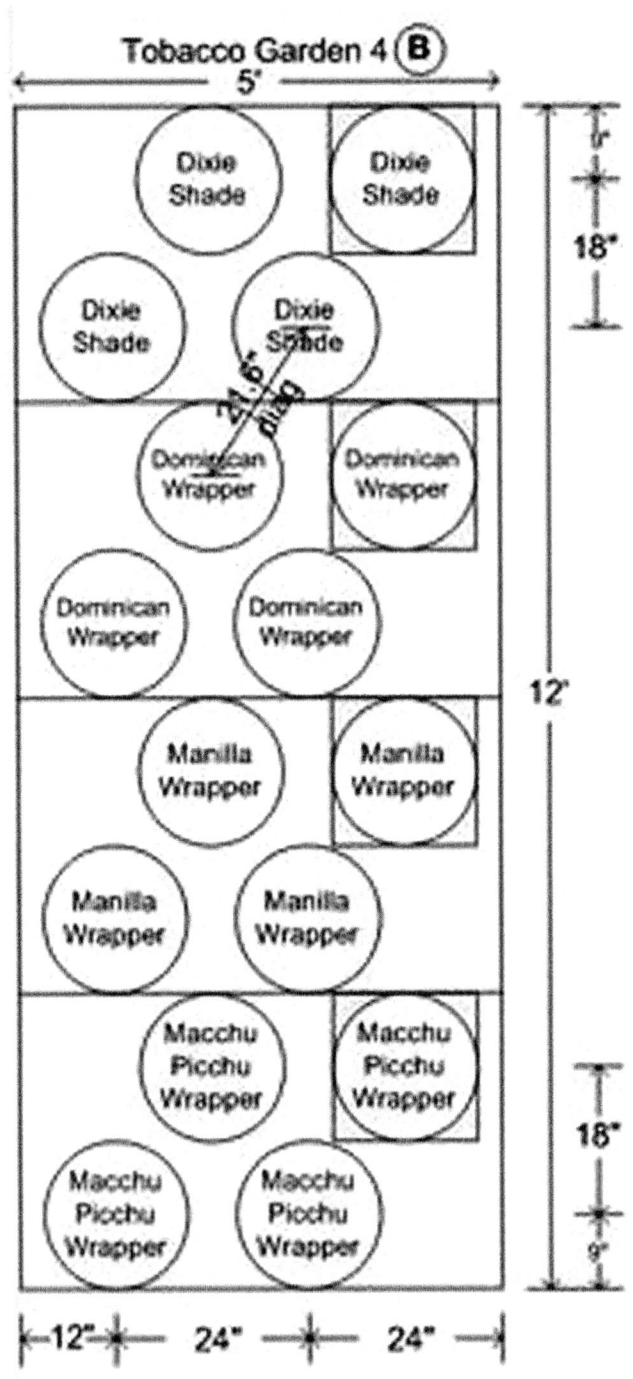

Four staggered rows in a 5' wide bed, showing distances for full-size tobacco plants.

While a raised bed, or even a flat bed that is "double-dug" produces a greater yield of vegetables, a disadvantage of double-digging for tobacco is that typical tobacco plants are 6' tall, with large leaves that act as sails during windy conditions. Tobacco in a double-dug bed is more likely to blow down during a wind storm, and require immediate re-standing, perhaps with a tall stake and ties. Tobacco puts out relatively shallow roots, but will stand better in wind if the bed is tilled down to only about 12".

One possibility, in a particularly windy location, or a newly dug bed with very soft and loose soil is to plan on placing a tomato stake at every plant, or a post at the end of each row, strung with cord or wire. Thin, bamboo tomato stakes are fairly inexpensive and more effective as support than their slight appearance might suggest.

For my own tobacco beds, each of which is tilled down 12" each season, and measures 5' x 12', typically with 4 staggered rows of full-size tobacco plants, I take no special wind precautions. Each season, out of the 130 to 200+ plants that I grow, I tend to have in the range of a half-dozen plants blow down. Once I can go outside again after a storm, I stand up the blow-downs, packing the soil around the roots, sometimes adding a 6" rock as a prop, and occasionally needing to place a stake.

If you plant tobacco on a slope that may be subject to soil erosion during the winter season, then consider planting a cover crop soon after harvesting the tobacco, and tilling it under in the early spring, allowing sufficient time for the plant matter to decay prior to transplanting the tobacco.

Another approach to managing a cover crop is to burn it with a garden torch, prior to tilling it under. The torch may not kill the roots, but the lack of upper leafage, together with being disrupted by the tilling should prevent any regrowth. Unfortunately, tilling exposes hibernating weed and grass seeds, so a second torching, just prior to planting may be required. Glyphosate can be used on a cover crop, or for weed intrusion, so long as it is applied at least a month prior to transplanting.

Planting a frost-sensitive cover crop in a location subject to freezing during winter can provide the benefits of a cover crop. By spring thaw, the cover crop may be well broken down, increasing the nutrients in the soil, while eliminating the need to promptly till it.

One additional benefit of a cover crop, beyond preventing soil erosion and adding nutrients to the soil, is that it tends to significantly increase the population of earthworms in the soil, enhancing aeration and organic matter. Shallower tilling also increases the earthworm population.

Soil Testing

Tobacco is able to adequately absorb required nutrients from the soil if the soil acidity has a pH in the range of 5.8 to 6.2 (max 6.5). Outside that range, the tobacco will show signs of various nutrient deficiencies even if they are present in adequate concentrations. Adjusting the soil pH, if required, needs to be done a month or more before transplant time, to give the sulfur or lime (depending on whether you need to make it more acidic or more alkaline) time to act. Some lime preparations may require one to two years to properly adjust soil pH.

For the average small tobacco grow, if vegetables have done well in the same bed during previous years, then you can just take a chance with the soil. But the only way to really know the nutrient and pH status of the soil is through lab testing.

Every state in the US, and each province in many other countries, provide agricultural extension services for soil testing. The cost may be free (or else it is under about $25 in the US). If you contact the nearest extension service, they will provide instructions, a form to fill out, and often the container(s) in which to submit the soil sample(s). By following their instructions, and submitting one or more samples of soil for testing, you will learn—in a few weeks—the pH, phosphorus, potassium, calcium and other measurements, and also be advised on what, if any, corrections should be applied.

Analysis	P (lb/A)	K (lb/A)	Ca (lb/A)	Mg (lb/A)	Zn (ppm)	Mn (ppm)	Cu (ppm)	Fe (ppm)	B (ppm)
Result	229	495	2485	359	6.3	15.1	1.1	9.2	0.7
Rating	VH	VH	VH	VH	SUFF	SUFF	SUFF	SUFF	SUFF

Analysis	Soil pH	Buffer Index	Est.-CEC (meq/100g)	Acidity (%)	Base Sat. (%)	Ca Sat. (%)	Mg Sat. (%)	K Sat. (%)
Result	6.9	6.38	8.4	1.4	98.6	73.5	17.5	7.5

A soil analysis report showing the soil is too alkaline. Lime had been added to the soil as a "general" recommendation, without prior testing.

Since extension service recommendations for soil amendment are usually provided to farmers, the amounts are often stated in pounds per acre. One of my 5' x 12' beds is a mere 60 square feet. That comes to about 0.00138 acres. You can do the conversions with a calculator, or ask the extension agent for help on doing the calculation. (See Appendix 5.)

Soil Supplements: composts and fertilizers
If you clear an area of otherwise healthy sod for your tobacco bed, then you can probably get by with little or no fertilizer application for that first season. Otherwise, tobacco, like corn (maize), grows a substantial mass of vegetation from the soil in a single growing season, and will rapidly deplete the available nutrients—unless you add more each year. Replenishing nitrogen is routine.

Most of the published recommendations available for fertilizers specific to tobacco growing are directed at tobacco farmers who often grow many acres of tobacco every year. The suggestions for burley vs. flue-cure varieties vs. dark tobacco vary, depending on the previous crop, the geographic region and the soil test results. Specific "tobacco" fertilizer is usually available only in prominent tobacco growing regions.

All of this is not particularly useful to the home-grower of tobacco. A commercial fertilizer recommended for tomatoes is perfectly fine, especially if blended as a "low chloride" fertilizer.

(Too much chloride in the fertilizer will adversely affect the combustion of finished leaf.) Application rates should be those recommended on the packaging for tomatoes. A standard, coarsely ground, 10:10:10 (N:P:K) fertilizer will grow excellent tobacco. It can be added as a single application during the final tilling prior to transplant.

Liquid fertilizer and powdered fertilizer can more easily be leached out by rain. In areas subject to frequent, heavy rains during the first few weeks following the last frost date, these preparations could be applied with 2/3 of the total in the week *after* transplant, and the remaining 1/3 a few weeks later.

Commercially sold compost mixtures can range in their NPK content from a usable 0.5:0.5:0.5 down to a nearly nutrient-free 0.05:0.05:0.05 or worse. Their analysis should be clearly stated on the packaging. For compost to serve as your only fertilizer, the 0.5:0.5:0.5 preparation requires 20 times as much as the 10:10:10 fertilizer, by weight.

Each of my 60 square-foot tobacco beds gets about one pound of low-chloride 10:10:10 vegetable fertilizer. That would suggest that about 20 pounds of 0.5:0.5:0.5 compost would supply an equivalent fertilization. But that was not the case. Using as much as *two* 40 pound bags of high-quality compost (Black Kow brand, during my testing) did not match the growth of using a pound of the low-chloride 10:10:10 vegetable fertilizer (Southern States Premium Vegetable Grower). And hefting two 40 pound bags to *each* bed, then dumping, dispersing and mixing the compost into the soil is a labor intensive exercise, though the earthworms were quite happy with it.

My one experience with the low quality compost (0.05:0.05:0.05) was to note that it did improve the texture of the soil. Other than that definite benefit, it resulted in a tobacco yield similar to using no fertilizer for that season.

Specific sources of fertilizer chemicals may affect the aroma and texture of finished tobacco. The Robaina tobacco plantation in Cuba's Vuelta Abajo uses cottonseed as a common fertilizer, and claims it increases the "oiliness" of their prized cigar leaf. [I'm not convinced of that. Choices of fertilizer in Cuba are limited.] But preparations like fish emulsion do worry me in that regard.

The Oriental tobaccos of the hills surrounding Xanthi, Greece, were historically fertilized by the feces and urine of goats that grazed over the fields during the early spring each year. This area is the source of their famed Yenidje tobacco (Xanthi Yaka). While the urine directly contributes its nutrients, the pellets of goat feces probably require most of a year to fully break down. Regardless, Xanthi Yaka tobacco never smelled like goats.

Bone meal and various blood preparations have been reported by several members of the Fair Trade Tobacco Forum to attract wildlife that digs up the surrounding seedlings, apparently searching for food.

To my knowledge, none of the liquid "super" supplements that have been touted as having been "shown" to improve tobacco yield have ever been documented to do so in a controlled demonstration. Trying a small comparison grow is reasonable.

You can, of course, experiment with "super" supplements. But nearly every year, at least one new grower on the Fair Trade Tobacco Forum asks questions regarding the abnormal plant growth they are seeing, after engaging in trendy or creative fertilizer application. At that point, even with careful photos, it's often impossible to diagnose the problem without current soil— and perhaps fertilizer—analysis. Don't risk your first grow.

A safer approach, if you wish to experiment with non-standard fertilizers for your tobacco, is to plant some tobacco as a test group, and other tobacco as a control that uses standard fertilizer practices, to provide a basis of comparison.

Soil Care Calendar	
After harvest	Continue to control weeds. Plant a cover crop, if desired.
Early autumn	Submit soil for testing.
Before soil freezes	Remove all residual stalks and roots, to minimize disease and pest carryover through winter. This debris should be burned or buried, rather than added to a compost heap.
Soil thaws in spring	Till under any cover crop, before it has a chance to go to seed. Remove intruding weeds or grass. A garden torch can be used to burn and kill weed plants, but tilling will expose well-insulated weed seeds, and these will emerge later. Add lime if needed.
30 days before transplant	Latest date to apply glyphosate.
Prior to transplant	Till all of the soil that will receive transplants. Add fertilizer. For weed control, you can use a garden torch to burn any newly emerged weeds.

Setting / Transplanting

From germination of tobacco seed, a minimum of 6 to 8 weeks of growth are required to produce adequately sized transplants.

There are two conditions that must be met before transplanting into the ground (or an outdoor pot). First, the growth tips should be at least 6" above the seedling mix. Secondly, there must be very little risk of frost by transplant date. If conditions are unusually chilly, tobacco seedlings will do better if transplanted one or two weeks late, but into warmer soil, than if immediately transplanted into cold soil after the last frost date.

Your specific last frost date can be easily found on-line, using your location or postal (Zip) code. But also it is wise to check a two week weather forecast as the last frost date approaches.

Sturdier transplants will be more likely to survive insects and birds (which sometimes use tiny seedlings for nesting materials), when compared to undersized transplants. Previously clipped transplants will also have higher nicotine levels (against insect predation) than transplants that have not been clipped.

If your seedlings have been raised under artificial light, or if they have received little direct sunlight during their growth to a transplantable size, then they should be gradually "hardened" to sun exposure, by moving them outdoors each day. Make sure they are well watered each time. Begin with 30 minutes of direct sun, and gradually increase this sun exposure period by 30 minutes to an hour daily.

When the time comes to put the transplants into the ground, carry them out to the garden in their 1020 tray inserts. Mark the location for each plant with a dibble or a spade. Bring along a bucket of water that holds 2 cups per plant, and include a cup for measuring. If you plan to use imidacloprid to protect your tobacco from insect predation for most of the season, the time to add it is into the bucket with the measured transplant water.

Place a seedling into a hole deep enough to accommodate all of its roots. If some of the stalk base is also buried, that is fine. Return soil to the hole with the transplant, and compress it around the plant and its roots. Add 2 cups of water (that includes imidacloprid, if you are using it). This water, depending on the weather, may last the seedlings up to a week, but you'll have to monitor them. If, each morning, you still see a damp spot where you added the water, then you don't need to water them that day.

As you plant them, transfer your label stick into the bed. Craft stores carry "giant" craft sticks that are 12" long, which can be used to make an easily readable variety label for an entire bed. Mark them with a Sharpie *on both sides, and tilt the stick in the ground so that one side slants away from the sun*, so that it will be slower to fade. By the time labels fade, you will know the names of your plants as you walk past.

Check them daily for the first couple of weeks, to check for drying soil, and to note failed transplants that will need to be immediately replaced (from your extras). If a seedling appears to be cleanly lopped off near the base of the stalk, and you see a small, circular hole in the soil nearby, this is probably a cutworm's handiwork. Before replacing the transplant, dig down at least 12", and look for a silvery, segmented cutworm.

If you discover multiple missing transplants, birds are likely to blame. Once you've replaced the transplants, cover the bed with Agribon AG-15 row cover, laying directly on the plants, and anchor it with a few stones. The Agribon can be left in place until the growing tobacco is literally lifting it well from the ground. If you need to water a bed covered in Agribon, just pretend the Agribon is not there, since the water will pass through easily.

Purchasing Ready Transplants

Chapter 1 discusses sources for ordering tobacco transplants. While some commercial tobacco growers may offer a wide selection of tobacco varieties (compared to what a typical tobacco farmer would produce), it is best to contact them by mid-winter, so that they will be certain to have available transplants of the varieties you wish. In a pinch, most commercial tobacco farmers who can ship transplants will have excess plants, but usually only of the varieties they intend to put into their own fields.

The plants typically cannot cross national boundaries, and are not allowed to be shipped into certain states in the US. Check your local and state laws.

Only when they are ready, will they be shipped, and only after the last frost date for the grower's locale—so they don't freeze in shipment. They may be wrapped in paper (for holding moisture) and plastic.

Because the plants will likely be laid onto their sides during at least a portion of the journey to you, their stalks will curve within the packaging. This is to be expected. When you transplant them, orient them so that the *roots are pointing directly down*, regardless of the curve of the stalk. The plants will then reorient their growth direction.

A shipped transplant, roots down, stalk curved, shown after adding 2 cups of water.

Field Growing

The easiest and by far the most productive way to grow tobacco is outdoors, planted in the ground, relying on soil, natural sunlight and rain to provide the basic needs required by the growing plants. The minimum requirement for producing *leaf* is 70 to 80 days of a growing season, temperatures above freezing, and adequate sunlight. Water can be provided, if rain is insufficient.

If your planting soil is adequately fertilized, then your final leaf number and leaf size will approach the maximum potential for the varieties that you grow. If constant, stormy wind is a problem (as is the case in parts of coastal Ireland, for example), then providing a fence for a windbreak, or even a hoop house of netting or row cover, will end up being less work than tending to plants grown indoors.

Poor soil conditions can be remedied, as can lack of rain. So long as you anticipate in your growing plans how you will deal with insect pests, insect herbivore depredation can be easily handled.

Perhaps the unique risk to outdoor vs indoor planted tobacco is blowdowns from wind storms. In most locations, this is a minor nuisance, though, like all weather phenomena, rare, unpredictable events (hurricane, derecho, flooding) can spoil a growing season.

Potted Tobacco

Tobacco will grow well outdoors in pots. But seldom as well as when planted into the ground. The standard recommendation of minimum pot size is 5 gallons, but this misses the proper considerations. Tobacco produces shallow roots, which may go as deep as 1 foot, but usually are shallower than that. And they like to spread out. So an "ideal" pot for a full-size tobacco plant would be about 1 foot deep and 3 feet in diameter. Since many growers who utilize pots do so because they want to be able to move them during the growing season, our "ideal" pot is useless for that purpose.

Smaller pots will grow remarkably nice tobacco, but the tobacco is typically about 2/3 the height of field-grown plants of the same variety, with leaves similarly about 2/3 the size. An exception to this is a small Oriental, which will often grow to full size in a pot the size of (or actually) a coffee tub.

When potting a tobacco transplant for outdoors, the same soil considerations apply as for field-growing: adequate fertilizer,

Havana 322, gracefully maturing

Havana 322 growing in a Folgers coffee tub on my porch steps. The ballcap shows the size.

reasonable drainage, sufficient watering, pest control. The pot must have drain holes in the bottom. Monitor soil temperature.

Do not add gravel or rocks to the bottom of the pot (as is often mistakenly suggested) for improving the drainage. This does just the opposite. The amount of liquid water (the water table) within the pot is determined by the capillary action of the soil. So if there are rocks at the bottom, it simply raises the water table within the pot. [This is known as the "perched water table".] A pot with rocks just ends up being a shallower pot.

If optimum productivity is not a particular worry, then pot-grown tobacco can be just as satisfying to grow as field-grown tobacco. Just remember that you pay for the pots as well as the dirt.

Even with the added height of the Folgers coffee tub, the pot-grown Havana 322 is clearly shorter, and has smaller leaves than the field-grown Havana 322 shown.

Indoor Growing: greenhouses and houseplants

A full-size tobacco variety may range in height from 3 feet to 12 feet. A leaf spread diameter of 3 feet is not unusual. A fully grown plant may weight up to 10 pounds, without counting the pot, soil and roots. Many of the smaller Orientals will range from 3 to 5 feet in height, and have a leaf spread of about 18 inches.

When planning to grow indoors as a houseplant, or within a greenhouse, lay out the available space as you would for growing outdoors, allowing sufficient room for you to pass between rows of plants, without snapping off leaves. Only a large, southern exposure window is likely to provide adequate sunlight indoors, and even then, the pot will need to be rotated to prevent its leaning toward the window. Somewhat diminished light leads to larger, thinner leaves. Inadequate light produces a runted plant.

In a greenhouse, sun is less of an issue, but allowing space for aisles between rows may be a challenge as the plants mature.

Since tobacco is self-pollinating, growing it within an enclosed space still allows for production of seed. If more than one variety is grown within the same enclosed space, then the blossom head will need to be bagged to prevent insect-mediated cross-pollination.

Insect and other invertebrate (e.g. snail) pests in enclosed spaces tend to be different from those experienced in an open field. Snails and slugs can be a particular problem in a greenhouse environment, and insects that benefit from the absence of wind can proliferate in both greenhouses and inside a house. These latter may be identical to insect pest on common houseplants (whiteflies for example), and not typical of the insects that cause problems for field-grown tobacco (aphids, flea beetles, hornworms, crickets).

I will not explore the intricacies and nuances of artificial lighting for growing tobacco. The fixtures are expensive, the energy required is expensive, and seldom do the plants grow to average size. The rich flavors of tobacco depend on season-long exposure to lots of solar-spectrum light. While the nicotine may or may not be sufficient under artificial light, other pleasurable attributes of tobacco leaf may be diminished or absent.

Growing Tobacco

The Course of a Growing Season
From the start of the growing season, until harvest, a succession of tobacco pests may damage your leaf or even entire plants. See Appendix 4 for a detailed discussion.

During the first two weeks after transplant, inspect the tobacco at least daily, to check for failed transplants, missing transplants and those sufficiently damaged (say, missing the growth tip) that may need replacing. Once neighboring tobacco plants have spread their roots sufficiently, they will suppress the growth of any new transplants, often to the extent that a replacement transplant may remain as a tiny runt for the remainder of the season. So put in replacements as soon as possible. After about 3 to 4 weeks, it's usually not worth the bother of doing so.

For the first two weeks after transplant, most tobacco seems grow very little. Their response to the process of being transplanted is what is often called transplant shock. But healthy transplants will be working to extend their roots during this interval.

Previously clipped transplants will require less water than those put into the ground with full leaves. If you've clipped your seedlings, be comforted by the results of a comparison grow which demonstrated that by about 3 weeks post-transplant, the clipped plants appear the same as non-clipped ones.

During your walks of the tobacco, scan the plants for insect damage or other injuries that may benefit from some further action. Common problems during the early weeks are damage from:

> **snails**: Slime trails and topped seedlings or blanched leaves. Sprinkle granules of an iron phosphate snail bait, like Sluggo, over the soil, and remove rocks and other surfaces where slugs shelter during the daytime.
> **crickets**: Ragged holes in the leaf. Mow down any nearby, tall grass.
> **flea beetles**: Multiple pinhead-size holes. These are entirely prevented for nearly the entire season by using imidacloprid in your transplant water. Otherwise, you will have to inspect each damaged leaf, and hunt down the flea-sized, jumping bugs, and crush each one with your fingers. Get them early, or they will riddle the leaf with holes.
> **birds**: Although nesting birds may steal a portion of a plant or all of it, to use as nesting material, they also can otherwise damage leaves by pecking bugs off the surface. This latter damage appears as 'V' shaped holes. The only remedy for either of these issues is to protect the young plants under row cover.

deer and other grazers: Occasionally deer or goats (especially very young kids that can escape through fencing) may nibble a tobacco plant or two, before deciding that it tastes horrible. Mammal herbivores don't eat tobacco. But simply wandering through a bed of young transplants (with tell-tale hoof prints in the soil) may break a plant. Unless this is a major problem, it's usually not worth more preventive effort than a momentary regret.

moles: Lifted "trails" of soil. Moles don't eat tobacco roots. They excavate for insects and worms. The voles that roam into mole traces, though they do feed on plant roots, don't seem to eat tobacco roots. The problem that moles can create is burrowing soil away from seedling roots, causing the plants to dehydrate in the sun. Usually just tamping the soil back in place remedies the issue, though the mole may return. Trying to kill moles is often a futile effort. Moles are more common in a tobacco bed with adjacent sod.

poultry: Most domesticated poultry will eat small greens, like tobacco transplants, and should be prevented from having access to tobacco, until the plants are at least a month in the ground. By then, they will eat pests from the leaf, and can be helpful.

pets: Both dogs and cats are prone to digging up young tobacco plants. I discovered, when a fox raised a family in a nearby brush pile, that fox kits love to do the same thing. And an older fox will naturally excavate anywhere that it senses a mole beneath the surface. I offer no remedies, other than fencing and training.

Watering

Tobacco should be watered only with non-chlorinated (or de-chlorinated) water. Excess chlorine will lead to finished tobacco that will not burn adequately. If your only water source is chlorinated, then rig a metal or plastic drum in which you can allow water to sit out, exposed to the air, for at least a day prior to using it for watering. If you need to use a hose with this arrangement, then you will have to come up with a way to elevate the drum, and attach a spigot to it.

While transplants settle in for the first two weeks or so, don't allow the soil to dry entirely. But in general, for most of the season, check in the morning. If the soil appears moist, then you don't need to water that day. By the time plants are four to six weeks old, you can go by the droopiness of the upper leaves. It's common to see drooping late in the day, during mid summer. Rather than water at that time, check them again the following morning. If the drooping has gone away, then you can skip watering for another day.

Four weeks after transplant.

As the leaf approaches harvest time, you may worry less and less about the need for watering.

In historic areas of tobacco growing, during the average season, the tobacco starts with its two cups of transplant water, then depends on rainfall for the remainder of the season. Home-growers in other areas of the world may need to pay more attention to watering.

Suckers

Primarily, new growth of a tobacco plant occurs at the growth tip (the apical meristem) at the top of the stalk. New leaves are created there, and eventually, as the plant matures, a blossom head will emerge from the growth tip. Tissue in the apical meristem constantly releases a plant hormone, called auxin,

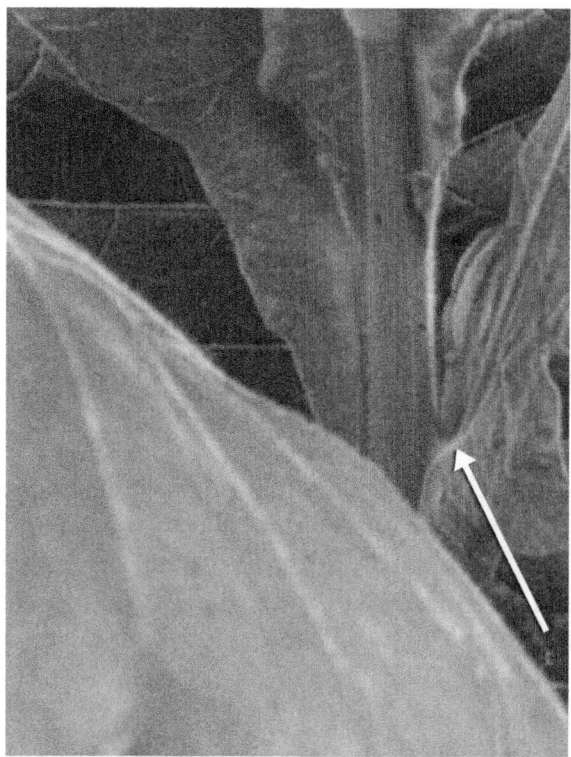

A secondary bud (a "sucker") emerging from a leaf axil.

which travels by gravity, down the stalk. As auxin moves down the stalk, it attempts to suppress any secondary buds from developing. [The effectiveness in suppressing secondary buds differs significantly from one tobacco variety to the next.] Secondary buds are common at the leaf axil, which is the point at which a leaf joins the stalk. They can also emerge from the roots. These are both referred to as "suckers". If suckers are allowed to grow, each one will attempt to create another stalk, complete with its own leaves and a bud head.

While having the one plant produce even more leaves seems like a bonus, the result is always that *all the leaves on the plant will be smaller, with lower alkaloids, and less flavor and aroma.* So suckers need to be removed, in order to achieve the largest and highest quality tobacco leaf. They should be removed as soon as they are large enough to be removed without damaging the main growth stem or the primary leaves.

In tobacco varieties with a wide leaf-to-stem angle, even tiny suckers can be easily pinched off. For those with a narrow leaf angle, waiting until a sucker is 1 to 3 inches tall makes removal easier and safer for the plant. If you wait too long, the sucker will develop a thick, tough stem (actually a secondary stalk) that may need to be clipped with pruning shears in order to remove it. Most suckers can be either pinched off, or snapped off with a twist of the wrist. With experience, this becomes a quick and easy process.

While walking the tobacco, looking for insect damage and other problems, get in the habit of removing any suckers you find. They can be well hidden. By scanning each individual plant from top to bottom or bottom to top, shift your head to visualize each leaf axil. If you go out to the tobacco with the knowledge that your hands will get sticky and dirty, then you won't hesitate to remove the suckers as you walk.

Weeding

During the first 6 weeks after transplant, the bare soil surrounding your tobacco plants will get full sunlight, and any weeds or grass capable of growing there will sprout and spread and grow, competing with the tobacco for water and nutrients.

With a flat-bladed hoe, you can easily scrape these away while remaining upright. This removes the weed top growth, but usually doesn't kill the roots, which will sprout again.

One approach to dealing with persistent weed roots is to wait until after a rain, before the soil fully dries out, and just squat beside the bed and pinch the base of each weed stalk, pulling its entire root system from the dirt. It's a lot of work, but those weeds will be gone.

Keeping the beds absolutely weed free is a pretty sight, but not necessary. Just suppress or remove them enough so that they are not impacting your tobacco. Once the tobacco leaves begin to approach full size near the base of the plants—by about 6 weeks after transplant, then the soil will be well shaded, and weed growth more anemic.

Topping

Topping tobacco is the removal of the top portion of the stalk. Don't top a plant from which you hope to obtain seed. But all the rest should be topped, *except for Oriental varieties.*

Topping has a number of effects. Topping removes the apical meristem, so immediately after topping secondary buds in the leaf axils will begin to aggressively sucker on most varieties. So expect sudden suckering. Topping reduces the final number of leaves. For the largest leaf, top low. To save the rich and potent top leaf, top higher. I usually top just below the "crow-foot".

Another effect is that the nicotine concentration in the actively growing leaves will increase, along with the fullness of the flavor. The reason Orientals are not routinely topped is because of the tradition of Turkish leaf to be as mild as possible, with low nicotine, and with smaller leaves (which bring the highest price per pound).

Topping also accelerates maturation of all the leaf. So an individual plant that is significantly less mature than its neighbors can be topped early, enabling it to catch up in maturity.

This Little Dutch plant has elongated its stalk, and is about to blossom. It can be topped now or later. Bagging for seed collection should be done before the first blossom opens.

When a bud head first appears, the plant still has a lot of height growth yet to complete. I usually wait until at least one blossom is about to open, to top an individual plant. For a large grow (and for commercial growers), topping is usually done when 10 to 50% of the plants have at least one open blossom, at which time all of the plants are topped.

For most varieties, the top of the stalk will snap like a celery stalk, and can be topped in the same manner you would remove a sucker. There are a few varieties in which the upper stalk is either too floppy or too woody to do this. If that's the case, just use a pair of pruning shears to top the plant.

Second Crop

Growers in some parts of the world allow a single sucker to continue to grow, so that, once the primary leaf has been harvested, a second crop can be produced from the same roots in a single season. Since tobacco is a sub-tropical perennial, in warm climates, the plants can live and produce leaf repeatedly, for years. Unfortunately, after the leaf of the first growth has been harvested, all subsequent leaf is of a lower quality, and is often a poor investment of time and nutrients and ongoing care for a home-grower. In a commercial production setting, a bale of lower quality leaf is worth a bit more than the cost of producing it (in low-wage countries), so the practice continues.

I have grown, saved, cured, kilned and sampled suckers from numerous varieties. Most of the finished tobacco from suckers ranged from mediocre to awful in quality. I believe it's not worth the effort, regardless of how promising some sucker leaf may appear as it matures.

Pests

In addition to the pests of early tobacco, discussed above, there are potential pests that tend to appear later in the season.

Hornworms: These notorious "worms" are the caterpillar stage of the huge Hawk Moth (*Manduca sexta*). In the southern tier states of the U.S., they appear in what are described as waves. In my location (southwest Virginia), the first wave usually begins in mid-to-late June, then recurs at intervals of about 3 weeks—so several waves per summer.

The moth lays its eggs at night, usually a single egg on the under surface of several nearby leaves, though they can also lay on the upper surface as well. A hornworm egg is a translucent, bright, almost iridescent green, and is the size of Abraham Lincoln's chin on a U.S. penny (~1 mm).

Hornworm egg & US cent

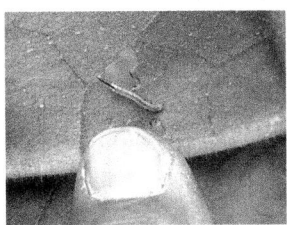

A newly hatched hornworm on the underside of a leaf. They can be spotted by identifying a small, smooth-edged hole from the upper surface. Just squish it with your finger.

hornworm on a cherry pepper

A voracious, fully grown hornworm.

From the time a hornworm egg is laid, it requires about 96 hours to hatch, depending on the temperature. Upon hatching, it immediately begins to feed, typically creating a small, smooth-edged hole through the lamina. As they grow, the divots of missing leaf become larger, while still exhibiting a smooth, easily identifiable margin. Hornworms avoid eating larger veins.

By the time a hornworm has reached its greatest size, it is capable of stripping all the leaf from half a tobacco plant in a couple of days. After that, it drops from the plant, burrows into the ground, and will eventually metamorphose into an adult moth.

A large hornworm, if simply tossed away from the tobacco plant, will slowly work its way back to the plant, from as much as 40 feet away—under a hot sun. Regardless of size, hornworms need to be crushed apart. For little ones, just use your fingers. For the big ones (You shouldn't allow them to get that big!), place it on a stone, and crush it with a second stone. They don't bite.

During prolonged rainstorms, a Hawk Moth may lay many eggs on a small number of nearby leaves.

Aside from manually hunting down and squishing both eggs and hornworms, it is possible to biologically prevent them from becoming a problem. A number of companies market preparations of BT (*Bacillus thuringiensis*). This is a bacterium that is harmless to humans, other animals, and even insects, but its ingestion is fatal to caterpillars of all sorts. It won't harm hornworm eggs, but once they hatch, and take a bite of the leaf, they die. BT is USDA rated as "organic". (It can be used on vegetables that are prone to caterpillar damage, such as cabbage, but the label instructions, as well as the minimum interval prior to harvest should be carefully followed. Since tobacco has many weeks post harvest to cure, the minimum interval prior to harvest is irrelevant.)

BT is washed away by rain, and naturally breaks down in about a week to two weeks after being sprayed on tobacco leaf. So it needs to be reapplied throughout the season, from the first sighting of a hornworm or egg, until harvest. It is not necessary to spray both the upper and lower surfaces of every leaf, but rather to disperse it over each plant. Hornworms eat full-thickness leaf tissue, so the BT can be on either surface.

Since hornworm eggs require around 4 days, from laying to hatching, you can wait a few days after a rain to spray again. During prolonged dry conditions, you can simply inspect carefully, starting about 8 to 10 days after the previous spraying, then reapply as soon as you see either an egg or a hornworm again.

In using BT in this casual approach, you can expect to find a few random, small leaf holes, as well as an occasional, small hornworm. But they will never become a serious problem. If you are growing prize cigar wrapper, then you may want to spray more thoroughly and more frequently.

Bud worms and army worms: These are smaller caterpillars. During the early season, bud worms may eat tiny areas of a tobacco growth tip. Subsequently, new leaves will develop from this damaged tissue, and show *expanding* holes, which are the result of missing leaf stem cells. So you need to find these early. The damage may appear minor at the time you should be hunting down the worms and killing them (with your fingers).

Using imidacloprid in your transplant water seems to have minimal affect on bud worms and army worms. But BT (see hornworms, above) is effective against these caterpillars as well.

When the blossoms begin to form, bud worms and army worms may burrow into the seed pods, and consume all the seed. If you don't spray with BT, then just prior to covering a bud head with an insect barrier, you should consider spraying just the buds with a relatively safe insecticide, such as permethrin. (Permethrin is what is applied to some clothing, in order to make it "insect repellent".) Do read the label precautions.

Budworms tend to be elusive. Search well. [NCSU]

Initially, budworm damage appears minimal.

Budworm damage after leaf growth

As the damaged leaf grows, it shows expanding divots.

Aphids: Flying, egg-laying aphids infest tobacco leaf.   They initially appear on young, tender leaf, either at the growth tip or, later in the season, on tiny suckers, and can be a nuisance for most of the growing season.   These are entirely prevented by imidacloprid used in the transplant water—until about the time that blossoms begin to form.   That late in the season, the imidacloprid is no longer present in significant concentrations (and seems to not appear in blossom nectar).

Aphids create three problems for tobacco.   First of all, the non-flying aphid offspring survive by inserting their mouth parts into the leaf tissue, and anchoring there, sucking the juices from the plant.   This reduces plant growth.   Secondly, their sugary excrement, know as honeydew, leaves a sticky goo on the leaf. This is not only annoying, but is hygroscopic (water attracting), and leads to localized mold in the curing shed. The final problem is that a significant number of dead aphids on a cured leaf can be a considerable bother to clean away, prior to use.

Aside from preventing aphids (using imidacloprid), there are several ways to deal with them. If you note only a small colony on one or a few leaves, then you can just smear them with your fingertips.

A second method is to dehydrate them using dish detergent. Add a squirt of dish detergent liquid (I use Dawn) into 4 ounces of water, and mist it directly onto the aphids. You've got to hit them directly, and there is no residual, preventive effect. It simply dissolves the waxy coat of those that are sprayed, causing them to dehydrate in the heat of the day. The detergent vanishes from the leaf within a few days (probably from its detergent action being consumed by secretions from leaf trichomes—hairs, and from dew and rain). The entire process must be repeated for several consecutive days, and will still be only a temporary remedy.

The spray from a garden hose can dislodge the aphids from their attachment in the leaf tissue, and wash them away. They won't crawl back up the plant. The spray needs to be forceful enough to accomplish that, but not so strong as to bruise the leaf lamina. To be effective, you'll have to inspect the underside of every leaf, and spray each individually. Again, this is only a temporary remedy.

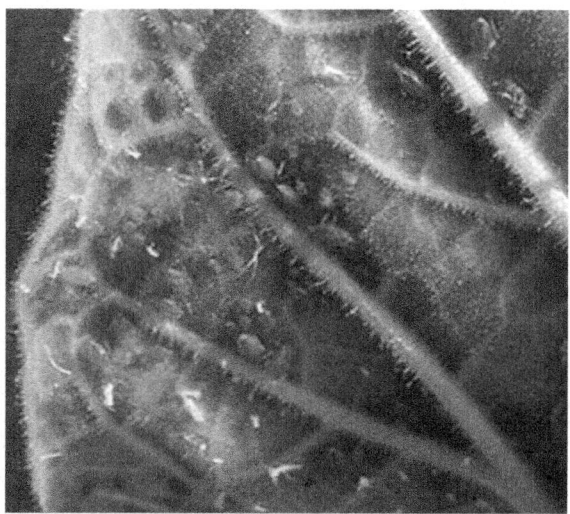

Aphid infestation.   *[NCSU]*

Later in the season, when the alkaloid (nicotine) levels are quite high, tiny, virgin suckers seem to be the preference of egg-laying aphids. If you keep the stalks clean of even tiny suckers, that will greatly reduce aphid populations.

Brown spot: This is a fungal disease (*Alternaria alternata*) of the leaf. It tends to be specific to particular areas of soil, and more of a problem in persistently humid growing seasons. Some tobacco varieties are highly prone to it, while others are more resistant.

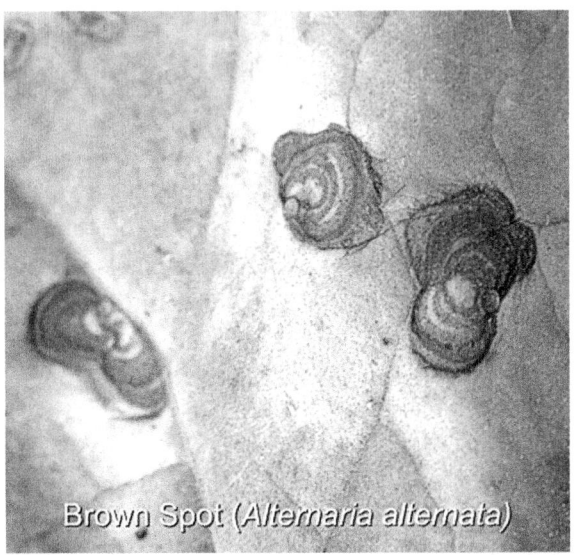

Brown spot shows concentric, brown rings, which gradually enlarge.

Initial infection and growth, from tiny spots of concentric, brown rings to large areas of leaf necrosis (death) is greater during humid conditions, while spore formation and dispersal occurs during dry spells. There is no treatment or prevention.

Viruses: There are a number of viruses that can affect tobacco. Though harmless to humans, these viruses reduce productivity of the plants, and can disfigure the leaf. Often, only a small portion (a leaf or two) of a small number of plants may be affected, though some viruses can dramatically stunt plant growth. Consider removing and burning any seriously affected plant.

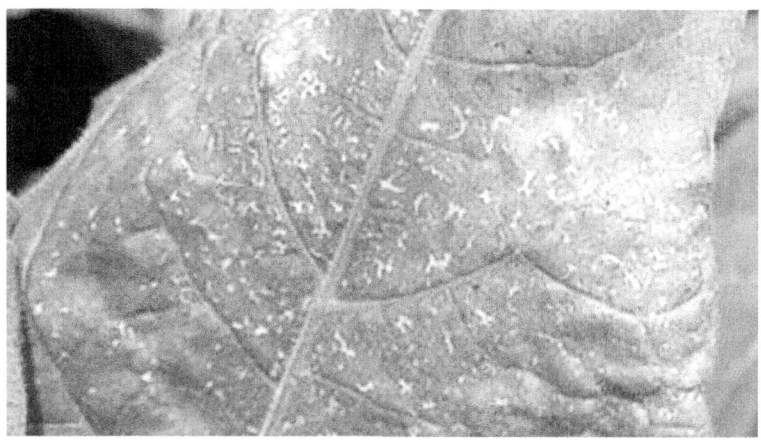

Tobacco Etch Virus [TEV] is transmitted by flying insects, and often spreads very little. Observe it, but remove the leaf or the plant only if it seems to progress significantly.

To identify specific viruses (sometimes not possible without a laboratory), consult IPM Images (see Appendixes 4 and 7). The more common viruses are Tobacco Mosaic Virus [TMV], Potato Virus Y [PVY], TEV and several others.

Nutrient Deficiencies

Among the many possible nutrient deficiencies that can affect tobacco, there are two that are quite easy to identify: Frenching and specific calcium deficiency.

Frenching: The term refers to a peculiar deformity and growth retardation that occurs at the top of an otherwise healthy looking plant. The new leaves form as narrow, pale and under-grown, with the lateral edges curling or rippling.

Frenching is caused by a generalized nutrient deficiency, which is often attributable to a soil pH that is above or below the range that is required by the roots to absorb nutrients from the soil. The nutrients are there, but the plant cannot access them.

Severe frenching. [Clemson Univ.]

Early frenching of Virginia Bright Leaf.

This should be a reminder to obtain a soil test. There are relatively inexpensive soil pH meters and colorimetry tests available from some nurseries and plant vendors on-line.

Calcium deficiency: Again, like frenching, this is often due to an inappropriate soil pH, rather than an actual deficiency of calcium in the soil. The visible sign is striking. Typically, the upper leaves all show a uniform cupping at their tips.

Cupping from calcium deficiency, seen on Shirazi.

Weather and other Friends and Foes

Friends? Yes. **Spiders** large and small, though they may be creepy in your tobacco, trap, kill and eat insects. The longer you can leave them doing their business, the more they help you.

Another friend is the assassin bug or wheel bug, which can poke a painful hole in your fingertip, but only if you mess with it. They use their saber-like mouth to puncture their insect prey, and suck away their juices. And of course, ladybugs eat aphids.

Junebugs and Japanese beetles: These rather inattentive bugs sometimes land on tobacco, and take a munch. But it's accidental. They just don't really eat it. You can flick them away, or mercilessly kill them, but it doesn't make much of a difference.

Wheel bug's saber-like mouth.

Flies, honeybees and gnats: These are unfortunate visitors to tobacco. If they land on the leaves, there is a good chance that the alkaloids from the leaf's trichomes will kill them. Honeybees typically do not pollinate tobacco, since they are too fat to get far enough to obtain nectar from narrow blossoms. (By contrast, bumblebees make a serious effort, apparently for the pollen.)

Hummingbirds: They seem to like tobacco nectar, and will visit tobacco blossoms about as readily as to a purpose-hung nectar feeder. I have seen them visiting year after year. A potted, blossoming Oriental placed on a sunny spot of your porch can serve as a delightful amusement for you.

Ants: The most likely reason you may see ants on your tobacco is if you have an aphid infestation. The ants collect the honeydew, as well as some aphid eggs, and carry them away to their underground nests. There is no need to do anything about the ants, but you should take care of the aphid problem.

Herbicides: Tobacco is a "broadleaf weed". It is exquisitely sensitive to contact with herbicides. After your transplants are in the ground, and throughout the entire growing season, if either you or a neighbor carelessly spray an herbicide, such as glyphosate, or use it on a day with even the slightest breeze, your tobacco may shrivel and die within a few days to a week.

Harvesting

Leaves on tobacco plants mature from the bottom of the stalk to the top. An immature leaf is relatively smooth and flat, with a uniform color over its entire surface. As it begins to *mature*, the surface becomes rough (sometimes described as an "alligator" texture), the coloration begins to mottle, and the very tip of the leaf begins to show yellow. Mature leaf may be a darker or a lighter green, when compared to immature leaf (depending on the variety), but the color always changes with maturation. Also, a mature leaf is more prone to breaking when gently folded, whereas an immature leaf will just fold. The stem of a mature leaf will snap off from the stalk with an abrupt twist of the wrist.

A *ripe* leaf is one that has taken on a yellow tint (or even a completely yellow color) over its entire surface. As a leaf becomes ripe, it becomes more brittle, and more subject to tattering from the wind.

Typically, signs of maturation may be seen on the lowest leaf prior to the plant's blossoming, but most of the leaf will not begin to mature until after blossoming time, or up to two or three weeks after topping.

Harvesting the leaf can be accomplished in three different ways.

Priming: Remove two to five individual leaves from each plant as they mature. These are "strung" on string or wire for color-curing. Often used for cigar leaf, as well as for leaf that will be flue-cured. This is the traditional method for harvesting all Orientals.

Columbian Garcia

Stalk-harvesting: Wait until most of the leaf is at least mature, then cut and hang the entire stalk for color-curing. This method is traditional for burley, Maryland, dark-air and dark-fire-cured, CT Broadleaf and various other broadleaf and seedleaf varieties.

Mixed harvesting: Prime the lowest leaves and string them. Then, when the remainder of the plant is mature enough, stalk-cut and hang the remaining stalk for color-curing. For a home-grower, this method saves the bottom leaf in good physical condition, while limiting the length of the stalk on very tall varieties, so that they might still be stalk-harvested, yet fit into a shed with a relatively low roof.

The reality is that, *other than for flue-curing*, you can use any harvesting method for any tobacco variety. I most often stalk-harvest everything, except the really tall plants, in which case I use a mixed method. My Orientals sun-cure *on the stalk*. My cigar leaf color-cures *on the stalk*. This approach works remarkably well, and is far less tedious than priming and stringing (and eventually un-stringing) all the leaf. The presence of a stalk also reduces the probability of leaf flash-drying green. Of course, for flue-curing, leaf must be primed.

Leaf Priming

Determining when a leaf is ready to prime (pick individually) is usually easy. When the very tip of the leaf begins to yellow, and the overall surface of the leaf is somewhat stiff and undulating, then it can be primed, with the expectation that it will color-cure reliably. If primed too early, then color-curing may be more difficult, depending on your temperature and humidity.

A mature leaf. Note the leaf texture and the lighter coloration of the tip and margin.

Stringing Methods

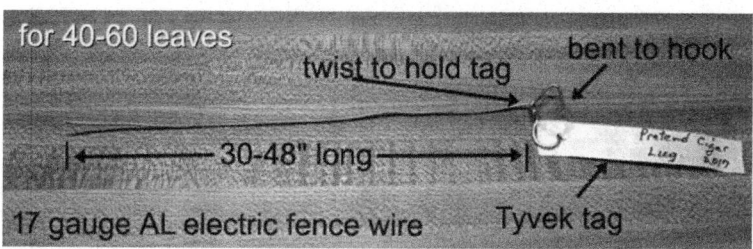

Primed leaf will need to be hung in some way for color-curing. A traditional method is to use a large needle to puncture the thickest part of the leaf stems, and collect them onto a heavy string. But using a single, 17 gauge aluminum wire is easier in both stringing as well as handling the strings later in the process.

I string my leaf back-to-back—front-to-front, with little or no added space between the stems. Since my beds typically contain 16 plants of a single variety, and I prime 3 or 4 leaves from each

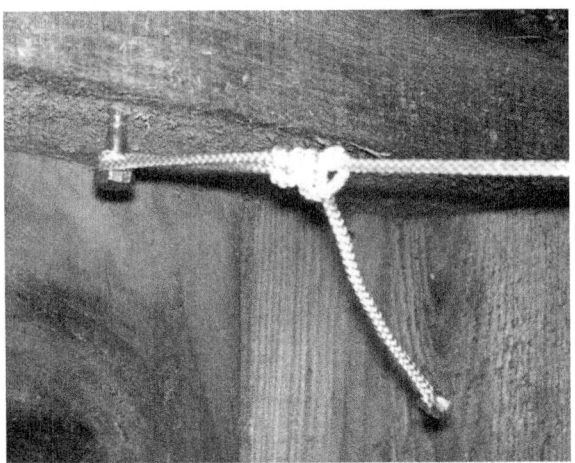

Braided nylon rope is tied to lag bolts anchored in the shed frame.

plant at each priming, I string 48 to 64 leaves onto a single wire. Each wire bears a Tyvek tag that indicates the variety, priming

A wire full of leaf, hanging on the rigged rope.

level and year. This tag follows the leaf all the way from the shed, into the kiln, and to its final storage bag.

My simple shed is strung with 1/8" braided nylon rope at the rafters. This rope allows me to hang both wires full of primed leaf, as well as entire stalks. The rope lasts for a decade or longer.

Stalk-cut

my stalk-harvesting tools
loppers
claw hammer
nails
Tyvek tags (pre-marked and pre-punctured)

To harvest every leaf at the same stage of maturation requires priming. But most tobacco will mature enough throughout the entire stalk to allow you to simply cut the stalk, and hang that to color-cure. The longer you wait to stalk harvest, the greater the likelihood that the very lowest leaf will become tattered by the weather, or otherwise damaged. Priming the bottom leaf, then stalk-cutting the remainder is a workable solution for that.

Deciding if the upper stalk (or entire stalk) is mature enough to cut is always something of a guess, unless you are allowing the entire plant to yellow (as is sometimes done with burley). If the very top leaves are showing signs of a thickening, undulated surface, then likely all the leaves below them are sufficiently mature. If you have primed the lower leaves, then the stalk can be cut immediately below the lowest remaining leaf.

With certain very tall varieties, I have primed the lower leaf weekly, until the remaining stalk would fit into my 7' high shed.

These 8' tall Corojo 99 plants show thickening and undulation of the leaf surfaces all the way to the top. The lower leaf has already been primed.

A large nail (with a Tyvek tag) is hammered at an angle, leaning away from the base of the stalk.

This allows me to stalk-harvest most of the leaf, which is considerably less labor intensive than stringing.

Each stalk is hung by its angled nail onto the rope.

Seed Collection and Preservation

With the current availability of pure seed for scores of different tobacco varieties from commercial vendors, you don't really have to save seed. You can just purchase each winter what you intend to plant during the next growing season.

If you decide to save your own seed (I save seed each year from each variety that I grow.), then you should bag the blossom head with insect barrier material, before the first blossom opens. A single plant will produce between a quarter and a half-million seeds. If you begin with a pure strain, then you need to bag only a single plant.

Unlike maize (corn), for example, which produces hundreds of seeds per ear, rather than hundreds of thousands, there is statistically no benefit to collecting seed from multiple tobacco plants of the same variety, and mixing them to preserve the variety. Even if you subsequently planted an entire acre from the tobacco seed, you would be randomly selecting a mere 1% of the seed from one plant. Pure strain tobacco is *homozygous*. That means that *there is no genetic variability from one seed to the next*. (At least, that's how it should be.)

Maintaining Pure Varieties

If you grow more than one variety during a season, then it is obvious that they may cross, and that you must use an insect barrier to prevent that. Not as obvious is that *even if you grow a single variety*, you should still bag the blossom head for seed saving. Unless you have unusually detailed knowledge of the gardens of each of your neighbors within a radius of 1/2 mile from your own tobacco, you need to bag your blossom heads.

Keep in mind that saving seed, cleaning it, properly storing it, then subsequently germinating it and raising a crop of tobacco from it is a lot of work to waste, if there has been cross-pollination of your collected seed. Bagging it requires only minimal effort in exchange for the assurance than the seed you save is what you think it is.

Types of Insect-barrier Bags

Because tobacco is not wind-pollinated, but rather is pollinated by insects, the material used to bag the blossoms does not to be pollen-proof, like the paper bags used in bagging corn ears. Any fine mesh can be used, such as organza, wedding veil mesh, no-seeum netting or even plastic window screen fabric. My own choice, and that of many professional growers, is to use a spun polyester fabric, which comes in various weights for uses as both insect barrier as well as frost protection. Agribon AG-15 is a lightweight insect barrier fabric suitable for not only blossom bagging, but also as a "floating" row cover—one which rests directly on the plants, and is easily lifted by them as they grow. Agribon AG-15 provides between 10 and 15% shade, is entirely water permeable, allows air to flow through, and dries rapidly when wet.

This size bud bag will accommodate the largest of bud heads. A small Oriental can be bagged with one that is as small as 15" x 12".

I purchase a roll of Agribon AG-15 fabric that is 118" wide (which comes folded in half). I cut sheets of it as row cover, if needed, to keep away nesting birds from plucking out newly transplanted seedlings. For bud bags, I cut a section that, when folded, will provide the dimensions of the intended bag, and stitch the top and sides (including a Tyvek tag in the side seam) on my sewing machine—three straight lines of stitching. Though pollen within a bag will no longer be viable by the next season, the bags get dirty, and should be replaced each season with new ones.

When and How to Bag the Blossom Heads

Ideally, the blossom head of a tobacco plant should be bagged after the stalk has elongated, and just prior to the first bud opening. If your bagging is delayed beyond that point, just remove any open blossoms, before placing the bag.

Remove any top leaves that may interfere with a snug tie around the stalk.

Remove some of the small, top leaves from the upper stalk. Spray the bud head with either BT (*Bacillus thuringiensis*) or with an insecticide such as permethrin, to deal with budworm eggs that might hatch inside the tied bag. Then roll up the length

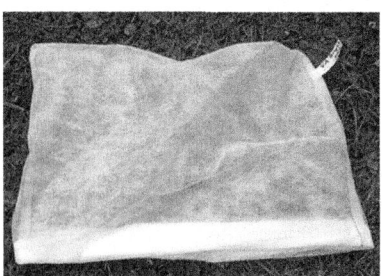

of the bag, if needed, to shorten it for the present length of the bud stalk—*but roll it to the interior*, so that it is protected from

stray pollen, and can then be safely unrolled, when more length is
needed as the stalk grows.

*Cover the entire bud head. Gather the rolled,
bottom margin of the bag about the stalk.*

Carefully place the bag over the entire bud head, so that the top
of the buds reach the top of the bag. This minimizes the wind-
sail effect of allowing the excess length to remain at the top. The

(usually rolled) lower margin is then gathered into pleats and
wrapped snugly around the stalk. This is tied in place with a
durable string. I usually cut 12" to 14" sections of nylon string,

and fuse the ends with a BIC lighter, to prevent them from unraveling in the wind.

The string needs to be firmly tightened about the fabric and stalk, and tied in a bow, since you will likely need to untie it to adjust the bag length by unrolling some of the fabric. The bag must remain in place for the remainder of the season.

Proper Collection and Storage of Tobacco Seed

When at least some seed pods are plump and brown, then the pod head can be cut and brought indoors. Leave the bag on it for some degree of protection against scavenging insects, like earwigs, which can damage the pods and eat the seed.

I usually wrap the stalk, on top of the string tie, with 17 gauge aluminum wire, and fashion a hook. I then cut the stalk just below this, using pruning shears, and hang the stalks (upside down) indoors with the wire hook. The bag still bears its Tyvek tag for identification of the variety and year.

My experience with hanging these still bagged seed heads in my shed was that mice were able to navigate the hanging ropes, chew open the bags, then eat everything in there, leaving nothing but fragments of dry pod husk. So I bring the seed bags into my enclosed back porch, where they are safer, and hang them.

Allow the seed pods to fully dry. This usually requires two or three months. Then, at my leisure, I can clean and store the seed.

The seed of *Nicotiana tabacum* is about 500 microns (0.5 mm) in size. To collect and clean the seed, I begin with a 5 gallon bucket (to catch debris) into which I nest a 400 micron, plastic sieve designed to fit a 5 gallon bucket. This sieve will catch the seed, yet allow dust and finer debris to fall into the bucket below. Nested on top of this is a 600 micron sieve, selected to allow the *N. tabacum* seed to fall through, and be caught by the finer sieve, while preventing any debris larger than 600 microns from being collected with the seed.

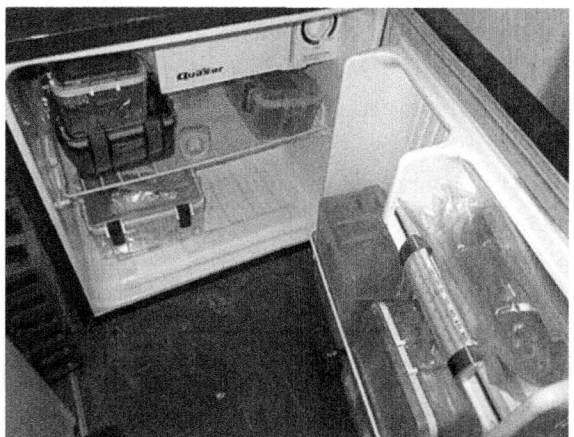

Small, labeled bags of seed, along with a bag of desiccant, are stored within latching dry boxes, in the little refrigerator.

I crush one pod at a time into the upper sieve, continuing until I have as much seed as I wish to collect and save. That clean seed is then transferred to a *labeled* 2" x 3" zipper-lock bag, which is placed into a latched, vapor-proof dry box, along with a bag of desiccant, and stored in a little "dormitory"-size refrigerator. Each box contains dozens of seed bags plus one desiccant bag.

The storage temperature is not as important as assuring that the seed is stored dry. [Studies in India have demonstrated viability of greater than 10 years for unrefrigerated seed that was kept dry.] Or course a very deep freeze (You can't afford the equipment!) will give you 40 or more years of viability.

If you grow many different varieties every year, and collect seed from each of them, then you should also create some method of cataloging them as to their location within storage. I have grown over 100 varieties, and sometimes have difficulty locating seed that I am certain I have in that tiny fridge.

Seed from *Nicotiana rustica* and some other species of *Nicotiana* *are larger than 600 microns, so the combination of sieves* *discussed above will not work for them.*

Plastic sieves (called "EZ-Strainers") are available from U.S. Plastics for 100, 200, 400 and 600 microns, sized to fit a 5 gallon bucket, each of which will nest within another one of the same or different specification. Metal sieves (or filters) are sometimes rated in U.S. Mesh, instead of microns. Metal sieves are available in a wider assortment of specifications, but you'll have to use a lookup table (for a specific manufacturer's product) to convert between mesh (number of holes per inch) and microns (the actual size of the holes), since the thickness of the metal wire varies.

Using just a simple piece of metal window screen will trap most debris, and allow the seeds (and anything smaller than the holes in the screen) to fall through to a container beneath. If you are unable to acquire a sieve, window screen will mostly clean your seed.

The fuss about cleaning your seed is because viruses are not present in the seed, but may be present in the chaff.

3. Curing and Finishing

Curing Tobacco

The word, "curing", can be confusing. Generally, when applied to tobacco, curing is the process better described as color-curing. A green, living leaf actively breaks down its chlorophyll, causing the mostly carotinoid (orange and yellow) pigments that have been there all along to now be revealed. The leaf turns yellow. If the leaf cells die before the chlorophyll is metabolized, then the green becomes a relatively permanent attribute of that leaf.

While chlorophyll is being broken down by the metabolism of the living leaf, leaf enzymes are also breaking down sugars and other carbohydrates, as well as albuminous proteins. Protein is made up of amino acids, and their break down (oxidation) releases the amino group as free ammonia. Technically, existing ammonia is not being "released" from the leaf, but rather is being created by the oxidation of the amino acids.

As the leaf slowly dies, its color transitions from yellow to brown. If a leaf becomes totally *dry* before that, then the leaf dies prematurely, and the active chemical changes of color curing are left incomplete. So, from the time of harvest, until the leaf has fully colored to brown, it should not be allowed to dry out completely. "Curing" should not be considered "drying".

For most tobacco varieties, chlorophyll breakdown and the breakdown of carbohydrates and proteins occurs simultaneously. So when "coloring" is complete, so is the primary breakdown of starches and proteins. [These processes will actually continue at a much slower pace for years after color-curing, since the oxidase enzymes are still active after cell death. We call this "fermentation" as well as "aging". Fermentation is primarily an aging process that has been temporarily accelerated by higher temperatures.]

The simultaneous clearing of chlorophyll together with starches and proteins is true for most varieties. It is not true for so-called white stem burley varieties, and for several other white stem varieties (such as the "Indonesian Besuki" sold by tabakanbau.de., which differs from green stem Besuki currently grown in Indonesia). The discordance between the two processes occurs because white stem varieties carry a genetic mutation that results in a reduced concentration of chlorophyll within the leaf cells. (I don't know if it is a reduced production of chlorophyll or an increased destruction of chlorophyll.) So these plants show a lighter green color to their leaves, as well as a nearly white-green leaf stem and stalk.

As a result, **white stem varieties** will color to brown *much more rapidly than they can clear starches and proteins*. These varieties will apparently color cure easily and quickly, but still need to be prevented from completely drying out for several more weeks, in order to allow the starch and protein breakdown to run to completion before the leaf is allowed to dry.

Once the leaf is dead, it can be subjected to freezing, without damage. The hazard at this point is if the three-day average humidity hovers well above 75% RH. Dead leaf held for many days above a relative humidity of 75% is prone to mold.

Air-Curing
This is the traditional method of hanging green or yellowed leaf in the shed, then leaving it there at least until it has color-cured. This usually requires a few weeks to a few months to complete.

For shed curing, the leaf can be primed, and hung in the shed on strings or wires. It can also be stalk-harvested, with entire stalks of leaf hung in the shed.

The advantage of primed, strung leaf is that each string usually holds leaf removed from a similar stalk level. So your tags for such strings can include the priming level (mud lugs, lugs, leaf, upper leaf and tips, or for cigar leaf, volado, seco, viso, ligero and corona).

By contrast, each stalk-cut plant will hold leaf from most or all the levels on that stalk. Stalk levels can, of course, be sorted later, while stripping the leaves from the stalks, but new tags or labels will be required.

There are two major advantages to stalk-harvesting for shed-curing. The first is considerably less labor than with priming and stringing. The second is that the presence of the green stalk will significantly slow the process of leaf drying and leaf death, which can be an advantage during hotter, drier periods of weather. Very tall plants (that is, plants too tall for your shed height) can be stalk-hung by priming the lower leaves, then stalk-cutting the remainder.

Historically, ambient conditions within a curing shed (or tobacco barn) were controlled by multiple ventilation slats in the shed walls. These were opened during the night, to lower the temperature and raise the humidity, then closed during the day to retain the nighttime conditions as long as possible.

Today, there are two methods for managing ambient conditions within a shed. Ventilation with one or more electric fans will help to equalize the humidity within the shed and among the hanging leaves. Without adequate air movement, enclosed pockets of high humidity, as one might find when several leaves are nested together, may lead to localized mold, even if the 3-day average RH remains below 75%. A thermostatically controlled window fan can also help to reduce high temperatures, by turning on whenever the temp rises above a set level. (I set mine to turn on above 70°F.)

Beyond ventilation, the only way to control humidity that tends to be too high is to add heat to the shed. Raising the temperature within the shed by 20°F will drop the RH by half.

Both of these solutions require that electricity be available within the shed.

In my relatively small shed, I have a box fan on the floor, tipped upward at an angle. This runs night and day, year round. And a dual window fan is activated only when the temp goes above 70°F. I leave my tobacco hanging in the shed from harvest time until the following summer. My climate in southwest Virginia is suitable for doing that. During the long winter, the humidity and temperature swing back and forth, allowing the leaf to continue aging whenever the temp is above 60°F and the RH is above about 60%.

Sun-Curing

Hanging harvested leaf or stalk-cut plants in the sun is suitable for Orientals, as well as for flue-cure varieties that will not be flue-cured. Most other varieties hung in the sun will not be able to complete their required chemical processes before leaf death.

A string of primed Xanthi-Yaka Oriental sun-curing on a clothes line.

Although traditionally, only primed and strung leaf is hung for sun-curing, I have found that stalk-cut Orientals sun-cure nicely, and are less prone to drying green.

The point of sun-curing is to kill the leaf after it has yellowed, but before it has consumed its sugars. This leads to leaf that is sweeter, and that produces a somewhat more acidic smoke.

In that regard, the goal is similar to flue-curing (a heat mediated, rapid curing method for flue-cure varieties, that requires only 5 to 7 days from green leaf to completed flue-cure). Sun-curing typically requires about 3 weeks of daily sun exposure.

Cyprus Oriental mw tops - sun-curing

These stalks consist of all but the very bottom leaf. A segment of 17 gauge aluminum wire has been twisted around the stalk, then wound over the clothesline.

So long as the leaf is green or yellow, it is not harmed by rain. But once some of the leaf has gone to brown, either those leaves need to be brought indoors if rain threatens, or the entire string or stalk brought in. Complete strings or stalks then have to be set again in the sun, after the rain has passed, in order to complete their curing.

Rajangan (Indonesian Shredded Sun-Curing)

In Indonesia, a uniquely cured tobacco, called rajangan, is often produced from leaf at mid stalk (while bottom and top leaf are usually simply sun-cured). The method, in short, is to shred green or yellowed tobacco first, then lay out the shred onto a mat to cure in the sun. In a tropical sun, this type of curing is even faster than flue-curing, though the quality of the results may vary with the weather and sun angle.

An American home-brew version of roughly the same method is to roll-up and shred green tobacco like a head of cabbage, then place it on the dashboard of a hot car, until it is fully colored. This approach is commonly referred to as the *dashboard method.*

The following four images are from Indonesia, illustrating the traditional rajangan method.

[https://mohdzawi.wordpress.com/2008/09/11/tembakau-darat/]

Rajangan: laying out green leaf.

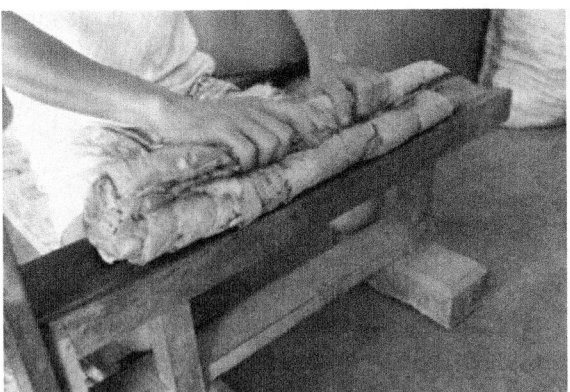

Rajangan: rolling the mat of green leaf.

Rajangan: shredding the roll of leaf.

Rajangan: spreading the green shred for sun-curing.

Fairtradetobacco.com member, *ChinaVoodoo*, explains his version of making rajangan in Alberta, Canada.

> *I used a flue cured tobacco [variety], Delhi 34. I picked leaves which were ripe, ranging from 20% to 100% yellow. I piled it in the garage for a couple days. I then sorted it, choosing leaves which were at least 80% yellow. I processed those, and left the rest to yellow for a subsequent batch.*
>
> *I frogged the leaves, removing about half of the mid ribs, only. I rolled them up into a cylindrical shape about 4" in*

diameter. I used the thinnest kitchen knife I had and shredded it by hand with said knife. It was about the same as shredding cabbage.

I used a 1020 tray, the 1020 basket insert, and the 1020 clear dome. I put the shredded tobacco on a bud bag in the basket, in the tray. I put some water in the tray, but not so much that it would get the tobacco wet. I put the dome on, and closed it's vents about 80% of the way.

I left this tray of tobacco in the sun on my lawn with a 2x4 leaned against it so the dome wouldn't come off in the wind. Every morning I would come and stir the tobacco. After 3 days, it appeared fully cured. I removed the tobacco after 4 days.

A month later, I weighed the tobacco and added water to bring it up to an approximate 30% water content. For example, if the sample weighed 100g, assuming it was already 15% water because it was in case, I added another 15 grams of water.

I then packed it as tightly as I could into a mason jar and put it in my kiln for two weeks at 131F.

[ChinaVoodoo]

As a sun-curing method, rajangan is likely suitable for curing similar varieties, Orientals and flue-cure varieties, and not well suited for cigar varieties, burley, Maryland and dark-air / dark-fire.

Flue-Curing

Flue-curing came about in the early 19th century, as an attempt to heat-cure tobacco (prevent it from molding during the curing process), but without imparting the heavy, smoky aroma that resulted from exposing the curing leaf to smoke of heating fires. The solution was to divert all the smoke of the fire out a closed chimney—a flue, which ducted the smoke-free heat into the barn.

Initially, flue-cures entailed about 3 to 4 weeks of modest barn heating. The perhaps apocryphal legend of modern flue-curing is a lapse of attention (around 1859) that allowed the heat within a flue-curing barn to climb to temperatures never before allowed during curing. The surprising result (according to the legend) was a barn full of the brightest, prettiest yellow leaf ever seen. This yellow leaf pleased all who smoked it, and brought the seller a high market price.

The fundamental task of flue-curing is to allow the leaf to mostly yellow, then immediately kill it, and dry the stems. Any apparatus that can enclose the leaf, raise the temperature in stages up to 165°F, and endure and vent the initial high humidity, followed by very low humidity, and can adequately circulate the air within the chamber, will get the job done.

For home flue-curing, the size of the flue-curing chamber should be adequate for holding one priming of your flue-cure leaf. If you put 30 flue-cure plants in the ground, and expect to prime 3 leaves at a time (typically at a weekly interval) from each plant, then your chamber should have a minimum capacity of 90 leaves at once.

The chamber can be constructed in any way you like (a can, a box, a shed). It will require sufficient insulation to reach the necessary temperature, without undue energy costs. The heat source can be whatever you like, so long as you keep the risk of fire in mind. You will need a temperature controller (digital or an old fashioned thermodisc water heater thermostat—a commercial one, not a residential one). The chamber must be capable of venting a lot of moisture during the early stages of the cure. And a humidity-resistant circulation fan is needed to maintain uniform conditions throughout the chamber.

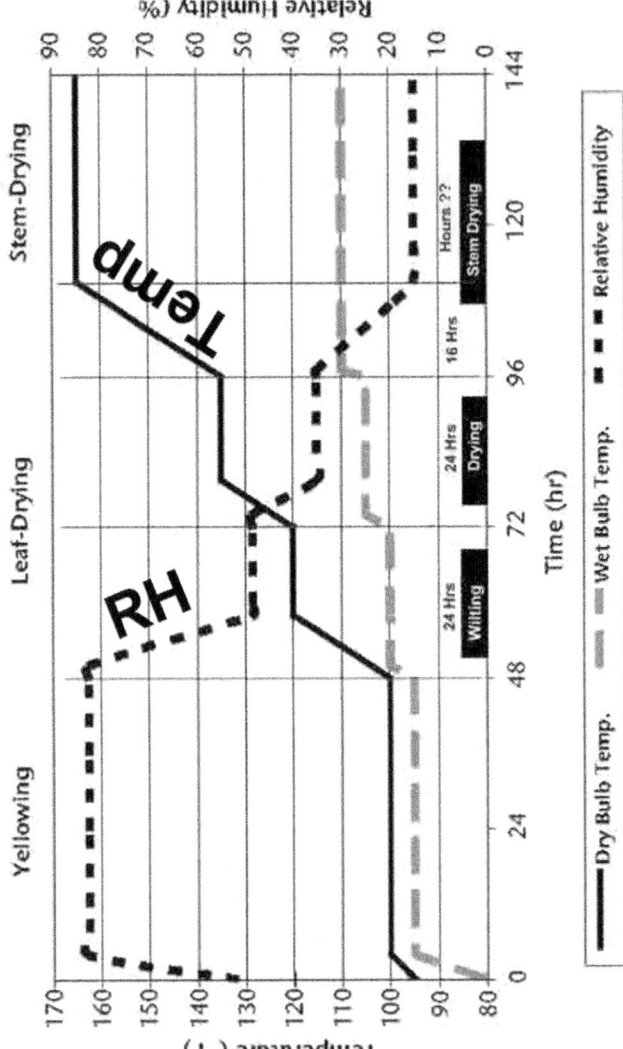

Most home flue-curing cannot control the humidity. By controlling the temperature along its curve (dry-bulb), the humidity will follow. The only alteration in the temp timeline is the duration of the initial yellowing phase. Upper leaf requires longer yellowing than lower leaf.

Leaf for a single batch is primed in a similar state of maturation. If some leaf is yellow, while other leaf is green, then it will not be possible to cure all of it suitably. So whatever stage of maturation you choose for a cure should be similar throughout that batch run.

Some folks systematically yellow their leaf prior to placing it into a flue-cure chamber. But you don't need to do that. Leaf of a similar degree of maturation is hung in the chamber, then the run is begun.

Begin the cure with the temp set to 95-100°F. (If you go much higher before the leaf has yellowed, then you may kill the leaf, leaving it permanently green.) For lower leaf, the 48 hours shown on the chart is about what is required to sufficiently yellow the leaf. The leaf should be *mostly yellow, though the stem and secondary veins may still be green.* **During the yellowing phase, you can briefly open the chamber to peek at the leaf, and judge its color from time to time. After the yellowing phase, you must never open the chamber, until the curing run is complete.**

As your primings work their way up the stalk, yellowing will take longer—sometimes up to five days. While checking the leaf color every 6 to 12 hours, hold the temp at 95-100°F until you see sufficient yellowing. Thereafter, close the chamber, stop peeking, and exactly follow the remainder of the flue-cure chart.

If you are manually adjusting the temperature during the required changes, a ramping rate of 2°F per hour is what the extension service experts recommend. But in a home chamber, the power of the heat element alters the chamber temp fairly slowly anyway. I have successfully flue-cured by making only two settings changes during each temperature ramp on the chart, at 6 hour intervals.

When a run goes from yellowing to leaf drying, you may need to open some ventilation, to allow the escape of moisture. For most home chambers, all vents will need to be sealed tightly in order to subsequently climb to the stem-kill phase. (165°F).

When a run is over, the leaf inside the chamber will be toasty dry, and will crumble if handled. Before removing the leaf, allow the chamber to cool, mist the leaf, then wait until it comes into case, before removing and packaging it.

A typical flue-cure season lasts about 6 weeks, and represents weekly leaf priming from the bottom of the stalks to the top. By designing a chamber that can handle both flue-curing as well as kilning, then the same chamber will find work to do year round.

CozyCan Flue-Cure Chamber DEMO
The CozyCan was a demo of the minimum chamber requirements for flue-curing. **It was only a demo. I don't recommend that you build this.** At the time that I built it, nobody had yet figured out how to scale-down commercial flue-curing equipment to be suitable for home-growers' needs. (At about the same time, *Leverhead*, a member of the Fair Trade Tobacco Forum, from Texas, was working on a 55 gallon steel drum flue-cure chamber.) Once those minimum requirements were determined, we could move on to building a more practical chamber.

[I include mention of the CozyCan in this book, only because several folks said that its simplicity inspired them to attempt flue-curing at home, using equally simple equipment.]

CozyCan is a 33 gallon, steel trash can. It was rigged with an angle iron bridging the opening (see the fire-cure chamber, discussed below), a barbecue grill thermometer, a 2.5 quart Crockpot as the heat source, and a mechanical (thermodisc) water heater thermostat. Since residential water heater thermostats in the U.S. typically max their temp setting at 150°, an "industrial" version (same price), is needed for this.

The water heater thermostat is attached to the exterior of the can, and wired to an extension outlet into which the Crockpot can be plugged in. CozyCan has no circulation fan, and relies entirely on convection to circulate the heated air among the loosely hung leaf. Ventilation is accomplished by setting the trash can lid ajar.

Each temp step along the flue-cure chart is adjusted on schedule by changing the water heater thermostat setting with a screwdriver. This is all painfully basic. The entire can and the lid are insulated using a fiberglass water heater blanket, attached using metal "flashing" tape.

CozyCan: A hole, lined with Tygon tubing, is cut into the can side, near the bottom of the can, for passing the Crockpot electric cord to the exterior. The industrial, water heater thermostat (black rectangle) is covered in the right photo by an open overlap of the water heater blanket, so it can still be accessed, using a screwdriver, to change the temp setting.

Since the yellowing phase of flue-curing requires a temp of 95-100°F, and the water heater thermostat was not capable of being set that low, two 17 watt seedling heat mats were placed around the bottom interior for yellowing, then removed prior to raising the temp for the next phase.

After two and a half years of using CozyCan for both flue-curing as well as kilning (constantly high humidity) during the rest of the year, the galvanized bottom of CozyCan rusted away. CozyCan was laid to rest at the local dump.

Fire-Curing

Going as far back as colonial days, small, open fires on the dirt floor of the curing shed were used, only when needed, to prevent color-curing tobacco from molding if the humidity was too high for more than a few days. There was no science to it, and no goal other than to color-cure the tobacco. In certain growing regions in the British North American colonies, this was a more common practice than in others. Of course, local wood was used for the fires. Eventually, the smoky aroma of "firing" with particular wood became associated with the cured tobacco of those growing regions, and became an expected character of them.

Today, marketed fire-cured tobacco is cured in barns specifically designed for fire-curing. The woods of white oak and black oak are most often used. One or more rows of small planks of wood are laid onto the dirt floor of the barn, and covered with a thick layer of oak sawdust. Then the row is ignited at one end, and allowed to slowly smolder its way through the covering layer of sawdust, toward the other end of the row, taking many hours to do so. When greater heat is required, both ends of a row (or of each row) are ignited at the same time, and burn toward the middle.

The vents of the fire-curing barn are manipulated to increase or decrease the humidity allowed into the barn between each firing. Ideally, for the final finish, the leaf is allowed to go into a higher case, so that more smoke particles will adhere to them—to get just the desired "finish". The process of firing goes on for about 3 weeks.

This method is not a practical approach for most small-scale home-growers. Instead, a small smoke shed, or a common smoker (used for smoking meat , fish or cheese) can be rigged in such a way that a relatively small batch of tobacco can be fire-cured.

The example below is a demonstration of such an arrangement. For the actual smoke chamber, it uses a 33 gallon, galvanized steel trash can positioned on top of a cylindrical, Brinkmann Smoker.

Holes are drilled into the bottom of the can. On the top land of the can (below where the can's lid rests), a hex bolt is attached on opposite sides of the can, with fender washers both inside and outside the can, and a pair of hex nuts tightened on them. These bolts serve as the supports for a piece of perforated angle iron that is cut exactly to the inside radius of the can at that level. The angle iron is removable, and provides a way to hang leaf within the can.

Grill thermometer.

A barbecue grill thermometer is attached through a hole drilled below the level of the angle iron. This allows monitoring of the temperature near the top of the can.

A small fire is ignited within the fire pan at the bottom of the Brinkmann smoker, then, instead of the lid that comes with the smoker, the steel trash can is placed atop the smoker barrel, and the trash can's lid is put on, slightly ajar. The two handles of the trash can are firmly tethered to the ground with bungee cords that are attached to 12" steel stakes, to prevent the tall assembly from toppling in a wind gust.

A typical, small fire will bring the temperature in the can up to about 130 to 140°F, and will slowly burn for about 1 to 2 hours. Two firings a day, for about 3 weeks, is sufficient to yield fire-cured tobacco, so long as you begin with fully yellowed leaf. But how long you fire the leaf is entirely your own preference for the result you hope to achieve.

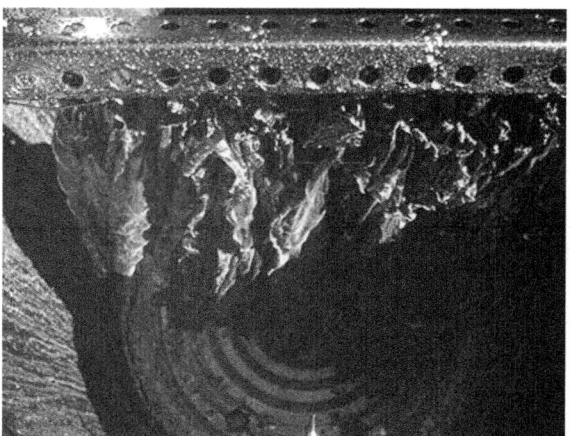

Leaf after 4 weeks of firing.

Each time the fire needs to be tended, the bungee cords are unhooked, then trash can is lifted off, and placed to the side. The barrel of the Brinkmann is removed as well. As soon as the fire is restarted, then both are replaced, and the bungee cords reattached.

After building the wood for a fire, complete with tinder and kindling and the main wood pieces, I ignite it using a propane garden torch. I've found that using the torch avoids a lot of burned fingertips.

Multiple wire strings of leaf can be hung from the angle iron, or you can hang stalks that are short enough to not touch the bottom of the can.

Your selection of wood can be whatever you like. Oak will give you a more typical fire-cured aroma. Hickory, maple, apple, mesquite, and a host of other firing wood choice will impart their unique character to the fired leaf.

Latakia

Latakia is fire-cured tobacco. The difficulty in making it in a location other than in the Mediterranean basin is that its distinctive scent, which is suggestive of a somber incense, and sometimes "soapiness", is found primarily in Mediterranean woods and herbs.

The use of traditional firing woods from the US, such as oak, hickory, apple, maple and mesquite create an aroma that is instantly associated with food or with barbecue, and is just not the right aroma for Latakia.

In Syria as well as Cyprus, from which authentic Latakia comes, the firing woods used are most likely scrub brush and the leftover stems of random herbs from the region, possibly acquired most abundantly due to their low cost.

Although traditionally, the variety of Oriental tobacco used in the process is a poorly defined "yellow Basma", the firing is so heavy and prolonged (at least 6 weeks or longer), that the choice of Oriental variety probably makes little difference. Whole leaf Latakia, if carefully hydrated and laid flat, can be seen as a Basma-shaped leaf with *no* petiole (lamina-free leaf stem at the base of each leaf).

Chemical analysis of the molecules emitted by true Latakia have not clearly identified its constituents. It is "cedar-like" in its general nature. This is not the aromatic cedar of the US, but more like Eastern Red Cedar, which is a variety of juniper. And it

Latakia Smoke Materials Source	Correct +Fragrance	Unpleasant or -Not Right	Availability
Apple Wood		--	
Ash Wood		--	
Bay Leaf (*Laurus nobilis*) [not Indian Bay Leaf]	++		easy
Black Tea		---	
Blackberry Cane (old, dried)	+	-	
Cloves (whole)	+++		abundant
Coriander Seed	+	-	
Forsythia Stem	++		abundant
Grape Vine (dried)	++		abundant
Gum Arabic		---	
Hazel Wood		---	
Hazelnut Shell	+	-	
Hickory Wood		--	
Honeysuckle [yellow] (*Lonicera flava*) Stem	+++		abundant
Honeysuckle [yellow] (*Lonicera flava*) Leaf			
Juniper Berries (from grocer)	+++		abundant
Lavender [English] Leaf	+	-	garden
Lavender [English] Stem	+		garden
Lilac (*Syringa vulgaris*) Leaf (dried brown)		--	
Lilac (*Syringa vulgaris*) Wood	++		abundant
Maple Wood		--	
Marjoram Leaf			
Marjoram Stem			
Mint Stem	+++		abundant
Oak Moss (*Evernia prunastri*)	+		abundant
Oak Wood		--	
Oregano Leaf		---	
Oregano Stem	+		abundant
Pine Needles, brown	+		abundant
Pine Wood	+	-	abundant
Pistachio Shells	+		expensive
Red Cedar [Eastern] (*Juniperus virginiana*)	+++		abundant
Rock Rose (Cistus ladanifer)			
Rosemary Leaf	+	--	
Rosemary Stem	+++		abundant
Sage Leaf		--	
Sage Stem		--	
Sweet Gum seed pod	+++		abundant
Tears of Chios (mastic gum)	+++		rare
Thyme Leaf		--	
Thyme Stem			
Xanthan Gum		---	

Materials tested for use in firing Latakia.

turns out that as a primary firing material, Eastern Red Cedar is quite compatible with the background aroma of Latakia. But its contribution must be supplemented by other, more exotic materials to approximate Latakia in its distinctive aroma.

Over a period of several years, I performed a simple test burn of the list of materials shown in the table on the previous page. Some likely candidates smell awful when burned. Others seemed like they offered an aroma that might contribute to a Latakia aroma.

The vague historical documentation of what is actually used includes:
- mastic (*Pistachia lentiscus*)
- Mediterranean pine—wood and sprigs
- Myrtle (not crepe myrtle)
- possibly Lebanese cedar
- "aromatic herbs"

While pure mastic resin (Tears of Chios) can be purchased, and when burned smells a lot like Latakia, it is expensive, and probably can not be justified as a major firing component for home-fired Latakia.

On a happier note, the stems of rosemary, when charred, strongly resemble the aroma of Latakia. And rosemary can be grown in abundance. Culinary bay leaf (not Indian bay leaf) is also a strong candidate, and readily available. This is also true of the prickly pods of the sweet gum tree, stems (not leaves) of mint, and whole cloves.

In home landscapes, lilac wood, forsythia stems and honeysuckle vine, when burned, give off subtle, compatible aromas, with no off odors. As for other herb stems that I have not tested, they simply need to be burned and smelled, to see what they offer.

Firing can be performed in a standard smoker, though it needs firing at least twice a day for a minimum of six to twelve weeks, in order to end up with black tobacco.

Using my trash can fire-cure chamber, the only modification that I made was to rig the removable angle iron with stiff, 14 gauge steel wires, so that multiple rows of leaf could be impaled onto them.

Wires for leaf, shown on the inverted angle iron, resting in the inverted lid of the trash can.

Finishing Tobacco

Sometimes tobacco is smokable as soon as it has color-cured. Usually it is not. It is "unfinished". Tobacco that has hung in the shed for a year has still usually not finished its primary oxidation tasks. One year old burley is notably better than at 2 months old.

The mantra for kilning (~125°F x 4 weeks @ >75% humidity) is that a month of kilning equals a year of aging. This is an over-simplification. Kilning is a forced fermentation. Fermentation is an accelerated aging.

My experience with cigar varieties is that after a year in the shed plus a month to 6 weeks in my kiln, only *some* varieties are ready to smoke after a few weeks of rest out of the kiln. Others may need another 6 months to a year of age (in low case), at which point they quite abruptly seem wonderful.

Cigar leaf growers in Cuba have opined that if they frequently sample fermented and subsequently aged leaf, many suddenly are perfect after 18 months of post-fermentation aging, while others need about two years or a bit longer. I have noticed that my Corojo 99 (original seed collected from the Robaina plantation in the Vuelta Abajo, the year before I first planted it) is delicious after a year in the shed, 5 or so weeks in the kiln, and about 2 weeks rest after kilning. But my Criollo (original seed from Cuba, via USDA ARS-GRIN) tastes quite raw at that point. After another 6 months of rest (at low case) after kilning transforms the Criollo to a wonderful, rich and flavorful cigar leaf. And both of these are from the same grow year, hung in the shed at the same time, and kilned in the same kiln run. I have experienced this in two consecutive seasons of leaf.

Aging

After completion of color-curing, most of the heavy duty oxidation of carbohydrates and proteins is done. The leaf begins to take on the aroma of tobacco, which it does not reveal before color-curing.

But the oxidizing enzymes (oxidase and peroxidase) are still active after cell death, and are, in fact, the primary agents of aging, fermentation and kilning. In later stages of finishing tobacco, especially during pressing or with the Perique process, microbes (bacteria and yeast) play a role. But during aging and traditional fermentation and kilning they do not.

Enzymatic reactions will occur above freezing temperatures, and below the temp at which the enzyme is destroyed (denatured). But the *rate of reaction is temperature dependent*. Significant oxidation of carbohydrates and proteins in tobacco leaf occur at temps above about 60°F, so long as there is adequate moisture present. As the temperature increases above 60°F, the rate increase is not linear, but is exponential. So at 125°F, the reaction rates may be 10 to 100 times faster.

The primary oxidase will denature at 149°F, and be gone forever, if that temperature is reached even briefly. Oxidase accounts for most of the oxidation activity. A secondary enzyme, peroxidase, is stable up to about 191°F, at which temperature it is also denatured. But peroxidase acts much more slowly than oxidase.

In flue-cured leaf (which reaches to 165°F or higher), the oxidase is gone, leaving only the slower, peroxidase to carry out any further aging of the leaf. Although we never know the temperature of the laminar cells exposed to weeks of sun-curing, its oxidase may or may not still be active. For both of these, kilning does bring about noticeable change in the leaf. So at least one of the oxidizing enzymes is still active.

Kilning vs. Pile Curing (Pilones)
A tobacco kiln envelopes all the leaf within the kiln at the set temperature (~125 ± 3°F) and its ambient humidity, and hold it there for the duration of the kilning—typically 4 to 6 weeks. This may be regarded as forced fermentation. *Kiln temperatures below 122°F risk growing mold in the constantly high humidity.*

Pile curing ("pilon" is the Spanish word for "pile"—plural "pilones"), as is done in sub-tropical and tropical climates, accomplishes the same thing. Despite the massive height and weight of the pile, it apparently serves only as thermal insulation so that the *center of the pile* is able to raise its temperature due to the enzymatic reactions within the leaf. These oxidation reactions release a tiny bit of heat. The pile traps that heat, and allows it to gradually raise the temperature. The weight (pressure) of the pile seems to play little role, since the vertical center of the pile reaches the highest temperatures, rather than at the bottom of the pile. A vertical cylinder pile is thermally more efficient than a square one. A long, rectangle is least efficient.

Tobacos Brasileiros 1977, showing massive square pilones.

Upon reaching the desired temperature (typically about 125°F), the pile is entirely taken apart, and rebuilt, now with the middle leaf on the exterior and the exterior leaf in the middle. The building and rebuilding is repeated until the spontaneous temperature rise slows. Even though portions of the damp tobacco in the pile are warm, but below 122°F, mold is apparently minimized by the airing and rebuilding.

Pile curing is labor intensive, requires a great deal of space, and is usually practiced only in sub-tropical and tropical locales. American growers who want their leaf pile-cured (for example, some of the cigar leaf grown in Lancaster, Pennsylvania) ship it to such a country specifically for that purpose, after which it is shipped back.

One has to wonder why kilning has not replaced the practice of pilon curing. In all likelihood, the energy cost and capital outlay of kilning such huge quantities of tobacco are simply prohibitive. Some commercial cigar leaf is kilned in Italy, for one example, in the relatively small production of Nostrano del Brenta cigars. My

Tobacos Brasileiros 1977. A long tube is placed into the center of the pilon, and a thermometer is inserted within it. The temperature of the pile is checked regularly, and recorded.

experience is that the quality of the finished leaf is similar for both methods of forced fermentation.

Pressing

Pressure greater than about 2 psi (pounds per square inch) can bruise and possibly rupture cells in the leaf lamina. The result is that some of the contents of the previously intact cells leak to the exterior, exposing them to higher concentrations of oxygen, and to ambient microbes (bacteria as well as yeast). Nicotine on the exterior of leaf oxidizes more, darkening it. Residual proteins and carbohydrates that become exposed are consumed by microbes, which leave their own reaction products—many of which are aromatic and durable. Some of the byproducts of these reactions are volatile, and dissipate with time. Altogether, this ensemble of effects changes the aroma, taste and color of the tobacco.

Pressing can be accomplished with whole leaf—either stemmed or left un-stemmed—or with shredded leaf. This can be done with a single variety or with a specific blend of whole leaf or shred.

In order to have some idea of how much pressure you intend to apply to tobacco during the pressing, you have to consider the width and length of the stack or packet. The thickness, so long as it is not more than say about 6 inches, will have little impact. For thicker masses of tobacco, its thickness mostly affects the time required for the applied pressure to be equally distributed.

Pounds per square inch (psi) are computed using a simple formula. Applied weight (in pounds) is divided by the area (in square inches). The area is simply the length times the width (both in inches) of the *upper surface* of the stack or packet of tobacco.

$$psi = \text{applied weight} \div (\text{length x width})$$

Using this formula will help you decide on a suitable length and width of your stack or packet, for a given applied weight. Keep in mind that the psi decreases significantly, as you increase the length and width of the stack to be pressed.

As an example, a 5 gallon bucket filled with water will weigh roughly 40 pounds. That sounds like plenty of weight to get over 2 psi. But applying that directly to a stack that has a surface of 6" x 6" (36 square inches) means that you will be applying only a smidgen over 1 psi. By contrast, a stack that is only 3" x 4" (12 square inches) will bring that up to 3.33 psi.

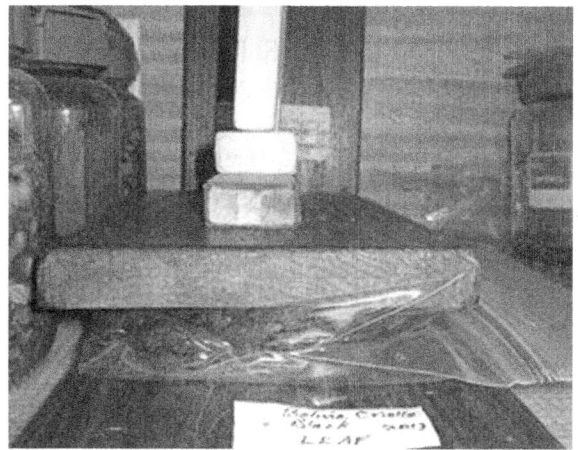

Pressing in a folded, open, freezer Ziploc bag.

This formula works for *applied weight*. If you use a lever-arm press, like a cheese press, then the fulcrum position, "piston" position and length of the lever will modify the actual weight to provide a greater or lesser *applied weight*. Without using math, you can easily determine the applied weight from a lever-arm press by placing a bathroom scale beneath the "piston" at various positions, and with various weights, to directly measure the *applied weight* in different scenarios. Write these down.

Typically, pressing needs to be performed with leaf in at least medium case, and to continue for at least 3 weeks to achieve meaningful changes in the tobacco. During that time, it's perfectly safe to interrupt the process from time to time, in order to smell the leaf and visually inspect it for desired changes. If your intent is to have the layers of tobacco adhere firmly together *after pressing and subsequent slicing*, then you may wish to apply an adherent casing solution to the leaf or shred prior to pressing.

Lever-arm cheese press.

A container for pressing leaf can be a sturdy, tightly constructed, wooden box, or as simple as a freezer Ziploc bag (folded over, and left "unzipped"). Given the fairly minimal pressure ranges used for pressing (except for the Perique method), there is not much lateral force applied to the container. When using cased (sticky) tobacco within a wooden pressing box, first line the box with bakers' parchment (available at grocery stores) before placing the cased tobacco into it.

Another approach is to roll the intended blend into a "cigar", and press that inside a tightly rolled freezer Ziploc bag. When pressing is completed, the "cigar" can then be sliced into square coins.

Perique (Pressure) Method

The perique method of pressure curing is a unique pressing arrangement in which tobacco is pressed beneath very high pressure—at least 5 to 30 psi, while being *blocked off from air by a liquid seal*. This requires a liquid-tight container capable of withstanding considerable side-pressure. The pressure and liquid seal are maintained for a minimum of three months.

Perique processed tobacco is a deep brown, with a prune-like, fruity, and somewhat barnyard aroma. It's smoke is more alkaline than other preparations of tobacco, allowing nicotine to be significantly absorbed from the mouth and nasopharynx. The nicotine content of the perique itself depends entirely on the variety of tobacco chosen, and the stalk level on which it grew.

Since the deep coloration of finished perique requires air exposure, for oxidation of the nicotine-rich juice squeezed out of its cells, all of the leaf is brought out of the pressing container after several weeks, and spread out to air for at least 15 minutes, before being re-packed, and the liquid seal restored. This may be repeated at intervals of weeks to months.

The process begins with fully yellowed (or even fully color-cured) leaf, that may or may not be stemmed. Thoroughly moistened leaf is firmly packed into the pressing container. A close-fitting follower covers the top surface of the leaf, then pressure is

*A home perique press. This $20 clamp can exert 400 pounds.
The container is an acrylic canister with its lid removed. The
follower is from a cylindrical cheese mold.*

applied. The pressure can be most easily applied at home using a
carpentry clamp with a twist handle for tightening. The exact
pressure applied is not particularly critical, but it must be
sufficient to squeeze out any air pockets, and to crush the leaf
tissue. If this does not result in the formation of a liquid seal at
the follower, then a bit of non-chlorinated water can be added to
assure a seal.

To get a rough idea of how much pressure a clamp is applying, use it to clamp a bathroom scale. For a 40 square inch surface of tobacco (approximately what you have using a 4" diameter cylindrical container), you will need to get between 150 and 200 pounds exerted by your clamp. That is not too demanding on a screw threaded clamp.

A wall-mounted lever-arm press can be used. You'll have to calculate the surface area and the required *applied weight* required to get above 3 psi. Keep the radius of the container small enough so that the *applied weight* is not so high as to cause the wall mount to lift your wall from the floor.

up force on the wall = down force on the leaf

You can certainly use a hydraulic jack or a shop press to apply the pressure, but these are capable of exerting truly massive pressure on a relatively small container, and may result in a consolidated, rock-hard puck of tobacco that can be cut only with a band saw. So if you use this kind of press or jack, be exceedingly gentle in applying the pressure. As a reference, the large, oak barrels used in making Perique in St. James Parish, Louisiana can be adequately pressed with a 3 to 5 ton jack or press. (They rely on massive timber framing to prevent the multiple jacks atop multiple barrels from ripping the building from its foundations.)

The primary microbe that transforms tobacco into perique is the yeast, *Pichia anomala*. It is fairly ubiquitous, and does not need to be intentionally introduced. Although it can grow in the presence of oxygen, it needs a relatively oxygen-free environment in order to dominate the random microbes that will also grow. It also is most effective in temperatures between 50 and 70°F. Below that temp, its action will take a very long time. Above that, the common bacterium, *E. coli*, will dominate, and create a fecal aroma that takes a long time to mostly dissipate.

Under the most ideal conditions, the pressed leaf will initially begin to stink, with a fecal aroma, but within a few weeks, the aroma will evolve to a deep, prune-like, fruity aroma.

After at least 3 months, during which you have removed and aired the leaf at least once or twice, and properly re-packed it, you can proclaim it "done". The finished perique can be stored soggy wet in well-sealed, doubled Ziploc freezer bags in the refrigerator for at least a year, with only a bit of additional, visible yeast growth possibly appearing on the surface. The double bagging is to prevent the perique aroma from permeating the refrigerator. It can also be stored indefinitely, soggy wet at room temperature, within a vacuum-sealed bag, like a FoodSaver bag.

Alternatively, you can spread out the leaf to mostly dry, then roll it into "cigars", and hand shred it. In low case, the shred will store indefinitely at room temperature, and also be readily available for blending.

Cavendish Method
Cavendish processed tobacco is cooked tobacco. The process reduces harshness, mellows aromas, and converts all but cigar leaf into a wonderful pipe-blending ingredient.

The simplest method for making Cavendish is to frog-leg the leaf, then pack it moist (not soaking wet) into one or more canning jars, like a Mason jar. The jar is then capped with a fresh, metal lid and a ring. This is put into a pressure cooker, and cooked at 15 psi (sea level) for about 5 to 8 hours. You may need to place a weight, such as a large, ceramic dinner plate, on top, to prevent the jar(s) from floating. The actual timing is not critical.

When done, allow the jar to cool. If you leave the seal unbroken, then it will store this way indefinitely, since the contents have been sterilized. Once you open it, the leaf should all be removed, and spread to dry to low case, prior to storing. Often, the color will darken significantly with exposure to air. But if you dry it down sufficiently to prevent mold, its final color *will not be black, but rather a shade of brown.* (Commercial black Cavendish is kept black and eternally squishy by the addition of mildly anti-microbial glycerin or propyleneglycol (PG), which adversely impacts both aroma and burn characteristics. (And some individuals can taste the presence of PG.)

Stemming

Tobacco stem burns as well as tobacco leaf lamina, but its nicotine content is lower. Cigars can be made sturdier with the inclusion of the thinner segment of stem on frog-legged filler leaf. Finely milled stem is sometimes used in making various smokeless preparations. The methods of stemming are discussed in the chapter on cigars.

Stoving Methods

"Stoved tobacco" means different things to different commercial manufacturers. It can mean toasting in a heated, rotating drum, dry heating between steam-heated press plates, steaming between press plates or even just gentle warming in a heated container.

One brand of cigarettes famously toasted its burley component at a high enough temperature to cause mild caramelization, which browns and burns some sugars (which are already minimal in burley). Others have used a somewhat lower temperature to bring about a Maillard reaction, which alters certain amino acids, thereby changing the smoking aroma.

For attempting stoving at home, you can spread shredded leaf onto a cookie sheet, and toast it lightly in the oven or toaster oven. Some recommend misting it with water or a casing mixture, and heating it only until the shred is once again dry, then repeating this several times.

Another approach might be a sealed jar of damp or totally dry tobacco that is simmered in a hot water bath for a few hours.

Twist

This is another method of pressing. Either partly yellowed leaf or color-cured leaf is moistened, then added to a spindle that continuously twists it into a tightly wound rope, and accumulates the rope around a spool or drum of some kind. The tobacco rope is left tightly twisted for several months, yielding tobacco that is dark brown to black. For use, a segment of the rope is sliced into coins, which are then rubbed-out for packing into a pipe or rolled into cigarette paper. The method is illustrated in the chapter on Pipe Tobacco.

Press Cake, Crumble Cake and Roll Cake

As the names suggest, these pressing methods differ only in the form of tobacco that is assembled for pressing, or the shape. These are discussed in detail in the chapter on Pipe Tobacco.

Press Cake consists of whole leaves (either stemmed or not) or rectangles of leaves that are layered, then pressed into a plank of tobacco. The leaf is comprised of all the components of a blend, in their proper ratio, and may be layered to a desired color pattern. If the ultimate goal is to create well adhered flakes, then a sticky casing must be applied as the leaf is layered. After weeks or months of pressing, the plank is cut into long, 1 to 2 inch wide bars, called plug. These can be sliced to produce flake, and the flake can conveniently be rubbed-out to a shred. Light rubbing of well adhered flake produces what is known as "Cavendish cut".

Crumble Cake is created in much the same manner as press cake, but begins with shredded, blended tobacco. It is most often used to prevent a blend of disparate particle sizes from separating during storage. For use, a corner of the plank of crumble cake is broken off, then crumbled into a pipe bowl. Latakia blends with greater than 50% Latakia are sometimes sold as crumble cake.

Roll Cake is actually just a very tightly rolled "cigar" of whole leaves that comprise a tobacco blend in its desired ratio. In a sense, it can be considered a long filler cigar of a pipe blend that is rolled too tightly to smoke. After weeks to months in this state, perhaps undergoing stoving along the way, the "cigar" is sliced into coins, for use. For well formed coins, a casing must be applied to the leaf prior to rolling. For home production, a large ring-gauge cigar clipper or a tuck cutter can cleanly slice the coins. For somewhat sloppier coins, the "cigar" can be simply sliced with a knife or chaveta.

Tying a Sailor's "Perique" Carotte

This is not the same as the perique pressure cure, which is carried out under pressure, beneath a water seal. Instead, this is a method developed by sailors during the age of sail, for finishing and preserving tobacco for personal use, over the duration of a long sea voyage. Although the method is known to Western historians as a method which sailors adapted from carottes of tobacco sold during colonial times from the French colonial city of New Orleans (and may or may not have been perique tobacco), the technique apparently dates back to pre-Columbian times, perhaps by thousands of years. (See Andullo, below.)

Leaf that has mostly yellowed, or has been fully color-cured is laid out thickly over a rectangle of canvas. This is then tightly rolled into a cylinder a few inches thick. Rope is wrapped around the canvas cylinder as closely and tightly as possible, until the canvas is encased within the coils.

As time passes, this carotte of tobacco darkens and dries. It can then be gradually used by unwrapping the rope and canvas at one end, and slicing off a chunk of tobacco. (An image of a carotte is shown in Appendix 1.)

Dominican Andullo ("andullo" is Spanish for "plug")

The origin of andullo—a tied carotte for fermenting tobacco leaf—is lost to history, though it seems to be related to pre-colonial Hispañola (known as Hayti or Saint Domingo among the British colonists of North America). The tradition is still carried on at a small scale today in the Dominican Republic, by La Aurora Cigars. [www.laaurora.com.do]

Yellowed, limp tobacco leaves that have air-cured for about two weeks (harvested from the mid to upper stalk of the plant), are first frog-legged, then laid out onto a huge leaf of royal palm, and assembled to a length of 3 to 6 feet. The tobacco leaf is then tightly rolled within the palm leaf, creating a tapered cylinder several inches in diameter.

Rolling the andullo in palm leaf. [La Aurora]

A heavy rope is coiled once around one end of the cylinder, and tightly stretched the length of the shed. As the andullo rotates, and traverses the heavy, compressing rope, a thinner rope is snugly laid onto the cylinder, from one end to the other.

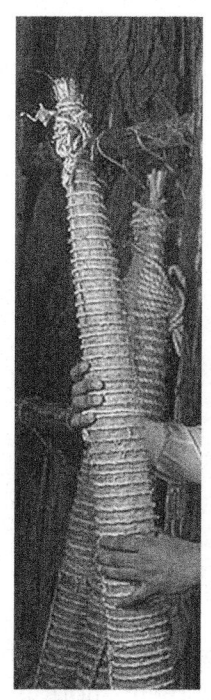

Pressing the andullo with a heavy rope. The thinner, wrapping rope is indicated by the arrow.   *[La Aurora]*

At intervals of about a month, the andullo is unwrapped, aired, much like airing in traditional perique pressure processing, then re-wrapped, tighter each time. After about a year of sufficient pressing, aging and airing, the leaf within the andullo cylinder becomes dry and rigid and nearly black. Tight compression is essential to preventing mold within the tobacco.

Andullo.
[La Aurora]

Common Problems Curing and Finishing

Even under the most ideal circumstances, things can go wrong during the curing and finishing processes.   These can be discouraging if they occur during your first attempt at making some nice tobacco. With more experience, you can catch them early on, or better yet, prevent them.

Problems in the curing shed

too humid or too dry: A hundred and fifty years ago, average humidity during the curing season served as a limit on the geographical areas in which tobacco growing was practical. [In the Ottoman Empire, it likely determined their most common method of curing—sun-curing, which in turn focused varietal selection on those varieties which sun-cure well.]

The typical air-curing barn in the U.S. during the mid-to-late nineteenth century depended on elaborate venting, that was adjusted several times each day—by hand, depending on whether or not the humidity within the barn needed to be increased or

Vented tobacco barn.   [Killebrew 1884]

decreased. Most often, an increase in humidity could be achieved by opening the vents more at dusk, and closing them more at dawn. Decreasing humidity required the opposite timing.

Vents might need to be closed because of blowing rain. The venting mechanisms were most often just hinges placed on the common planking of the barn sides, augmented with vents high above, and some near the ground.

Tobacco barn with horizontally as well as vertically hinged planking.   [Killebrew 1898]

Today, much the same adjustments can be accomplished with manually or digitally-controlled fans. But this only works if the 3-day average humidity hovers in the range of 50 to 75%.

In very dry climates, a humidifier can be used during dry spells or during the warmest temperatures of the day. Another approach to very dry color-curing conditions is to construct a "tent" of tarp or plastic sheeting—such as a drop-cloth, that is draped closely over the hanging tobacco, capturing some of its moisture.

If prolonged conditions are too humid, the most effective method for reducing the relative humidity is to heat the shed. Raising the ambient temperature by 20°F will drop the relative humidity by half. In humid conditions, it is especially important to circulate the air effectively within the shed, to prevent trapped pockets of higher humidity from allowing mold growth in those areas. Stalk-harvesting retains more moisture in the leaves, when compared to primed leaf that is hung on a string.

leaf won't yellow: For novice growers, the most common cause of leaf failing to yellow is harvesting leaf that is not yet adequately mature. Waiting until the tips of the leaves show a bit of yellow increases the success rate.

If the problem is that the leaf dries green before it yellows, yet has reached maturation prior to harvesting, then one solution, though quite labor intensive, is to layer the newly harvested leaf within a box, and conscientiously air and rearrange it at least daily, until it is yellow. Once adequately yellow, it can then be hung, to complete coloring.

As leaf begins to yellow, it releases ethylene gas, which tends to accelerate yellowing of that leaf and its neighbors. Boxing concentrates that ethylene gas, speeding the yellowing of all the leaf in the box. The risk, if not tended to daily, is that the leaf will mold or rot. Any leaves that have sufficiently yellowed within a box of still-green leaf should be removed and hung.

aphids: The risk presented by aphids in the curing shed is that they will proliferate on any green leaf, and leave a residual of honeydew, which becomes a site for mold. Aphids that die on the leaf, without leaving a patch of honeydew mostly fall off in the shed, and can also be easily brushed away when handling the cured leaf.

Aphids should ideally be controlled in the garden, rather than in the shed. If, at the time of priming a leaf, you see aphids (most often on the under surface, near the stalk), then rub them with your fingers, to kill them. You don't need to remove them, since they will mostly dry to dust during curing.

The greatest risk of introducing a lot of aphids into the curing shed is with stalk-harvesting. The preventive approach is to quickly inspect each plant for aphids, just prior to cutting the stalk, and rubbing away the aphids, to prevent them from being carried into the shed.

If you spray with sudsy water, just prior to placing leaf into the barn, there will be no rain to wash away the detergent. That may or may not present a problem. In addition, leaf is ideally harvested only when their surfaces are dry, in order to reduce the total water that is carried into the shed, since green leaf itself already contains a huge weight of water that will need to slowly dissipate. And wet leaf allows soil organisms to cause barn rot.

If, during the later stages of color-curing, you notice an aphid infestation, typically on the youngest leaf of stalk-harvested tobacco, you may as well just remove those leaves from the shed, rather than trying to cope with the aphids directly. Using any insecticide on leaf in the shed is not something that I would recommend.

A fairly common outcome of stalk-cured leaf is that, upon completing curing, and while proceeding to strip the leaf, you discover an occasional plant heavily infested with aphids (by now, dead) and their honeydew. This is usually just on leaf from the top of the plant. You can continue to finish such leaf, and clean away the mess as you go, though this is tedious and frustrating. My practice is to just write-off those leaves as a loss —at the time of stripping them from the stalks, and toss them away, never to look at them or think about them again. Honeydew that makes it through kilning is still sticky.

hornworms: Sometimes, when harvesting leaf, you miss spotting a tiny hornworm or hornworm egg. Within a few days, the egg will hatch. A hornworm in the shed will eat any green leaf, leaving large divots (usually in your best leaf), and will move from leaf to leaf.

You may or may not see the leaf holes appearing, and likely won't see the actual hornworm during a cursory check on the curing tobacco.

A sure sign of a hornworm is their droppings. With hanging leaf, either on strings or by the stalk, these hornworm droppings fall directly to the floor of the shed. They appear black, barrel-shaped, and the size of grape seeds. The thicker the dimensions of the droppings, the larger the worm. Although they are dry enough to bounce away on a wooden shed floor, their greatest concentration will be directly beneath the current location of the hornworm. Look for the hornworm there, until you find it, which is sometimes difficult. Remove it from the shed, and kill it (squish it with a rock), so that it does not burrow into the soil to pupate into next year's moth.

dealing with mold in the shed: Even with ideal conditions of temperature and humidity in the shed, a small amount of mold is not unusual, especially on the thicker portions of the more succulent stems. Most often, this does not progress onto the lamina—so long as shed conditions remain appropriate.

The first thing to consider is the temperature and ventilation of the shed. Maintain a circulation fan. If need be, heat the shed.

You can actively kill mold by spraying with 50:50 solution of hydrogen peroxide and water. If the leaf has finished coloring, you can alternatively spray with a 50:50 solution of distilled vinegar. In either case, spray only the affected areas. Vinegar on yellow leaf will alter the curing process, and lead to discolored patches.

A second approach is to remove mostly cured leaf from the shed, and lay it as a flat stack on a seedling heat mat, to complete drying of the stem. The temperature needs to remain below 104°F, and the leaf stack needs to be rearranged daily.

A third remedy is to remove the affected leaf from the curing shed, and frog-leg it (remove the thickest 2/3 of the stem). With any removal of leaf from the shed, be sure to keep track of the identity of the leaf.

Problems Sun-Curing

flash-drying green: Leaf that sun-cures green (flash-dries) will retain its chlorophyll indefinitely. So you want to prevent this from happening. There are a number of ways to keep the leaf from drying too fast.

With strung leaf, pack it closely together on the string or wire. Clear plastic sheeting (drop cloth) can be used to construct a tent, to increase humidity, as well as shield from rain. The leaf can be hung closer to the ground, taking advantage of available ground moisture to moderate the conditions of humidity.

Alternatively, stalk-harvesting and sun-curing on the stalk will slow leaf desiccation. On the stalk, leaf from the bottom of the stalk will complete sun-curing before upper leaf. (With the thickest portion of the stalk hanging upward, your fastest curing leaf will be above the slower leaf.) As the leaf progressively sun-cures along the stalk, you should remove those leaves that are done, before they can be tattered by the wind.

rain: Growing plants are rained upon all the time. That is not a problem. Leaf hung to sun-cure, either on strings or on the whole stalk, is not harmed by rain, so long as the leaf is still alive. But any leaf that has begun to transition from a bright yellow, living leaf to the duller brown of a dead leaf will be spoiled by any significant rain. Nicotine is leached away, and the quality of the leaf begins to rapidly deteriorate.

The simplest solution is to bring sun-curing leaf indoors, whenever rain is likely, then return it to its place in the sun as soon as possible afterwards. This can be a lot of work, and also requires somewhere to hang it in the shed or house.

wind: Sun-curing leaf that is closely strung is usually not harmed by winds below about 30 mph. Leaf on stalk-cured plants do not enjoy much support from their neighbors, and, once the stem dries, may be carried away in much softer wind gusts. These leaves are ready to be removed, and should not be left hanging on the stalk. Regardless of hanging method, if stronger winds are forecast, just bring all the sun-curing leaf indoors until it passes.

Leaf that blows off during sun-curing may still be worth locating and collecting. Even with fallen tree leaves scattered about, tobacco leaf usually stands out, because of its unique color and shape.

pests: Aphids, flea beetles and hornworms may appear on your sun-curing leaf. Just be aware of the possibility, and deal with these as you would in the garden.

Problems Flue-Curing

Every flue-curing chamber has its own quirks. You may need two or three runs to become accustomed to them.

won't yellow: Leaf that is not primed until it shows a yellow tip *will yellow* promptly during the flue-curing process. Leaf that is entirely green may require holding at the yellowing phase of the flue-cure chart for an extra day or three. Leaves from the lower stalk yellow more rapidly than those from higher on the stalk.

For a single batch of flue-curing, prime only leaf *of a single variety* and that is all at a similar stage of maturation. Otherwise, some will yellow, while others stubbornly remain entirely green. So long as the batch consists of a similar priming level, you can just relax, and keep peeking at the leaf, not moving on to the wilting phase until it has yellowed sufficiently.

finishes mostly green: This will happen if the temperature of the chamber is allowed to go above 104°F prior to adequate yellowing. This leaf has been cooked while green, and will stay that way. You have made candela. This process releases asparagine, which causes the aroma during processing to resemble that of cooking asparagus.

The remedy, before this happens, is to control the temperature more diligently. Once you kill a green leaf with too much heat, it cannot yellow.

finishes with some green: If you have minimal spots of green, or a greenish tint adjacent to the veins, this will likely resolve with a little exposure to sunlight. More green than that most often results from ending the yellowing phase too soon. Allow the leaf to become *mostly* yellow, before raising the temperature.

If only some leaves are tainted with green, while others are golden, then the batch may have consisted of leaf from different priming levels or different degrees of leaf maturation. A more homogeneous batch will yellow in synchrony.

If green leaves are appearing only toward the corners of your flue-cure chamber, then the heat is not being circulated uniformly. If your circulation fan seems to be doing its job adequately, then you may need to leave more space between the leaf and the side walls of the chamber, or improve insulation.

finishes too brown: If you hold leaf in the yellowing phase until every bit of every leaf shows no green, then most of the batch may come out brown. That tells you that the magic of killing the leaf as soon as it is sufficiently yellow failed to occur. Wait for *most of the leaves of a batch to mostly yellow,* then move on to leaf wilting. This works if the batch is all from the same priming level, and at pretty much the same stage of leaf maturation. Mixed batches (whether matured to a different degree, primed from different stalk levels, or if the leaf of a single batch comes from more than one tobacco variety) only rarely come out nicely.

But this is entirely about the yellowing phase of the flue-cure. One way to get around these restrictions is to yellow the leaf outside of the kiln, and select for a batch all the leaves (regardless of priming or stalk level or even variety) that are sufficiently yellowed to allow you to start them in the chamber with a ramp up to leaf wilt—skipping the yellowing phase. The remainder of the flue-cure temp chart never changes from batch to batch. This approach can be tricky, but some folks have succeeded at it.

Problems Kilning

cool areas of the chamber: If leaf in the corners of your kiln, or leaf along the sides or floor exhibit mold, while the remainder of the leaf does not, there are two aspects of the kiln that will need attention. Mold localized to the periphery of the kiln volume suggests inadequate insulation, or inadequate air circulation. This assumes your heat source is capable of maintaining its set temperature.

My own present kiln has walls of 2" thick extruded polystyrene foam (XPS foam). At an R-value of about 5 per inch, this gives me insulation of R-10. It could use a bit more, but is unlikely to get it. My present insulation and muscular ventilation fan will have to get the job done.

If your fan seems adequate, then the insulation problem can be addressed by providing an air passage, within the kiln, that separates the leaf from the kiln walls and floor. Something as simple as a wire baking rack, placed on the kiln floor, will permit circulation of the heated air between the leaf and the floor. More practical for the door and walls are "disposable", aluminum grilling pans, which come with perforations (to allow grill drippings to pass through). These can be taped with Tyvek tape to the interior surfaces of the kiln, so that their perforated bottoms are closest to the leaf. (See Appendix 3.)

too much condensation: Any condensation *inside* the kiln is the consequence of inadequate insulation, which results in cool areas (see above). Condensation at seams on the *exterior* (joins or the door) are vapor leaks.

Taping of the interior (with Tyvek tape) can eliminate vapor intrusion into the joins of the kiln. The more careful the taping, the more effective it is. If this kind of condensation is minimal, it can usually be ignored, by placing a plastic lid from a food or coffee container beneath the corners (or other seams), to catch the occasional drip, and allow it to evaporate.

If the primary source of external condensation is along the door closure, then then kiln's door gasket may need attention. The gasket should make firm contact with the body and the door around the entire periphery of the closure, with no gaps.

Aside from being a mess, this condensation is being delivered there by your electric energy bill. It takes extra electricity to evaporate water that vanishes from the interior space of the kiln. That condensation also carries away heat, causes the heat source (your Crockpot, for example) to cycle on more of the time, and allows the correct temperature of the kiln, when reached, to promptly drop, rather than remaining as stable as the insulation would allow.

water refills are too frequent: See the above discussion on condensation. Check your taping of the walls, and the integrity of your door gasket.

leaf too moist at the end of the run: So long as the leaf is kept at kiln temperatures (122°F or higher), damp leaf cannot mold. When the kiln run is done, if any or all of the leaf is too wet, just continue the run until the Crockpot has been dry for a day or two. If you humidify with another method, just turn that off, and continue the normal kiln heat for another day or two.

leaf too dry at the end of the run: If you can safely remove the dry leaf from the kiln, then remove it, and mist it with water to bring it into low case for packaging. If the leaf cannot be removed without damaging it, then, for hanging leaf, mist it with water, close the kiln door, and check back in a few hours. Or, you could replenish the kiln's humidity source (perhaps a Crockpot), and run it for a day, to soften the leaf.

Problems with Press Cakes

mold: During active pressing, mold will not grow when the pressure is adequate to exclude air. After pressing, mold may appear on the surface of the press cake if it is not promptly allowed to dry-down. If you intend to have a persistently "moist" press cake, then you will need to use an anti-fungal agent, such as propyleneglycol (PG) in the casing. Keep in mind that most casings are more hygroscopic (moisture-drawing) than the tobacco alone. So once the press cake has dried-down to a storage condition, it will need to be protected from absorbing ambient moisture.

too hard: Too much pressure applied for too long can lead to a press cake that consolidates into a dense, solid slab of material that is nearly impossible to cut without a band saw. This most often happens when using a hydraulic press or shop press, both of which are capable of applying excessive psi.

falls apart: While it is relatively easy to press tobacco into a nicely consolidated press cake, it may not stay that way after pressing. Unless you use some manner of adherent casing, the press cake may de-laminate, and fall apart. The chemical alterations of the pressing will remain, but the physical form may not be what you had hoped for.

won't compress: You will need to generate about 1 to 2 psi to compress tobacco into a press cake. Higher pressures will work, but may bring about other changes. The most common explanation for inadequate pressure is that the top surface of your press cake is too large for the applied weight. You can reassemble the cake to provide a smaller surface, increase the weight, or use the same weight on a lever-arm press to generate greater *applied weight*.

sticks to container: A press cake that contains casing that is even slightly sticky may stick to the bottom, walls and follower of a pressing container. This is not an issue with pressing in a polyethylene bag, which allows you to easily peel the cake from the plastic. But for some other containers, especially wooden ones, you should assume in advance that it may stick. Sections of baking parchment, available in most grocery stores, can be cut to fit the bottom and sides, and used to separate the tobacco from the follower.

Problems with Twists and Ropes

mold: Mold is always the result of too much moisture. If starting with green or yellow leaves, allowing them to wilt, or frog-legging them, or both, will significantly reduce the starting moisture. The pressure of the twist (how tightly it is twisted or bound) can compress moisture out of the center.

For techniques that bind the tobacco within a coiled rope, such as a sailor's perique carotte, the rope can be removed from time to time, and the contents then re-bound more tightly. Doing so also allows further oxidation of the nicotine, darkening the tobacco.

Once the rope or twist has cured sufficiently, it should be relatively dry. If not, then prolonged, gentle heat will allow it to dry-down.

smells raw: Either a "grassy" or ammonia smell is an indication that the fermentation of the twist or rope is still unfinished. It will require more time.

too hard: It is difficult, when twisting tobacco, or when binding it to wrap it so tightly that it becomes too rigid and solid to cut. If using a binding rope that is passed through more than one pulley, to increase the force of binding, don't overdo it.

Problems with Flakes and Coins

crumbling: Flake or sliced coins will often crumble apart if no casing is used to bind the layers together. If your intent is to just rub out the slices for subsequent blending or use, then it doesn't make much of a difference if it crumbles or not. If, instead, you hope to produce intact slices, then you will need to consider using an adherent casing.

For producing a Cavendish cut from the slices, a casing may or may not be needed, depending on the extent of pressing and the nature of the tobacco varieties.

crushes when cut: This results from inadequate pressing of a press cake, or insufficiently tight rolling of a rope.   More compression will remedy this. Be sure to use a very sharp edge to cut flake or coins. For coins, a tuck cutter with fresh blades may work well when slicing the "cigar" or rope.

cut flakes or coins stick together: Only casing will make slices stick to one another. The casing may not have sufficiently dried, or the casing is so hygroscopic that it soaks up ambient moisture after initially drying.

Problems with Perique Fermentation

not enough liquid for a seal: If you initially pack the container using moistened leaf, that moisture, together with the juices crushed from the leaf during initial pressing is usually sufficient to provide a liquid seal surrounding the edge of the follower. If it does not, or if with time the liquid seal begins to recede, then just add only enough non-chlorinated water to restore a seal. For a relatively small container (say, 4 inches in diameter), a liquid seal of a quarter inch is plenty. If you add too much water, it may reduce the osmolarity (the concentration of fermentation chemicals) in the solution, and allow undesired microbial growth.

smells bad: The mix of microbial inhabitants in the solution of fermenting perique changes with time, eventually reaching a point where the yeast, *Pichia anomala*, becomes dominant. This yeast produces a prune-like, fruity aroma. Before that happens, other microbes may produce unpleasant smells. *E. coli*, which is commonly present in the early weeks of fermentation, may emit a fecal aroma. This is normal.

What is not normal is for a fecal aroma to persist into the second month of fermentation. Higher fermentation temperatures (80°F or above) favor *E. coli* over *Pichia anomala*. So a perique batch that is allowed to spend too much time in high temperatures, such as a barn in summer, or an attic, may still produce a strong barnyard aroma at the end of fermentation. Performing the fermentation in comfortable indoor temperatures will usually clear the stinky *E. coli* after the first month.

leaf not darkening: Darkening of perique leaf is mostly the result of oxidation of nicotine. Although perique can be left under compression for the duration of the fermentation, and yield a lovely perique in the end, its color will not begin to darken until it is removed, and spread out to air.

Traditional practice is to release the pressure, and remove the leaf—for spreading out to air—after the first 3 or 4 weeks. After a brief airing (~15 to 60 minutes), the leaf is repacked, and put under pressure again, with its liquid seal restored. This airing procedure may be repeated two or three more times during the course of the fermentation.

finished perique is too bland / too strong / too weak:
This issue comes down to the variety of tobacco you choose for making perique. Nicotine concentrations are unchanged by the process. Richly flavored varieties will make richly flavored perique.

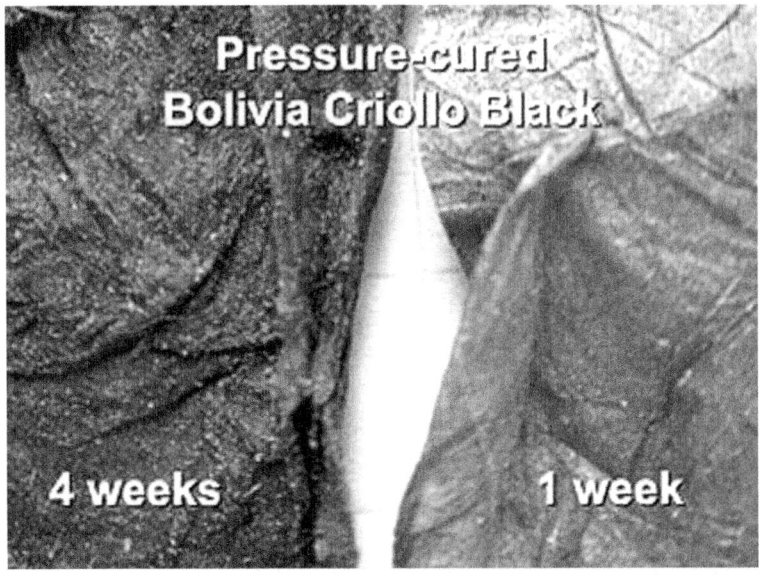

In making perique, the leaf (and juice) darkens with each "airing" of the leaf. Nicotine is oxidized in the air.

Chapter 4. Storing Tobacco and Tobacco Problems

Totally dry tobacco will never "age". What we consider to be "aging" changes are chemical changes that are mostly accelerated (on the order of ten to one hundred-fold) by enzymes within the leaf lamina. And those chemical changes require water molecules. No moisture allows no aging.

The water vapor equilibrium (within a closed container) above a saturated solution of sodium chloride—table salt—is useful for calibration. That solution is made initially by dumping non-iodized salt (I use rock salt when I do this.) into a small vessel—cup or tray—of water. You add enough salt so that some of it remains undissolved. At typical room temperature, the relative humidity above the salt will remain at ~76%RH. Use this phenomenon to accurately calibrate a hygrometer.

If you have adequate room within a humidor, you can add an open bag (like 12-16 ounces) of super-cheap, unflavored, commercial black Cavendish tobacco. It will have been literally soaked in propyleneglycol, and will dramatically stabilize the humidity within the humidor in the mid-to-high 60s RH. If it is aromatic, then the humidor will smell just like the ones at a tobacconist shop, and doesn't seem to seriously affect the tobacco or cigars within the humidor.

If you use canning jars (with sealed lids), make sure the moisture within the jar is not too high (tobacco should be flexible, but not "moist"), to prevent mold. Otherwise, if you actually "can" the tobacco as you would home-canned green beans, it would be sterile, and will never mold, regardless of the moisture content, so long as it has not been opened after sterilizing.

For pipe tobacco containers that are regularly opened, the tobacco will eventually become too dry. Just dip your fingertip into some water, and flick a few drops onto the tobacco prior to re-closing the container, check it again the next time you open it.

After a few trials, you will become an expert at adding just the right moisture to keep the tobacco nicely packable in a pipe. [More information is in the chapters on cigars, pipe tobacco, etc.]

Tobacco Problems

Mold

Risk of mold
Cured, finished tobacco can support mold growth in a humidity range somewhere between that of leather and that of cheese. If the relative humidity (shown as percent in the chart) is kept below 76%, the risk of mold growth is quite low. As the humidity

TABLE 4. *Mold growth on materials after one year at different humidities with added nutrients*

MATERIAL	PER CENT HUMIDITY						
	100	96	92	88	85	80	76
Leather...............	5*	5	5	5	4	4	4
Cheese...............	5	5	5	5	5	2	1
Wood...............	5	5	4	4	3	0	0
Wool...............	5	5	4	4	1	0	0
Cotton...............	5	5	0	0	0	0	0
Glass Wool..........	5	2	0	0	0	0	0

* Visual scale of mold growth: 0-None, T-Trace, 1-Very light, 2-Light, 3-Extensive, 4-Heavy, 5-Very heavy.

S.S. Block, 1953.

is increased above that (in typical home temperatures), the risk increases dramatically. Tobacco that is damp will usually not mold over a span of a few days, but after that may suddenly bloom with common molds. Since mold spores are ubiquitous, their control is generally limited to manipulating the humidity, in order to inhibit them (in the absence of chemical anti-fungal agents).

Mold typically appears on the thicker parts of the stem first, since this region of whole leaf is most likely to hold the most moisture, and release it slower than the leaf lamina. In stemming a leaf for use, if there is slight mold only on the stem, then it can be ignored once the stem is discarded.

Mold health concerns

Mold on the lamina creates two issues. The most obvious is its impact on the smell of the tobacco. If it smells moldy, it will be unpleasant to smoke or use in a smokeless preparation.

A more important issue with mold is its potential to create toxins within the tobacco on which it grows. Of greatest concern is aflatoxin (commonly produced by species of *Aspergillus*, which may be white, black, gray or yellow). Aflatoxins can permanently damage human tissues, including the liver—and can cause liver failure.

When aflatoxin is burned, during the combustion of tobacco, no toxin is detectable in the smoke. By contrast, aflatoxins that are in non-burned tobacco (e.g. snus, snuff, chew, and the wrapper of a cigar in the mouth) are absorbed into the tissues of the mouth and nasopharynx.

So if there is any concern about using tobacco that might be moldy, its use in cigar filler or a cigarette or in pipe tobacco is probably safe. Such tobacco should not be used in smokeless products or as a cigar wrapper.

Control of mold

Very slight mold can be inhibited by misting the tobacco lightly with diluted (50:50) hydrogen peroxide. But by far the wisest policy is to prevent mold in the first place, by controlling the ambient humidity.

With regard to controlling humidity, one factor that is often ignored is storage of a closed container of tobacco in ambient temperatures that swing back and forth. If, for example, a sealed bag of tobacco is exposed to a 20°F increase in temperature, the internal relative humidity drops by half. If the ambient temp decreases by 20°F, then internal humidity will likewise rise.

That in itself is not a major issue under most circumstances. But a container of tobacco exposed to swinging temperatures does not alter its internal temperature uniformly—some parts of the contents becoming warmer than other parts of the contents. This causes a heat pump effect, by driving moisture from the warmer areas, and then condensing that excess moisture within the cooler areas. The result of this heat pump effect caused by swinging ambient temperatures is to create favorable conditions for mold growth in portions of the contained tobacco. The easiest way to avoid this is to store tobacco containers (bags, tubs, etc.) in living areas of a home that are the most stable with respect to ambient temperature. In large tobacco containers (5 to 10 pounds), periodically inspect the tobacco within the most interior regions.

Moisture control

Whole leaf shipped by on-line vendors usually comes in sealed bags. The poly-nylon bags are entirely vapor-proof, and the heavy gauge polyethylene bags are nearly so. It is sealed within the bags at low to medium case (somewhat to fully pliable, but not damp) at controlled, warehouse temperature—like a typical home. If the sealed bag is shipped or stored at a significantly lower temperature, the internal relative humidity will increase.

These shipping bags should be carefully opened with scissors, cutting a clean line across the seal at the top, so that the top edge can subsequently be rolled, flattened and clamped, to retain humidity. Each time the bag is opened, for inspection, or to remove some leaf, the humidity of its contents drifts toward that of the room environment in which it is opened. If the ambient environment tends to be more humid, then the leaf's moisture content may increase toward it. If the ambient environment tends to be drier, then the leaf will gradually dry.

If the leaf in a container becomes too moist (risking mold), that can be reduced by gently warming the open bag, to drive off some of the excess moisture, then sealing the bag again. If the leaf is too dry, its contents can be lightly misted with non-chlorinated water, then sealed again. Light misting will disperse its humidity into all the leaf in the bag over a period of a few hours to a day.

Tobacco Beetles

Lasioderma serricorne, the tobacco beetle, first became a pest of cured tobacco over a century ago. It initially was a problem in tobacco warehoused in the Philippines as well as other areas of the Far East. But subsequent world trade, coupled with poor pest control measures, led to its spread throughout the world. It is now a ubiquitous pest.

The tobacco beetle is a brown, pinhead-size (2-3mm) beetle that can fly. It is its larval forms that like to tunnel through cured, finished tobacco leaf—both lamina and stems—leaving easily identifiable holes as well as "dust". Tobacco warehouses everywhere today regularly inspect for it, and fumigate their tobacco to eliminate it. But it nonetheless persists. The adult beetles can be successfully wiped out, but then return when its eggs hatch and mature.

Lasioderma serricorne can hitch a ride into a house in any tobacco or tobacco product (including commercial cigarettes), as well as in purchased, dried grains and cereals (including breakfast cereals), flour, commercial bread crumbs, and a host of other items. If they get into a cigar humidor, they may tunnel through wrappers on expensive cigars, and otherwise create damage to tobacco, and to foods in the pantry.

Once tobacco beetles have been detected within a home (in a humidor or pack of cigarettes, or in stored tobacco or pantry foods), they are quite difficult to eliminate. The beetle and its eggs can be killed in stored tobacco by placing the closed bag in the freezer and leaving it there for a week to 10 days. (The adults die within 6 days at 4 °C [39.2° F], and eggs survive 5 days at 0–5 °C [32°F].) Individual bags, cartons or boxes of pantry foods can be kept within closed Ziploc bags, and tossed if seen to be infested.

Characteristic damage pattern of tobacco beetles (Lasioderma serricorne).

5. Tobacco Varieties

Tobacco Before Columbus

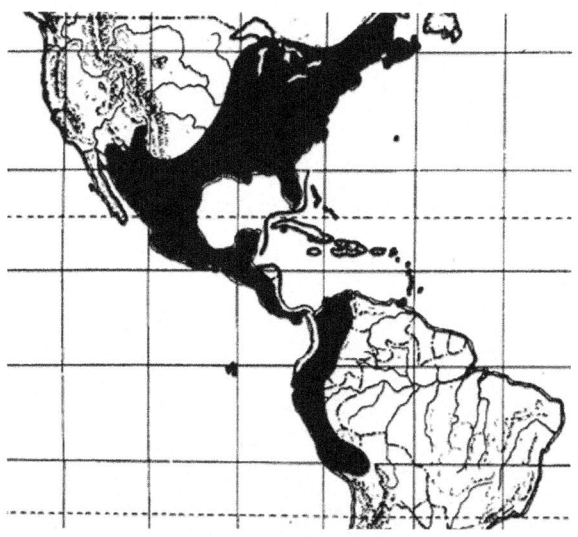

Range of cultivated Nicotiana rustica.
[Spinden: Tobacco is American, 1950.]

From the book, Tobacco is American (1950), by New York Public Library. Only 500 copies of Spinden's book were ever printed:

"It should be kept in mind as regards commercial tobacco: the straits of Yucatan and of Florida separate the two domesticated tobaccos of pre-Columbian times so that north and west of this line only *Nicotiana rustica* was available, and south and east of it only *Nicotiana tabacum*, while the two species mingled in the general region of Panama."

"The old tobaccos of Mexico and the United States were essentially pipe and cigarette tobaccos. The South American species with a larger and broader leaf gave rise to our cigar, or bundle of smaller leaves wrapped in a larger leaf of the same material."

"Perhaps cigars, in our sense, were known and used already to a limited extent by Maya and Aztec smokers when the Spaniards arrived, but cane or cornhusk cigarettes certainly were more usual."

"...in 1528, we must assume that the people of the Valley of Mexico had at least some trading knowledge of the large-leaved *Nicotiana tabacum*, which already had penetrated the northern continent as a contribution of recent immigrants from South America."

"It now seems likely that *Nicotiana rustica* must have spread south from Mexico as a domesticated plant, certainly over Colombia and Ecuador, possibly as far south as Chile."

Range of cultivated Nicotiana tabacum.
[Spinden: Tobacco is American, 1950.]

Use Classes

Nicotiana tabacum varieties were assigned by the USDA during the mid-to-late nineteenth century to specific "use classes", based on geography of production, typical commercial use *at that time*, and methods of curing.   It's really not scientific, and can be confusing, especially for classes named for their one-time geographic area of production.   But we continue to go by these classes. A small sampling of examples follows each class.

Flue-cured ("Virginia")

Flue-cured varieties tend to produce relatively large leaves that contain higher levels of natural sugars when they ripen.   It is these sugars that are "fixed" into the leaf by the rapid heating of the flue-cure process.   Used commonly in cigarettes and pipe blends.

Flue-Cured		
African Red	Golden Harvest	Spectrum
Amarillo Parado	Golden Wilt	Stolac 17
Awa	Goyano	Symbol 4
Banana Leaf	Helena	Ternopolskii 7
Bamboo Shoot	Hickory Pryor	Ternopolskii 14
Big Gem	Jaffna	Thailand
Bonanza	Kasturi	Virginia 15
Brown & Williams Low Nic	Lemon Bright	Virginia 24
Bucak	Lizard Tail Orinoco	Virginia 116
Cherry Red	Manilla Wrapper	Virginia 647
Coker 213	NC 82	Virginia Bright Leaf
Coker 371	No. 3666 Deli	Virginia Gold
Costello	Ostrolist	Vesta 64
Crimean	Oxford 207	White Gold
Del Gold	Paris Wrapper	White Mammoth
Dixie Bright 27	Polish	White Stem Orinoco
Dukat Crimean	Reams 158	Yellow Leaf
Frog Eye Orinoco	Red Rose	Yellow Gold
Gold Leaf 939	Silk Leaf	Yellow Orinoco
Gold Leaf Orinoco	Southern Beauty	Yellow Pryor

Dark Air-cured and Dark Fire-cured

These overlapping groups produce large, heavy, thick leaves with sticky surfaces.   They are used as condiment in a number of different applications, especially for pipe tobacco blends and for potent, smokeless products. Any of these varieties can be either air-cured or fired.

Dark	
Adonis	Madole
Bolivian Criollo Black	Negro Black
Goose Creek Red	Rot Front
Greenwood	Shirey
Indian Black	Small Stalk Black Mammoth
Little Yellow	Stag Horn

Burley

Burley varieties tend to be high in alkaloids, very low in sugars, and present a quite distinctive burley aroma. They are usually stalk-harvested and air-cured. Their uses range from cigarette and pipe blends to various smokeless preparations.

Burley	
Baldío Vera	KY 8635
Bravyi 200	Li Berli 21
Burley 9	Moldovan 456
Burley 21	Monte Calme Yellow
Burley 64	Sobolchskii
Chillard's White Angel Leaf	Sobolchskii 33
Gold Dollar	Sobolchskii 193
Golden Burley	TN 86
Green Brior	TN86 LC
Harrow Velvet	TN 90
Kelly Burley	TN90 LC
KY 10	Virginia 509
KY 14	Virginia 510
KY 15	Warner
KY 17	Yellow Twist Bud
KY 190	

Maryland

A seedleaf type of tobacco, Maryland varieties—all air-cured—produce large leaves with little sugar, and moderate to high

Maryland	
Catterton	MD 609
Keller	Pennbel 69
MD A30	Thompson
MD 201	

alkaloids. The aroma is neutral. They are particularly favored for absorbing casings for various uses.

Cigar Filler

Cigar filler and binder varieties overlap in their characteristics. Those with a more or less "square" vein angle are usually classed as binder, though not always. Consider this an indistinct group of cigar leaf.

Cigar Filler	
Ahus	Little Cuba
Amarello Rio Grande	Little Dutch
Bahia	Long Red
Brasil Dunkel	Machu Picchu Havana
Colombia Garcia	Matsukawa
Coroja (Cuba) Pi 405643	Matsukawa Kantu 201
Corojo 99	Nacional
Corojo (Honduras)	Mont Calme Brun
Criollo (Cuba) Ti 1376	Native 10
Criollo 98	Nostrano del Brenta
Criollo Missionero	Ohio Dutch
Diamantina	One Sucker
Dominican Republic Olor	Pennsylvania Red
Hacienda del Cura	Pergeu Brazil
Havana 38	Piloto Cubano
Havana 142	Punta De Lanza 1
Havana 263	Punta De Lanza 2
Havana 322	San Andrés
Havana 608	Selección Olor (1543)
Havana Z299	Uruguay
Habano Colorado	Vallejano
Jalapa	Vuelta Abajo
Kanburi	Walkers Broadleaf
Lancaster Seedleaf	Zimmer Spanish

Cigar Binder

Some cigar varieties that provide a large leaf, with a "square" vein angle and good tensile strength are classed as binder. These are often indistinguishable from many filler varieties, and they often make excellent cigar wrappers, depending on the stalk level and the grade (quality and color consistency) of the leaf.

Cigar Binder	
Comstock Spanish	Havana K2-24
Glessnor	Swarr-Hibshman
Havana 503b	Wisconsin 901
Havana K2	Wisconsin Seedleaf

Cigar Wrapper

The cigar wrapper class includes those varieties that have been traditionally used in that role. The shade-grown varieties are quite thin, when grown beneath shade cloth, but may be too thick, small and undulating for use as wrapper when grown in full sun. Florida Sumatra, Sumatra Deli, Besuki and Timor produce excellent wrappers when sun-grown.

Cigar Wrapper	
Besuki (Ambulu)	Jamaica Wrapper
Besuki (Kesilir)	Java Besuki
Connecticut 49	Magnolia
Connecticut Broadleaf	Metacomet
Connecticut Shade	Moonlight
Dixie Shade	Poquonock
Florida 17	Scantic
Florida Sumatra	Suifu
Galickii	Sumatra Deli
Habano 2000	Timor

Hungarian

This class is a geographic hodgepodge of varieties grown within the bounds of the former Austro-Hungarian Empire. Beyond that consideration, there is no rhyme or reason to their being classed together. Some a mild and Oriental-like, while others are burley-like, and still others similar to members of the Dark Air/Dark Fire class.

Hungarian	
Baiano	Kumanovo
Bitlis	Simox
Colon	Szamosi
Haskowo	Tekne
Herzogovina	

Oriental

This class encompasses, like the "Hungarian" class, a geographic notion. But within the bounds of the Ottoman Empire, selection of desirable tobacco traits tended to focus on smaller, milder, slightly sweet and slightly floral tobaccos. So in that regard, they do make sense as a distinct class. Most are planted with very close spacing (*as little as 6 inches between plants*), are grown on non-irrigated land, and receive minimal fertilization. Though loosely categorized by leaf shape and the presence or absence of a leaf petiole (lamina-free leaf stem), they are often interchangeable in pipe blending, offering only subtle differences and nuances of aroma and floral quality.

Oriental		
Adiyaman	Ege	Rejina
Alma Ata 315	Harmanli	Samsun
American 14	Harmanliiska Basma 163	Samsun Maden
American 26	Incekara	Shirazi
American 3	Izmir / Lebanese	Smyrna
American 572	Izmir-Karabaglar	Sultansko
American 63	Izmir Ozbas	Tasova
Anatolian	Japan 8	Tekkekoy
Bafra	Krumovgrad 58	Trabzon
Balikesir	Lattaquie 92	Turkish 1
Basma	Meechurinski	Turkish 2
Black Sea Samsun	Mutki	VA Gustolistnaja
Bursa	Native 9	Variegata
Canik	Nevrokop 5	Vavilov
Çelikhan	Okinawa	White Flower
Chilean	[Perique]	Xanthi-Yaka 18A
Citir	Prancak N-1	Xanthy
Cyprus Oriental mw	Prilep P66-9/7	Yayladag
Djebel 174	Prilep 79-94	Yenidje
Düzce		

The following is a list of Oriental varieties that are considered sub-strains of Izmir, and may or may not be distinguishable after curing and finishing. [Provided by Fair Trade Tobacco Forum member *Istanbulin*.]

Ege 97, Saribaglar, Otan 97, Akhisar, Karabaglar, Usturali, Ligda, Milas, Resatbey.

Primitive

The underlying assumption in placing a variety in this class is that, though persistently cultivated, it appears to have undergone little agronomic improvement. They often exhibit long stalk segments between leaf nodes, lower total leaf count, higher tendency to sucker prolifically, and sometimes odd aroma characteristics.

Primitive	
Bosikappal	Mopan Mayan
Chapeollo	Mostrenco
Chichicaste (712)	Mt. Pima
Clevelandii	Orinoco
Costa Rica 589 Iztepeque	Papante
Cuba 4	Pretinho
Daule	Tabasqueño Prieto
Guácharo	Tobaco Colorado
Hyang Cho	Yumbo

Documenting your own variety data

At the end of your first season of growing tobacco, you will recall a lot of detail about each variety that you grew, and how they differed from each other. The more varieties you grow, the fuzzier that recollection becomes. After several years of differing varieties, it become impossible to remember, for example, the different leaf counts or leaf sizes of what you have grown.

Over the years, I have grown over 100 different varieties of *Nicotiana tabacum*. Starting with my very first year, I documented detailed measurements and impressions. Of the varieties that I have grown for multiple years, my data on those specific varieties contain more *series* of complete data per variety than that held by ARS-GRIN in their GRIN-Global database. GRIN has, of course, data on thousands of varieties, but that is usually limited to a single grow-out, or at most three different grow-outs. The more *series* of annual data you collect on a specific variety, the more you can see the range of variation in measurements from year to year, or under differing conditions of weather or fertilization and tilling. (See GRIN in Appendix 7.)

Plant Variety Data: *Nicotiana tabacum*	
Variety Name	
Plant length Untopped (to crowfoot) - cm/in	
Plant length Topped - cm/in	
Leaf length (length of 10th leaf from bottom, at maturity) - cm/in	
Leaf width (width of 10th leaf from bottom, at maturity) - cm/in	
Leaf number topped (exclude 2 bed leaves)	
Days at maturity (transplant to 50% plants 1 flower)	
Plant form (pyramidal, columnar, inverted cone, other)	
Flower color (white, pink, red, other)	
Flower head habit (closed, intermediate, open)	
Leaf attachment (sessile, petiolate)	
Leaf carriage of midrib (arched, not arched)	
Leaf color (light green, green, dark green)	
Leaf margin (wavy, not wavy)	
Leaf angle (upper angle between stalk and 10th leaf) - degrees	
Leaf margin (recurved, not recurved)	
Leaf surface (smooth, puckered)	
Stalk diameter - cm/in	
Tip shape (acute, acuminate, obtuse.)	
Venation pattern (square, angular)	
Yield (cured weight) - grams per plant/lbs per plant	
*Auricle configuration	
*Spacing - sq. ft. per plant	
*Variety Comment 1st hornworm eggs: 2nd wave:	
germination start date	
transplant date	
bagging date	
number of seedlings required	
number of seedlings to start	

This section of a spreadsheet shows (in the rows) the data that I collect each year for each variety of tobacco (one column per variety) that I grow. Although the detail might seem tedious, it comes to about 15 minutes per variety each year. With this level of documentation, I find it easier to determine if specific modifications of my techniques actually make any difference. My data, over many years, has shown me that the similar data provided by ARS-GRIN is a mere snapshot, and not gospel. I print the blank data sheets in "landscape", onto as many pages as required for all the columns (varieties) of a particular year's grow. I fill it in by hand, on a clipboard carried to the garden. At the end of each season, I transfer the data into the spreadsheet on my computer, and save that year's file permanently. "" fields are data not collected by ARS-GRIN.*

Although you certainly don't need to track information that is of no interest to you, do take the time to document what is important to you. It's value to you will become more apparent as the years pass.

On my own spreadsheet, the size of my "Variety Comment" section increases year by year. I simply make it a taller row. It's a handy place for unstructured thoughts and observations.

If you are fluent with the use of spreadsheets, you can embed formulas within cells that expect both centimeter and inch values, so that you never need to actually do the arithmetic. Otherwise, just record the unit that you commonly use. The spreadsheet is for your eyes only.

Measuring board showing a comparison of leaves from different stalk positions.

Another valuable bit of documentation is a photo of the mature plant, as well as one of a single leaf.

6. The Whole Leaf Trade

Whole leaf tobacco is an agricultural commodity, rather than a "tobacco product", as far as US federal taxation is concerned. Tobacco farmers can grow however much tobacco they wish, and can sell it without the encumbrance of tobacco "excise tax". If the leaf is being sold to a consumer, then state sales tax may apply. Otherwise, it is simply not taxed any more than, say, ears of corn.

Once the central vein (or stem) of the leaf is removed, or if the leaf is processed in a number of other ways, it becomes a "tobacco product", and falls under numerous laws and taxes (both federal and state) that regulate its sale. So far as the question has been tested, fire-cured tobacco (and therefore Latakia as well) is considered whole leaf. Pressure-cured perique (with the stem still intact) is considered whole leaf. And frog-legged cigar leaf is still considered whole leaf, even though part of the stem has been removed.

By contrast, Cavendish processed tobacco is regarded as a "tobacco product", even with the entire stem present. In order to

---

Tobacco Barn Mishap

A vignette provided by Larry Butcher, a member of the Fair Trade Tobacco Forum *(BigBonner)*, and a commercial tobacco grower in Kentucky.

When I was way younger, I helped a lot of farmers around to house their tobacco. There was a farmer who had a barn full of tobacco and a Farmall Super C tractor parked in and under his tobacco hanging in a barn. The tobacco was cured and ready to strip and bale. When the farmer went to start his tractor to move it out of that barn, it backfired up through the exhaust, catching the hanging tobacco on fire. They say fire went all the way up to the top of that barn, and that the tobacco burnt like kerosene, and destroyed the whole barn to ashes.

produce and sell a "tobacco product", an individual or business must obtain a federal permit, track all the sales, and pay the various applicable taxes to one or more taxing bodies.

Birth of a Business

Don Carey, owner of Whole Leaf Tobacco, in Akron, Ohio, began his journey by deciding to simply grow his own tobacco. He obtained tobacco seed, germinated it, transplanted it to his field in Ohio, grew, harvested and cured it, and eventually sold it to individuals—as whole leaf. It was a tiny enterprise, run from his home. Around the same time frame, he founded a forum for home tobacco growers, *www.fairtradetobacco.com.*

Within a few years, he was no longer growing his own tobacco. As he sought out commercial sources of whole leaf, for both domestic and imported tobacco varieties, his sales, and his new website, *www.wholeleaftobacco.com*, generated enough business that he needed to move the leaf sales into an industrial

A view of some of the huge cartons and bales of tobacco at the Whole Leaf Tobacco warehouse.

warehouse. With growth, the warehouse filled, and the required space steadily increased.

Today, Whole Leaf Tobacco is a successful and growing business, located in several adjacent warehouses in Akron. Don receives samples from leaf wholesalers from across the globe, and evaluates the quality of each one of them, selecting and purchasing only the leaf varieties and qualities that his worldwide

A bale of cigar filler leaf.

customer base demands. While the offerings shift from one crop year to the next, or with the final exhaustion of a supply of a scarce variety, he can always boast a broad selection of whole leaf for use in cigarettes, pipe tobacco, smokeless tobacco and cigars. These are sold to individual home-rollers and home-blenders for their personal use.

A Matter of Scale

The difference between what Don Carey does at Whole Leaf Tobacco, and what most home-growers of tobacco do is mostly *a matter of the scale of operation, and the need for efficient fulfillment* of purchased leaf. Every home-grower is familiar with bringing leaf into case, grading it for use as filler or wrapper, storing it in a state and container that will maintain it over time, and managing its "inventory". With Don, all of that can be accomplished only with the help of paid, skilled staff—now numbering between six and eight.

When cartons or bales of leaf arrive at the warehouse, they need to be inspected for their general condition, then unpacked and brought into proper case. For leaf intended for use as wrapper, meaning that it has already been graded as wrapper prior to being shipped to Akron, each leaf, nevertheless, needs to be inspected and graded again. Don's quality standards demand it.

Misting the leaf, to bring it into case for inspection.

Before leaf can be unfurled and examined for holes or other damage, it needs to be carefully removed from its bale, then

Spreading a leaf over the light table.

misted with water, to bring it into case. Once the leaves are pliable, they are unfurled, one by one, and held over a light table. Leaves with significant holes or damage, are placed into a "filler" pile, and those that are intact are moved into a "wrapper" pile.

Sorting the graded leaf.

The result of this careful grading is that leaf that might make a purchaser of wrapper unhappy is excluded from wrapper bundles, even though the leaf that fails that inspection costs Don

Adam Rimer (left), Warehouse Manager and long time employee, discusses a bale of bright leaf with Don Carey.

as much as those that pass. Maintaining the quality of the leaf he sells is part of his cost of business.

Each bale or carton of leaf must be initially inspected on arrival, and either moved to a spot for longer-term storage, or immediately broken down for meeting current needs. With certain leaf varieties, such as perique, only some of it will be divided into retail parcels, while the remainder will stay under a seal within its original container.

The lid of an oak, perique barrel is held in place by the compression of the barrel staves. Each time the barrel must be opened, the metal hoops holding the top half of the staves are knocked off with a hammer, then a small pry bar is used to lift the lid away.

Inside the partially used barrel of perique, the dense mat of damp and hand-staining leaf must be teased away. Adam Rimer says that whenever he has to handle the perique, he always goes ahead and repackages an ample supply for shipping to customers.

A remarkable attribute of good perique is that it can remain fairly soggy, and at room temperature, without molding. This is true so long as the air exposure is minimal, and its wrappings are tightly replaced after each access. It is likely the relatively higher pH of the perique that limits microbial growth to its dominant member, *Pichia anomala*, a common yeast, and prevents growth of mold.

Another tobacco type that appears to inhibit mold growth, from the nature of its curing process, is Latakia. This Oriental leaf is heavily fire-cured, and maintains a coating of aromatic combustion products over its surface.

Bales of smoky, fire-cured Latakia, from Cyprus.

Leaf is usually packaged into one-pound bags, for retail sale. The bags are vapor-proof, so that once at the proper case for storage

Pre-bagged leaf fills the shelves of the shipping room.

and shipping, it remains that way indefinitely. Retail-ready bags are shelved in the shipping room, ready for immediate shipment when an order arrives.

A package awaiting the arrival of the shipper.

Many orders ship the same business day, while the rest is usually in the hands of shippers by the following business day.

Shipping Manager, Alyssa Kline, handles most of the on-line orders.

Alyssa Kline, Shipping Manager for Whole Leaf Tobacco, makes sure that orders are handled promptly, and arrive in the customers' hands as quickly as possible. Her desk is tidy.

She also handles a lot of the headaches, like unclaimed international parcels returned by customs. This usually happens because customs incorrectly designates a shipment as a "tobacco product", and charges an exorbitant tax, which the customer, of course, refuses to pay.

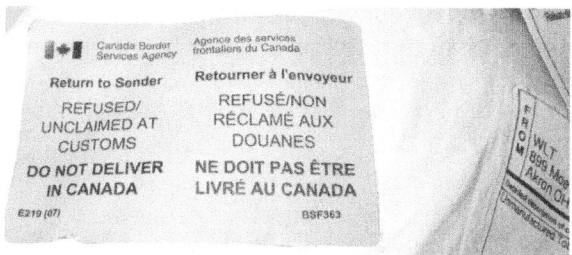

A bright orange refusal sticker from Canada Border Services Agency.

In addition to tobacco, Whole Leaf Tobacco also carries a number of tobacco-related accessories, as a convenience to customers, and often at minimal or no profit. These include shredders, filter cigarette tubes, chavetas, casings, etc.

Just a fraction of the inventory of cigar molds, for every conceivable size and shape of cigar.

Whole Leaf Tobacco also sells whole leaf in wholesale quantities of 25 to 50 pounds, depending on the type of tobacco. An individual can also purchase at the wholesale price, if she or he buys in that quantity.

Don Carey pulls all the strings to keep the business running, and his customers satisfied. He has a sensitive finger on the pulse of

Don Carey at his warehouse desk.

changing demands and preferences. As commercial cigars have gone from relatively balanced blends to intimidating, one-cigar-a-day, overpowering blends, he has been able to offer cigar leaf to match the trend, while still offering more traditional, milder leaf.

Fronto and Grabba

With the increasing legalization of cannabis, there has been a growing demand for *grabba tobacco* to blend with cannabis, and for *fronto* leaf in which to wrap cannabis. Don created his own line of just such tobacco, sold prepackaged *by the leaf.*

While Whole Leaf Tobacco created these various *grabba* and *fronto* brands, Don has sold them to a third party, and now simply supplies the prepackaged leaf on a wholesale basis to this vendor.

A poster of the brands of by-the-leaf fronto created by Whole Leaf Tobacco.

Tobacco Seed:

Paul Wicklund [skychaser], a long-time member of the Fair Trade Tobacco Forum, operates **Northwood Seeds**, *in eastern Washington state, near the Canadian border. His tobacco seed is produced in quantity, and according to the best genetic practices. He is regularly visited by a government inspector in order to maintain the phytosanitary certificate that accompanies seed shipment to destinations that require it.*

Northwood Seeds offers for sale—both retail and wholesale—the largest selection of tobacco varieties available anywhere. In addition to traditional heirloom and commercial tobacco varieties, he carries some that are not even included within the USDA's ARS-GRIN germplasm bank.

He produces seed for every USDA class of tobacco, and currently maintains the former Fair Trade Tobacco seed bank.

Bales
A vignette provided by Larry Butcher.

They are between 80 lbs. to 100 lbs. My average hits in the 90s lbs. per bale.

This year I have sold some that weighed 120 lbs. The bales were high in case when stripped. I made some bales light to keep my average below 100 lbs.

When I unload these small bales at the contract station, **they place 8 of them on each basket, and band them together***. If they average over 800 lbs., they reject the basket of tobacco.*

I have hauled over 10,000 pounds on that trailer a few times. If the days are rainy and the air full of moisture the leaves will come in a high case. Each rain will be different in moisture in the air. I have seen it rain and thinking tobacco should be in a case to put down in my barns, but the tobacco will still be crumbly dry. Warm fine, misty rain and the tobacco may be in a high case and too high a moisture for putting down tobacco.

If the tobacco is put down with a live green stalk then we have to make sure to strip it quickly or the moisture from the stalks will make the leaves too high of a case, and the pile will get hot. Tobacco with well dried stalks can keep easily in a pile (We call a bulk) on the stalk for a week or more.

The June and July sweat, the tobacco will be in case from morning up to noon or more before it gets too dry to handle. No rain just high humidity.

Buying Flue-Cured Leaf at Auction

For nearly 200 years, tobacco has been sold in tobacco auctions located primarily in the major tobacco growing regions of the US south-east. The city of Danville, Virginia was built around its massive and economically important tobacco auction houses. These are all gone now.

Today, the northernmost surviving flue-cured tobacco auction is located in Rural Hall, North Carolina. It is the Old Belt Farmers Co-op auction, held weekly, starting with the tobacco harvest season, and continuing into late fall.

Their warehouse is about the size of a football field, under one roof. On the day that I visited, they had 1.2 million pounds of flue-cured tobacco, in single-stacked, large bales, spread across the floor in enormously long rows.

The agents of tobacco buyers inspected each bale, prior to the start of the auction. They knew the exact grade of leaf that their clients wished to purchase that day, and how much they would be willing to pay.

Old Belt Farmers Co-op tobacco auction. Each bale weighs between 500 and 700 pounds. A narrow aisle between each row allows buyers to closely examine every bale.

Rick Smith (left) and Don Carey discuss what grade of flue-cured leaf he is hoping to buy.

The general appearance of each bale tells a lot about the timing of the harvest, consistency of the cure, and the care used by the grower to sort and pack the leaf. The oldest generation of current growers still clings to the tradition that one should be proud of his crop, and that the bales should demonstrate that. The comparison was obvious.

Don Carey examines a bale of flue-cured leaf, before the start of the auction.

The different bales that day ranged in quality from what appeared to be debris from raking a previously harvested tobacco field (weed stems, broken and deteriorated leaf, dirt, etc.) to the finest flue-cured leaf that I've ever seen. The former was likely destined to be shredded and packaged into bulk bags of discount "pipe tobacco"—and explains why that product sometimes seems so disappointing in quality and aroma.

But Don Carey was looking for the best flue-cured leaf on offer. Of the 1.2 million pounds auctioned that day, Don paid the highest price for any bale, and managed to purchase a mere five bales of the very best leaf. (That represented the best 0.625% of the leaf for sale that day.)

In accordance with the longstanding tradition of tobacco auctions, a seller (often the actual grower) could reject the final price of individual bales, and those bales would go unsold that day. As soon as a seller's tobacco was sold, he could go to the auction house office and collect his payment, even though not a single buyer had yet paid a dime. On that one day, over 1-1/2 million dollars changed hands on trust.

The auction itself lasted only a little over two hours. Once it began, the auctioneer walked slowly and continuously down the long aisles, chanting as he went, while selling tobacco at a rate of about 10,000 pounds of leaf per minute.

Now that growing contracts from large manufacturers are scarce, due to imported leaf, auctions like these are the only route many tobacco farmers have to sell their production.

A tobacco auction in Wilson, North Carolina, in 1926. All tobacco was transported and sold as tied hands. [Univ. NC Chapel Hill Library]

Adding water to a bale
A vignette provided by Larry Butcher.

We spray dry tobacco with a hand sprayer well before stripping, if needed, to get a good handling case. Stripping tobacco too dry makes the work a little harder, and it also crumbles the tobacco up. I Use a water hose with the sprayer nozzle on mist or similar, and spray as we put down, if the tobacco is a little on the dry side.

Back when tobacco was first put into bales some farmers was setting the bales up on their ends and pouring a gallon of water down the ends of the bales. Then the next day they would turn them over and pour another gallon down the other end. Water turned to money is the thinking behind that. Two gallons of water weighed 16 pounds, and times that by 50 bales and you made yourself an extra 800 pounds of tobacco.

After the tobacco companies found the tobacco was over moist they started the moisture checkers, and would only buy tobacco that was 24% or less with moisture. This put a stop to over moist tobacco from farmers. This also caused tobacco stored by the companies to overheat and start rotting, if stored for a long period of time.

I know one farmer who would buy 50 pound bags of salt and add salt to bales. The salt would draw moisture, and salt was cheap. Some farmers put rocks and other junk into bales for weight. This was called "nesting tobacco". The USDA finally started the farmer ID system, and they knew which farm each bale came from. Some farmers lost their quotas by nesting tobacco.

Twenty lipa coin from Croatia, depicting tobacco, one of Croatia's major crops.

7. Cigars

"Cigars" are a broad category of smokable tobacco items that can be loosely defined as "tobacco wrapped in tobacco". This includes the use of reconstituted tobacco sheet (paper made of tobacco) as a wrapper, or as a binder beneath a natural leaf wrapper. Cigars range from tiny cigarette-sized ones with filters, to chair-rung size, Caribbean-style premium cigars made of full-length filler leaf bound in natural leaf, and wrapped in natural leaf. This discussion relates exclusively to tobacco—either long filler or scrap—wrapped and bound in natural leaf.

A perfectly smokable and delicious cigar can be rolled from well-aged, whole leaf tobacco of just about any variety. The wrapper does need to be mostly free of holes, but otherwise, can be from any *class* of leaf. That is to say, that a stack of leaf from a variety considered to be "cigar filler" may provide some nice wrappers— if you just look through the leaves carefully. Experimentation is what makes rolling your own cigars such a pleasure.

Learning to roll a cigar is a relatively easy skill to acquire. It usually takes a complete novice about 10 cigars (rolled and smoked one at a time, *not made in a batch*) to begin to consistently roll a cigar with proper draw. Rolling a nice looking cigar may, of course take longer. But the skill will come naturally with time. [Keep in mind that a novice cigar roller at a cigar factory will roll 100 or more cigars per day. So your first 100 cigars could be considered only 1 day of practice.]

An ugly cigar that offers a good draw, and burns properly is a far better result than a work of art that is too loosely or too tightly rolled. Free-hand rolling, without using a cigar mold, is easier for a novice to accomplish in a way that draws properly, than by using a mold. Learn how to roll, then consider improving the appearance with a mold, if you desire. In the same vein, rolling a cigar that smokes well does not require a chaveta or tuck cutter, or even glue or a rolling board. So long as you have a decent, straight-cut cigar cutter (clipper) and decent leaf, you can roll a smokable cigar

The only important *secret* is to bring the leaf into proper case (moisture content). You can just hand-tear the stemmed filler to a suitable cigar length, and wrap it in a half-leaf on any surface. It may not be pretty, but with practice, it will draw well and will smoke well. And you will be gratified at having rolled it yourself.

Once you have a feel for rolling a cigar by hand—one that draws well, then adding the tools of the trade can allow you to create perfectly artistic cigars—give one to your father-in-law quality— as well as duplicate an exact length and ring gauge. The tools and their use will be discussed in the sections that follow.

Cigar Tools

Chaveta
A chaveta is a flat, steel blade with a curved cutting edge (usually 6 to 8 inches long), but no handle. The chaveta is held by its flat, upper edge, and rocked over the surface to be cut. It is used to trim the outer edge of a wrapper for wrapping a cigar, and is also used to shape the wrapper to the size and contour of the filler bunch.

While any knife (or even scissors) can perform the same function, using a chaveta or similarly curved blade that can be rocked makes the required cuts more effortlessly and more precisely.

Chavetas are not mass produced for the commercial supply chain. They are niche blades that are usually custom made by small

Steel chaveta.

craftsmen. (In 3rd world countries, they are often made from the worn-out blades of circular saws.) Those made of carbon steel are far easier to sharpen, but will dull more rapidly from use, and will rust, without taking precautions to prevent it. Stainless steel chavetas will never rust, and will require sharpening less frequently, but are more difficult to sharpen, because of the hardness of the steel.

Board

Any type of cutting board of adequate size (14" x 11" is large enough to roll a very large cigar) can be used for rolling cigars. While some rollers like to use a stone cutting board, because a moist wrapper can be spread on it more easily, the stone surface will rapidly dull a chaveta. Wood cutting boards are what the cigar factories regularly use. An inexpensive, relatively thin, bamboo cutting board will last for many years of cigar making.

A kitchen cutting board that is concurrently used for food is a poor choice, since the tobacco will pick up food flavors, and food will acquire tobacco dust. A dedicated cutting board, used only for cigar rolling is ideal. After each rolling session, just brush the surface with your hand or a paper towel over the trash can, to clean away the tobacco bits and dust that may have accumulated.

Glue

Cigar glue is used to prevent the wrapper from coming off the head of the cigar after it is opened (clipped). If you roll one cigar, and immediately smoke it, then moisture from your mouth will prevent unwrapping. If you instead roll multiple cigars at a time, or intend to "rest" the cigar for a time in a humidor, then using glue will allow the cigar(s) to behave like a factory cigar—and not unwrap itself, even though fairly dry.

Any natural glue can be used. Each of these is a complex carbohydrate that becomes sticky when moistened, and holds two surfaces together when dried. These include most natural, non-latex gums, such as gum acacia, gum Arabic, tragacanth, xanthan gum, and even pectin. Bermocoll (a cellulose polymer) is most commonly used in cigar factories. The various gums are used as thickeners in many foods, from commercial salad dressings to chocolate milk to canned chili.

Every gum has a taste. Most cigar smokers can taste only some of the gums, while other cigar smokers can taste others. If you use a

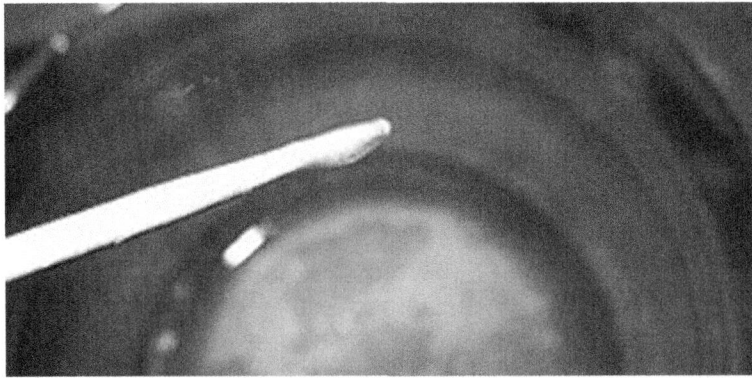

Cigar glue. This mixture is barely thick enough for use. If it is too runny, then it will not hold. Aim for a thin paste.

cigar glue that has a noticeable taste, just switch to another one.

Most of these gums come as a powder that must be hydrated for use. Since only a minuscule amount is used on each cigar, mix only a tiny batch at a time. Add the powder to a very small container (like the size of a custard dish or smaller), then add a couple of drops of water at a time, mixing it to achieve the particle-free consistency of a thick, smearable paste. If any of the prepared gum is left over after you have finished using it for the time being, cover it with plastic wrap, and refrigerate it. If the prepared gum dries out between uses, you can try adding a few drops of water to reconstitute it. (Some, such as xanthan gum, may require rehydration with warm water.)

Cigar glue is used only at the head end of the cigar binder or wrapper, extending no more than an inch along the outer edge. If you are adding a cap to the cigar, then glue is used as needed to attach it. In applying the glue, wrap the cigar—starting at the foot, wrapping toward the head—to near completion, then use the tip of a finger to very thinly smear a tiny amount of glue to the interior surface of the wrapper, at the outer edge, prior to completing the wrap. There should not be enough glue to squish out and be visible. Use of too much glue may allow the wrapper to unwrap before the glue dries sufficiently.

Properly mixing and applying cigar glue requires a little practice. But only a little.

Cigar Molds

A cigar mold has two major purposes. The first is to allow any cigar roller to produce a cigar of a very specific size and shape—important for a cigar factory, which will need to pack the cigars produced by different rollers into the same box. The other is to produce many identical cigars at one time—also important to a factory, which offers only a limited selection of possible sizes and shapes.

For the home roller, the only real advantage is that a mold makes it easier to wrap a perfectly smooth cigar, if that is an important consideration. For the complete novice, a mold encourages

Cigars that were wrapped after using molds. [Waikikigun]

rolling many bad cigars at once, and is probably not a good idea. Once the basic skill has been learned of consistently rolling a cigar that draws well, then using a mold can improve their

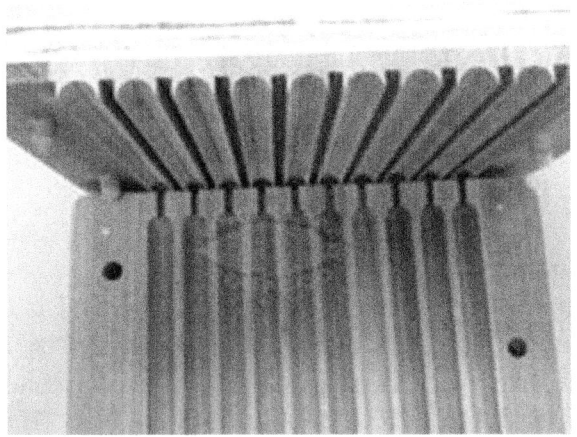

8-inch x 50 ring, 10 stick cigar mold.

appearance. But rolling a cigar bunch for placing into a mold is a separate skill that will need to be learned. *The lid of a cigar mold is different from the bottom of the mold. The bottom is crafted with deep wells into which cigars can be placed, while the lid indentations for cigars are much shallower.* Cigar molds are commonly made for 1, 2, 10 and up to 20 cigars, and come in *figurado* (curved or shaped) as well as *parejo* (parallel or cylindrical) forms. Another consideration is the ring gauge of the mold. If you prefer a cigar of a particular thickness, then select that ring gauge mold. The wells of p*arejo* molds are usually fully open at the foot end, allowing them to be used for any length cigar of a specified ring gauge.

Using a mold is fairly simple. *A properly sized* bunch of filler is wrapped in a binder, and glue applied at the head. Usually, the binder is left with its twisted pigtail at the head. The bound

A 2-stick mold with its own clamping screws. Hand-made in Slovenia, by forum member rainmax.

bunch is then placed into the mold so that its head is toward the closed end of the *bottom* mold well, with its pigtail extending through the narrow slot at that end. The fit should be snug, but not truly tight. Once all of the cigars intended for the mold have been placed into their bottom mold wells, the mold lid is placed on top of it, and either clamped or weighted, so that it completely mates with the bottom.

A mold tends to leave a linear crease in the binder on either side of the cigar, where the mold top and bottom meet. To minimize this, the mold is opened after about 15 minutes, and each bunch is carefully lifted out, rotated 90 degrees, and returned to its mold well. The lid is again placed on top, and clamped or weighted for the remainder of the pressing time—30 minutes or even overnight.

With a wooden cigar mold, excess moisture in the cigar bunch(s) is slowly drawn out. This does not happen with a plastic mold. But a plastic mold will have a longer service life. Cigar molds are available for a vast number of different cigar sizes and shapes.

Tuck Cutter
The "tuck" of a cigar is the same as the "foot" of a cigar—the end at which wrapping begins, and the same end that the smoker will eventually light. The term, "tuck", comes from the process of

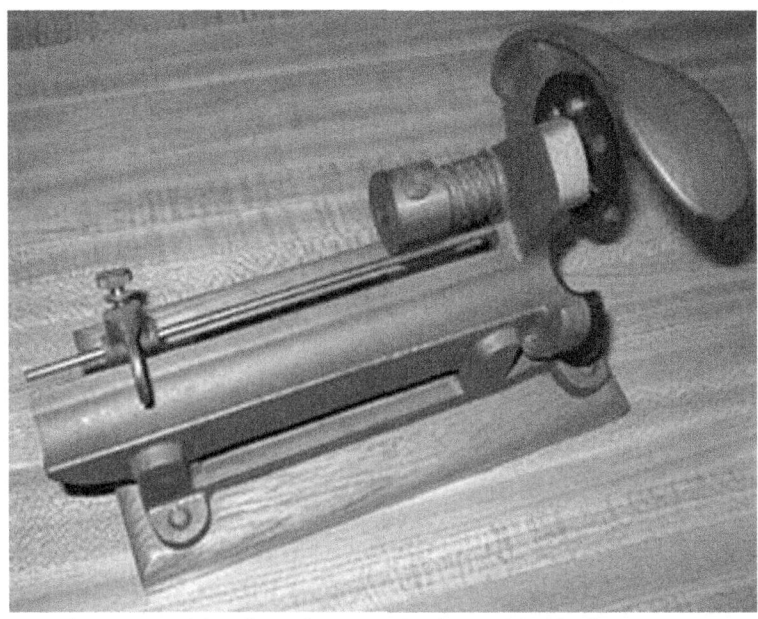

A tuck cutter with a length set and adjustable blades.

tucking the starting tip of the wrapper, as you begin to wrap the bunch. The purpose of a tuck cutter is to cut the foot of a cigar to a specified length, which is set as a set-screw stop along the tuck cutter's length. When mass producing identical length cigars, a tuck cutter saves the time required to precisely measure the desired length on each new cigar.

For a home-roller, the primary use of the tuck cutter is simply to obtain a clean, 90 degree cut at the foot. In the absence of a requirement to produce multiple, identical length cigars, any flat blade cigar clipper can perform that job just as well, and for only a fraction of the cost of a tuck cutter. Whether or not a tuck cutter is attached to the cutting board, or rests on its own stand, a tuck cutter occupies more space in your rolling area, whereas a simple cigar clipper is a tiny, mobile thing.

Tuck cutters are available with differing blade types. Some have a simple guillotine blade, some a blade that can be progressively rotated to a fresh edge, and some with a choice of cutting arcs for differing ring gauge cigars. On some, the cutting edges are easily replaceable (if you can locate the parts), while others must use the same blade for the life of the tuck cutter.

Cap Cutter

When creating a triple cap at the wrapped head of a cigar, the final piece is a circular disc of wrapper leaf about the same diameter as (or slightly larger than) the cigar. A cap cutter is a sharp edge that will "punch-out" that disc from a scrap of wrapper. They are usually hand made from a 1 or 2 inch length of metal water pipe of a suitable diameter, which is then sharpened at one end on a grinder. Many cigar rollers maintain a selection of two or three different diameter cap cutters.

Some commercial cigars are packed in individual tubes, some of which are metal. In a pinch, either the sharp, top edge of such a tube, or even the cap of the tube, can be used for a time as a cap cutter, though it won't last very long.

Rectangular Cigar Mold

To create a cigar with a rectangular or square cross-section (sometimes called box-pressed or square-pressed), a bound bunch—filler bound in just the binder, still round, is fitted into a wooden mold that squares the sides. After pressing to the desired

Multi-place box-pressing cigar mold.   *[MarcL]*

degree of angularity, the bunch is removed, wrapped in its wrapper, then very gently re-pressed for rounded corners, or firmly re-pressed for sharp corners.

Leaf Selection for Cigars

Wrapper

A wrapper is made from half of a stemmed leaf. So there will be roughly equal numbers of right-hand wrappers and left-hand wrappers. For a home-roller, that makes no difference, other than needing to practice wrapping from both directions. For a cigar factory, all the cigars in a single box are either right-hand or left-hand wrapped, just to increase the visual appeal of the box full of cigars. (Their bands are also applied at an identical distance from the head, for the same reason.)

The wrapper leaf selected should be sufficient for the length and girth of the planned cigar. Aligning the leaf half so that its secondary veins are perfectly horizontal (the leaf strip lies at an angle), the length of the required wrapper is at least the *horizontal distance* represented by the length of the planned cigar.

The width of the wrapper required for a cigar of a particular ring gauge is measured at a 90 degree angle to the secondary veins, and must be greater than the *circumference* of the planned cigar,

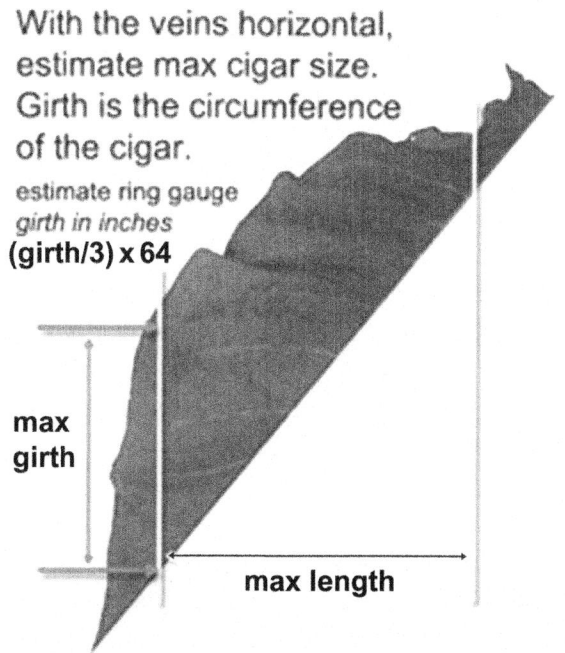

With the veins horizontal, estimate max cigar size. Girth is the circumference of the cigar.

estimate ring gauge
girth in inches
(girth/3) x 64

max girth

max length

since the wrapper will need to overlap itself while wrapping. Make these measurements of the selected wrapper leaf *after* any trimming of the outer and inner edges.

The wrapper is mostly what you taste with your tongue, even though it is contributing only a relatively small portion of the cigar's overall aroma. A very mild and tasty wrapper can render an otherwise overly strong filler more enjoyable.

Binder

A cigar binder serves two purposes. It is the binder that maintains the compression of the filler bunch. So it needs to have sufficient tensile strength, along with some degree of stretch, to accomplish this without tearing or "popping". Secondly, the binder should serve as the primary barrier to air leaks through the sides of the cigar. If a selected binder has some small holes, but in wrapping around the filler, these holes will not overlap, then it can likely do that job.

The combination of a binder and a wrapper must, together, burn well. A slow-burning wrapper will burn well with an efficiently-burning binder *or vice versa*. If both burn well, that is not a problem, but if neither burns well, then the finished cigar will maintain a margin of black char at the start of the ash, and is more likely to burn lopsided, or create a tunnel down the middle of the filler.

Cigar binder contributes very little to the tongue taste of a cigar, and only contributes to the aroma in proportion to its mass.

Sometimes, a quick cigar can be adequately rolled using a nice, sturdy binder, and no wrapper at all.

Filler

There are no particular criteria for what tobacco qualifies for use as filler. Any variety of tobacco can be used, depending on your preferences. Leaf from any level of the stalk can be used, though its nicotine strength increases as you move up the stalk. Filler leaves can have tears and holes and missing pieces, and still serve perfectly as cigar filler. Dissection of premium cigars has shown that "long filler" *may* mean that each piece of filler leaf runs the entire length of the finished cigar. Another interpretation of "long filler" is more aspirational—merely a contrast to scrap or short filler, in which all of the filler content consists of scraps of various length, or even entirely of tiny pieces or shred.

Hand-rolling with long filler is easier than hand-rolling with short filler. The opposite is true of machines—they are much more efficient at using short filler than using long filler. It is a fact that production of long filler cigars (nearly always by hand) yields a bounty of short cutting scrap of fine cigar tobacco. That scrap tobacco is used to make less expensive cigars.

The reputation issue with short filler cigars is that they are not as enjoyable a smoke as long filler cigars. In truth, if the leaf varieties are the same, if the cut or shred of the short filler is fairly uniform, if the binding of the bunch is properly calibrated, and if the blending is as carefully managed as that of long filler cigars, short filler cigars—even machine made ones—can be created to draw just as well, burn just as well, and taste just as enjoyable as a similar long filler cigars. Those "ifs" are seldom met in commercial short filler cigars.

Leaf Preparation for Cigars

Bringing into case

Acquire a heavy plastic bag that is at least 24 inches wide. A gallon or 2-gallon Ziploc bag can do. At least an hour or two in advance of rolling, heavily mist one or several wrappers and binders with non-chlorinated water. The stems will absorb some of the moisture with adequate time, leaving the lamina (the part of the leaf that you will use) in medium to high case.

Filler leaf can be stored in low case, and always ready for cigar rolling. If it is too dry, then the day prior to rolling, lightly mist non-chlorinated water into the leaf's storage bag, and re-close and clamp it. The added moisture will generally distribute among the leaves in the bag after 24 to 48 hours. Doing this on several different bags of filler that is too dry will give you a sense of how much to mist any particular bag of filler. You want it to be still somewhat noisy, but pliable enough not to crumble when handled or when the stem is removed.

Removing the stem (stemming)

For both wrapper and binder, the central vein, or leaf stem, must be removed prior to their use in binding or wrapping a cigar. The leaf should be in case. It will crack and tear if too dry. The simplest and most reliable method of stemming that will not risk significant tearing of the wrapper or binder is to turn the leaf so that the tip is toward you, and the underside of the leaf (generally a lighter color than the upper surface, and always with more prominent or visible veins) facing upward. Fold the leaf in half

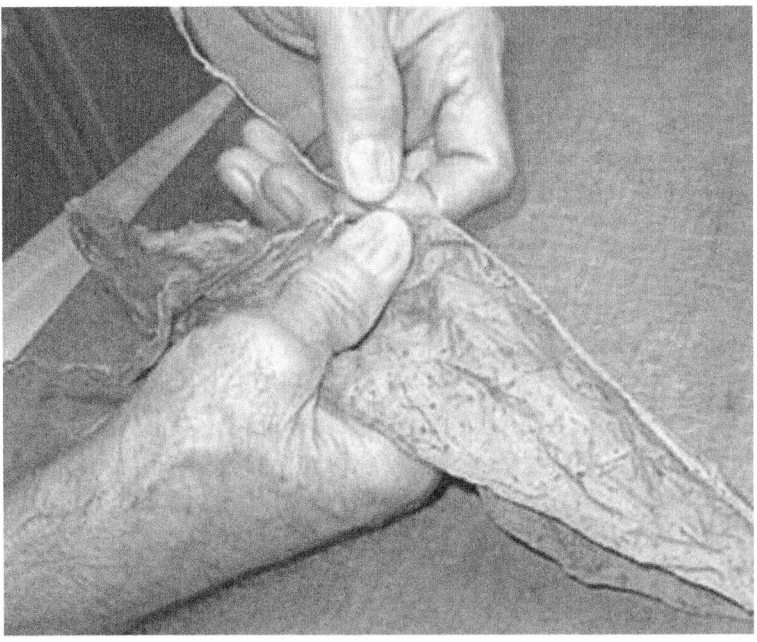

Stemming a folded leaf.

along the stem. About one to two inches from the leaf tip, firmly grasp the folded leaf alongside that portion of the stem, and with the other hand, carefully tear away the stem, extending the tear toward the leaf tip. Once this is free, move the grasping fingers away from you, still alongside the stem, to the next pair of secondary veins, and with the other hand, grasp the now thicker stem, and carefully tear it from the lamina and secondary veins that you are holding. Slowly work your way toward the butt of the stem, grasping at each pair of secondary veins, to prevent them from ripping into the lamina.

You will see in videos every manner of "expert" stemming techniques that may include wrapping the leaf rapidly about the hand, as the stem magically comes away. With practice, this can work with some varieties of tobacco leaf in certain conditions of case. But be warned that you may or may not be happy with the outcome. And you will save only about 10 seconds per leaf—if it works.

The unused halves of wrapper and binder should be promptly returned to their bag or container, so that they don't dry out.

For filler, not as much care is required, since a broad tear into the lamina is not a fatal flaw. For filler with full-length stems, the stemming technique is the same as for wrapper or binder, with the exception that it is usually more convenient in handling the filler leaves if you retain a segment of stem at the tip—usually slightly shorter than the proposed cigar—to keep the two halves

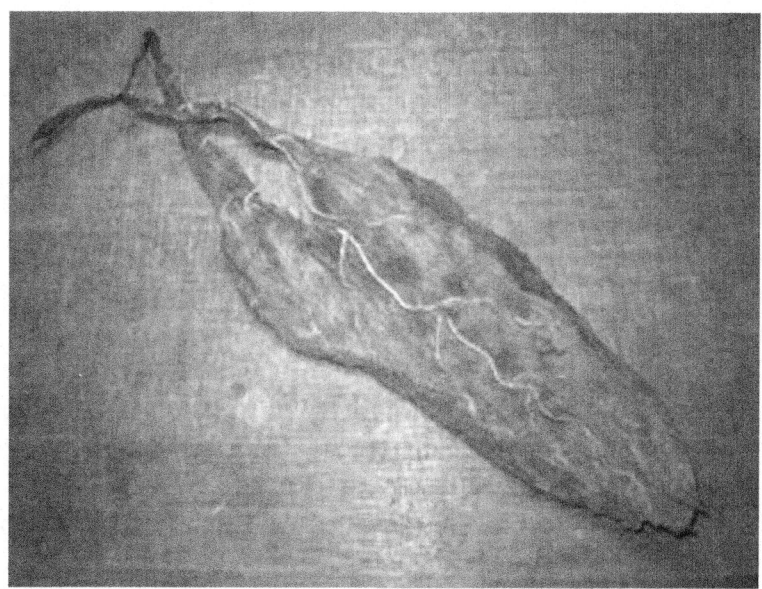

A frog-legged filler leaf.

joined, and to add a bit of rigidity to the final cigar. (Stem is lower in nicotine than the leaf lamina, but burns equally well.)

Some whole leaf filler is shipped partially stemmed, in a state known as "frog-legged." The frog-legging is performed on the premises of the tobacco producer or fermenter. In the process, the thickest half or more of the stem is removed, leaving the thinnest portion of the stem joining the two leaf halves. (Leaves from some factories are frog-legged in a tidy fashion, but other factories may ship fairly sloppy frog-legged filler.)

If the remaining stem of a frog-legged filler leaf is longer than the intended cigar, it is usually easier on the cutting blade (tuck cutter or cigar clipper) if it does not extend all the way into the head of the cigar. A shortened stem also eliminates the possibility of a stem protruding from a cigar head when it is opened for smoking. To shorten the stem of a frog-legged leaf, again fold the leaf so that the under surface is out, tear a small area of lamina where you want to snap the stem (this makes snapping it easier if the stem is tough), snap it, then work your way toward the thicker portion of stem. This is usually a very quick process. For stiff stems in frog-legged leaf, select a length of stem to preserve that does not curve toward the side. You want the stem remnant to be easily embedded within the bunched leaf, and not sticking a sharp end sideways, toward the binder, where it can easily puncture a hole.

Cutting and Trimming
Filler: Depending on the nature and initial length of your filler leaf, it will likely need to be shortened in some manner. The simplest approach, if you are planning to quickly hand-bunch the filler randomly, is to align the tips in one hand (say, with them pointing upward), then tear the bottom to your desired length. The remaining leaf is then aligned with the tips, compressed, then torn again to the same length. Repeat for the length of the remaining leaves. This bunch is then well compressed with both hands, prior to rolling in the binder.

With the more complex, accordion method or tube method, the filler length is cut to an appropriate length using a chaveta. Some even use a ruler or template to measure the length to cut.

Binder: Most binders, after removing the stem, require no trimming. If the thick ends of the remaining secondary veins appear to pose a threat of puncturing the binder as it is wrapped, then use a chaveta to cut a thin arc along that back edge of the binder leaf, removing all the thick vein ends in the process.

Wrapper: If, when the wrapper half-leaf is laid out flat, a crinkled or curly outer edge remains, then trim that away with a chaveta, so that the wrapper will lay well as it is wrapped. That issue aside, an untrimmed wrapper is somewhat more difficult to lay well on the cigar, because of the excess lamina on the back edge. The wrapper strip needs to be wide enough so that, given the ring gauge of the planned cigar, there will be at least a quarter to a half-inch overlap as the bound bunch is wrapped.

Wrapper trimmed for a figurado.   [MarcL]

For a cylindrical cigar (so called *parejo* or parallel), no arc is required in the wrapper. So it can be trimmed as a *straight strip* of leaf. (With a large wrapper leaf, the leftover leaf may be adequate to wrap another cigar, though the secondary veins will be a bit thicker in the cutaway strip.) For making a triple cap, a flag can be left attached to the wrapper strip, or can be cut separately. With a triple cap, the "third" cap is the circular disk

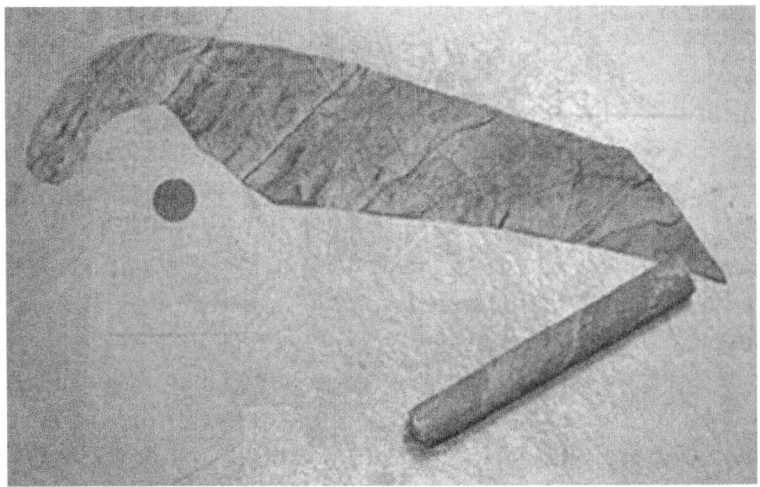

Wrapper trimmed with cap flag and 3rd cap for a parejo. [MarcL]

that tops the head. For a shaped cigar (e.g. torpedo), different portions of the wrapper may require a differing arc to be trimmed. If you are using a figurado mold to produce identical figurado cigars, you may want to make a paper template of the 'S' shaped wrapper, once you find just the right size and arcs.

Kinds of Cigars

American-style cigars

For well over a century and a half, the majority of cigar smokers in the US smoked what may be considered American-style cigars. Originally all hand-rolled, by the early 20th century, most of these cigars were being machine-bunched as well as machine-wrapped, which kept their retail prices below about 10 cents per stick. (Marsh-Wheeling Deluxe Stogies were 11 cents in 1970!) Their fillers used American variety tobaccos, such as Pennsylvania Red, Little Dutch, Lancaster Seedleaf, Glessnor, Swarr, Maryland and even burley varieties. The binders tended to be American binder-class tobaccos, such as Wisconsin Seedleaf, Comstock Spanish, Pennsylvania Broadleaf and Connecticut Broadleaf.

American preferences for wrappers were focused on light-tan *claro* leaf, with thin, Indonesian Sumatra wrappers taking the lead in the late 19th century, soon replaced by the newly developed Connecticut Shade Grown. There were also Florida Sumatra, Dixie Shade and several others. Dark wrappers were nearly all Connecticut Broadleaf or Pennsylvania Broadleaf. Following World War II, the popularity of green wrappers, called *candela*, increased (presenting the image of a "cleaner" cigar habit), and displaced nearly all natural wrappers for about a decade in the 1950s. [*Candela* wrappers are flash-cured while still green, retaining the leaf's chlorophyll, and completely lacking in any natural cigar flavors.]

Most American-style cigars are delicious and enjoyable, but fundamentally different in taste and aroma from cigars made with predominantly Central American and Caribbean varieties of leaf. The introduction of Honduran and Nicaraguan cigars in the late 1960s and early 1970s began to make inroads into the popularity of American-style cigars (in the US), but only among a niche clientele. They did, however, eliminate the popularity of *candela*-wrapped cigars. "Natural" and soon, "Cameroon" wrappers became the favored wrapper on American-made cigars. [Cameroon wrappers are a variety of Indonesian Sumatra Deli leaf grown in the African country of Cameroon.]

The so-called cigar boom of the late 1990s—with its celebrity-endorsed reviews and numerical cigar ratings, spelled doom for the American-style cigar, and eventually, by about 2017, for the entire cigar manufacturing industry in the US, which has nearly ceased to exist, with the exception of the mega companies owned by Swedish Match and other multi-national corporations, Some are still smokable, but most of the sales go to flavored and scented cigars.

Caribbean-style cigars
Since the late 19th and early 20th centuries, cigars from Havana, Cuba have been blessed with an aura of being the best cigars in

the world. This is despite the fact that, until the early 1920s, tobacco grown in Cuba was a collection of random, poorly selected, varietal cultivars. Seedling suppliers there were careless and haphazard in what they produced and distributed, and growers planted whatever they received, performing "selection" of leaf on the maturing plants, and sorting the resulting leaf for various, different uses. But the combination of soil and climate in Cuba, especially in the Vuelta Abajo, is ideal for the production of cigar tobacco, and the majority of what was grown was loosely derived from prototypical *Habano*-type tobacco, later named the *Vuelta Abajo* variety. Most subsequently developed strains, Corojo, Criollo, Criollo 98, etc. were derived from the Vuelta Abajo variety.

Much of the credit for transforming that production into world famous cigars was due to the talents of the cigar blenders and the skilled rollers (*torcedores*) of Havana's cigar factories. They performed the most polished blending and the most consistently beautiful and smokable cigars available anywhere.

With the US embargo of Cuba—extended to cover everything, by President John F. Kennedy in 1962, as well as the nationalization (appropriation) of the Havana cigar factories by Fidel Castro's government, many of Havana's finest cigar experts migrated to Florida, Mexico, Honduras, Nicaragua and other countries, taking their talents and knowledge with them. While premium cigar manufacturing has since languished in Tampa, Florida and Miami, the "Cuban" cigar industry as gained a second life in Central and South America.

All the output of these reborn "Cuban" cigar manufacturers in countries outside of Cuba has focused throughout their existence on producing Cuban-style cigars. A similar style of cigar has been made in the Dominican Republic, and for a while, in Puerto Rico and even the Canary Islands. All of these—true Cuban cigars, Central and South American cigars, as well as those made on various other islands of the Caribbean, can now be globally considered as cigars of the Caribbean Basin, or Caribbean-style cigars.

Their general characteristics are darker wrappers, relatively stronger fillers—most from Habano or Habano-derived tobacco varieties—having a broad, somewhat rounded leaf, and a highly polished appearance. While the possible combinations of components and size and cross-section are infinite, they all unmistakably resemble one another.

European-style cigars
Although Caribbean-style cigars are popular throughout Europe, traditional European-style cigars remain. These are typically small cigars—cigarillos—that are intentionally manufactured to be stored and smoked dry. They are usually not intended to be stored in a humidor. These cigarillos often come in small tins of 10 cigars, and are machine-made.

Methods of Rolling Cigars
For the complete novice, it is worth understanding that a long-filler cigar is not made by twisting the tobacco. A better image is that of a bundle of sticks wrapped from top to bottom with a ribbon. The process of gathering the filler leaf into a bundle is called bunching, which can be approached using one of several different methods, discussed below. The bunched filler is compressed together by wrapping it with a sturdy strip of leaf, known as a binder. Sometimes, this *bound bunch* is set into a cigar mold, in order to make its surface smoother, and perhaps to shape it further. The bound bunch is then wrapped again with a second strip of leaf, known as a wrapper, selected usually for its appearance.

Bunching
Simple bunching: Simple bunching is fast and effective, after a little practice. Grab some leaf, and squeeze it into a cylindrical form with your hands. Excess length can be torn off, and added to the thickness of the bunch. The objective is to avoid any knots or clumps of tobacco that may obstruct air flow within the filler

bunch, to avoid multiple layers of nested leaf, and perhaps to distribute different components of the blend in a particular arrangement within the bunch. If flat leaves are simply placed on top of each other, then rolled up like a beach towel, the flow of air and combustion will channel only through the center of the cigar, leaving the exterior unburned. The leaf within the bunch should be equally crinkled and equally compressed.

Accordion bunching (sometimes called booking): Accordion bunching is relatively fast, but requires quite a bit of practice to perform consistently. With this method, individual— or even stacks of individual—leaves are tightly folded back and forth, like an accordion. Many cigar factories use this method. Compared to other methods, the final compression of the bunch is not as uniform, and sometimes leads to an inconsistent draw. Placing accordion-bunched cigars into a cigar mold may minimize the asymmetry that it sometimes produces in the cross-section of the bound bunch.

***Entubado* (tubed) bunching**: Tubed bunching is the most tedious and time consuming approach to bunching, though it may theoretically provide the most consistent draw in the finished cigar. Using this method, each segment of leaf within the bunch is snugly rolled into a "tube". The tubes are then assembled into a complete bunch of many tubes. This is then bound. Some rollers cut the leaf segments prior to rolling the tubes, then carefully roll an actual tube. Another approach is to start at the leaf base end of a frog-legged filler leaf, and loosely roll it onto itself in a helical form, along an axis parallel to its secondary veins, so that once the top of it is grasped, it remains wound. Each of these helical tubes is added to the accumulating bunch. When using uncut filler leaf, excess length can be torn off, and added to the thickness of the bunch.

While the tightly rolled, carefully cut tubes present a striking visual pattern at the open foot of a finished cigar, and certainly permits adequate draw (if not too tightly compressed), the air flow improvement rationale of this method may exist only in theory, and depend mostly on degree of compression of the bunch. Entubado filler is no doubt more effective at providing adequate draw compared to accordio-pleated filler.

Long-scrap and short-filler cigars: Long scrap can usually be bunched using simple bunching, and bound in the same fashion as a long-filler cigar. Short scrap or even shred is more troublesome, in the absence of a specialized bunching device, such as a Lieberman. A Lieberman is a lever-arm rolling mat that traps a pocket of short filler, much like a manual cigarette roller,

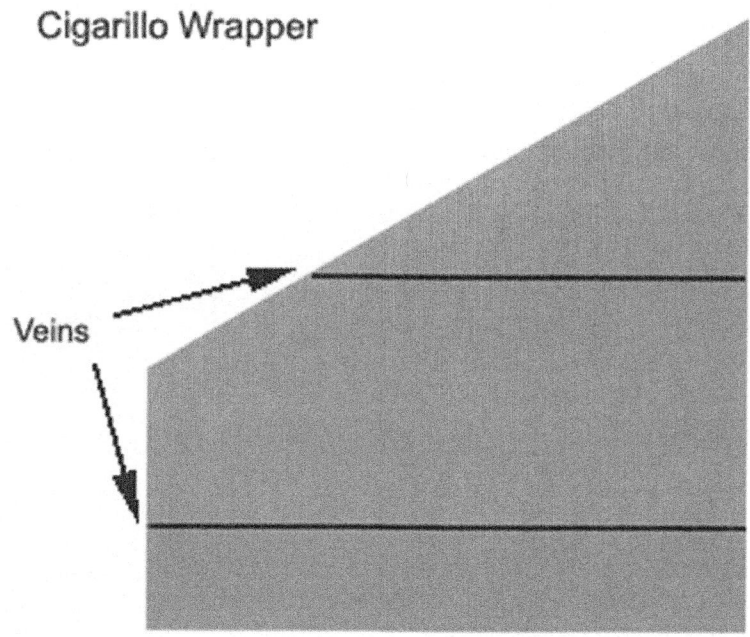

Cutting a binder/wrapper for use in a hand-roller for a cigarillo. The wide, square end (bottom) is inserted into the rollers, after the filler has been formed into a cylinder by the roller mat.

and compresses it into a cylindrical form, while allowing a binder to be inserted and wrapped about the filler. There are little, hand-held cigarillo rollers on the market that are just enlarged versions of a manual cigarette roller.

It is possible to lay an ordinary binder strip on the rolling board, then add little piles of short filler, as the binder is slowly wrapped, inch by inch. A more effective hand-binding approach is to use a broad binder leaf that is cut in half, across its full width, parallel to a secondary vein, so that there is a cigar-length straight edge at the start of rolling. Two or more smaller such binder strips can be combined to comprise the full length of the cigar at the start of rolling.

Bunching short filler in this manner may yield a limp, spongy, bound bunch. In that case, add a standard binder, to stiffen and further compress it solidly.

A temporary "Lieberman" can be created by taping a plastic mat (a common 7 to 10" wide leaf bag) to the countertop, laying a

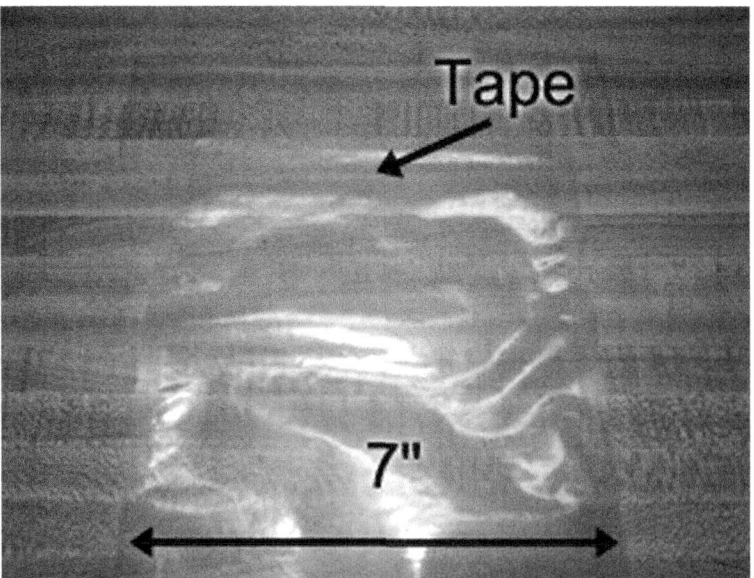

A 7-inch wide tobacco bag taped to the counter.

binder leaf on it lengthwise, and then piling short filler in a row across the far end of the mat, and on top of the wide start of the binder. Fold the mat over the pile of filler, then compress and drag the hump in the mat toward you, so that the binder strip is wound about the filler as the filler is compressed.

Two pieces of binder leaf laid near the taped end of the mat.

Short scrap filler is piled onto the binder.

The loose end of the mat is folded over the tobacco, then a dowel is used to compress the bunch, while drawing it away from the taped end of the mat.

With a little practice, this works reasonably well, though it sometimes requires a second binder to be manually wrapped onto it, before the wrapper is applied in the usual fashion.

Appearance of the scrap filler, after a wrapper is added.

Binding

Single binder: For a bunch that you plan to place into a mold, a single binder is usually sufficient. Lay the binder half-leaf so that the leaf tip is closest to you on the rolling board, the under surface of the leaf (most prominent veins) is facing up, and the veins are horizontal to you. Place the gathered bunch of long filler parallel to the veins, with the "foot" end near the closest tip of the binder. Bring the bottom tip of the binder toward you, and then over the bunch—like wrapping a scarf around a neck, and tuck it under the opposite edge of the bunch. Begin wrapping it by compressing the bunch beneath your fingertips, and very slowly rolling it away from you, while keeping the binder taut and smooth. This takes a little practice. When you reach the "head", and the bunch is entirely wrapped, you can apply a small amount of cigar glue to hold it wrapped, or simply twist the end of the binder well, and clamp it with a clothespin.

The binder can appear sloppy, so long as it compresses the bunch adequately and uniformly, and does not leave gaps. Its sins will be hidden by the wrapper.

Double binder: When using relatively delicate binder leaf, or when rolling free-hand, without a mold, a double binder reduces the risk of the filler puncturing through to the binder, increases

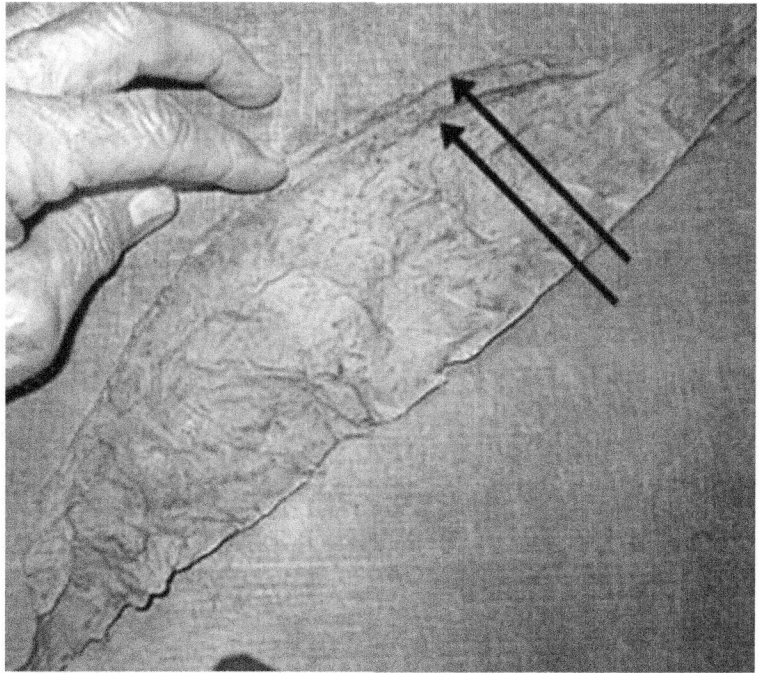

Double binder, one on top of the other.

the stiffness of the bound bunch, and allows for better compression of the bunch. *A double binder is easier for a new roller to learn to use effectively*, since it requires less of an understanding of how much stress a particular variety of binder can handle.

A single binder is laid flat on the rolling board. A second binder half-leaf is laid on top of it, with its veins oriented the same, and with its outer edge slightly "inside" the outer edge of the first binder. If you create a double binder with the two halves of a single leaf, one strip will have its prominent vein side facing up, and the other's facing toward the board. Wrap the bunch within the double binder as though it were only a single leaf strip. If you use glue, glue the final edge of both binder layers.

Reinforcement cap: If the "head" (the mouth end) of the bound bunch does not feel as sturdy as you would prefer, you can often use the remainder of the unused binder strip to reinforce

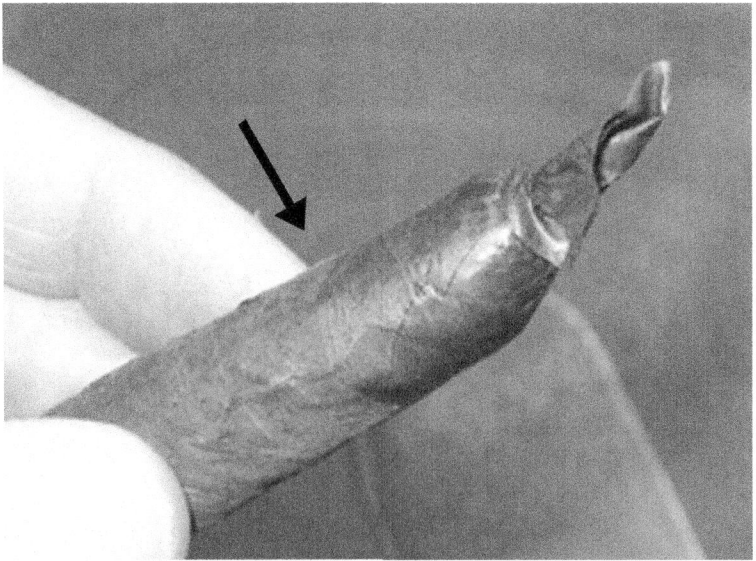

A reinforcement cap added to a binder. [MarcL]

the head. Trim the lower margin of this scrap perpendicular to the veins, so that you have a straight edge. Mist it lightly with non-chlorinated water, then start wrapping the bound bunch 1-1/2 to 2 inches below the head. This will add an additional layer to the binder at the head, and the seam it creates will be hidden under the final wrapper.

Wrapping: If you begin with a nicely bound bunch and a properly trimmed wrapper strip in high case, this is the easiest aspect of making a cigar. Wrapping an aesthetically flawless cigar requires experience. Wrapping one that you can be proud of does not. The wrapper should be in high case, so that it is fully relaxed, and its secondary veins limp and straight. The leaf strip is laid out in the same manner as for a binder. Begin closest to you, with the "foot" of the bound bunch about an inch from the tip of the wrapper strip. Bring the tip of the wrapper toward you, then carefully wrap it over the foot of the bunch, and *tuck* it beneath the far edge of the foot. [The foot of the cigar is sometimes called the "tuck", because in starting the wrapper, you wrap then tuck it under at the foot.]

Wrap the bunch by rolling it away from you, while gently applying tension (and smoothing) to the underlying wrapper strip. Keep veins parallel to the bunch. Don't hesitate to back up and try a section again. Aim for a snug fit to the outer edge of the wrapper, and a wrinkle-free lay. As you near the head, apply a tiny smear of glue to the outer edge of the wrapper. Or you can just complete the wrap, and close the head with a twist.

Capping (closing the head)

Adding a simple or complex (for example. a so-called triple) cap requires that you use cigar glue. Add the first cap using remaining wrapper leaf in the same manner as applying a reinforcing cap on the binder (see above), and glue it. For a more complex cap, an oval or teardrop shaped segment of vein-free wrapper leaf is cut from wrapper scrap using a chaveta. It needs to be long enough to wrap more than one complete wrap around the head, and must be glued on. Any protruding bits of the head must be trimmed and tucked toward the center of the cigar head. Cut a third cap (a circular disc), using a cap cutter, apply glue to it, then hold the cigar vertically above it, head down, and stick the head onto the glue-covered disc. Tidy it with your fingertip.

Approaches to Cigar Blending
Spanish names for stalk positions—their significance

Volado: *Fliers.* These are leaves from the very bottom of the stalk. They are often large and thin, have little flavor or aroma, and burn quite well. Volado usually contains very low nicotine concentrations. They seldom appear in the whole leaf market. Their purpose is simply to enhance the burn of a filler blend that otherwise might not burn adequately.

Seco: These leaves are from the lower stalk positions, just above *volado*, and up to about half-way up the stalk. They are thicker than volado, often quite large, their flavor and aroma are distinctive of the variety, though they are mild, with moderate nicotine. They usually burn well. They comprise the bulk of the filler in *milder* cigars.

Viso: Viso is leaf from about the half-way point of the stalk, for another quarter of the length up the stalk. Viso leaves tend to be somewhat smaller than seco, are darker, somewhat thicker, and usually have higher nicotine. They don't burn as easily as seco. Their flavor and aroma are richer than seco. They are commonly added to a filler blend to enhance the aroma.

Ligero: Ligero leaf is most of the upper quarter of the stalk. They are dark, thick, tend to be small, their flavor and aroma are intense, their burn relatively poor, and their nicotine quite high. They are conceptually used to provide *fortaleza,* or strength, though many current, premium cigars utilize ligero heavily.

Corona: Corona leaves (sometimes called tip leaf) are the topmost four or so leaves on the stalk, below the start of the blossom head. They often ferment to nearly black (*oscuro*). They are quite thick, very small, and have an exquisite aroma. Their nicotine is very high. They do not burn well. Corona leaf seldom appears on the whole leaf market. Their use is for very dark wrappers on specialty, small cigars (Petite Corona and smaller), and as a minor blending component. [Commercially, tobacco plants are often topped—the stalk cut off—below the level at which corona leaf grows. This increases the strength, thickness and size of all the remaining leaf.]

Spanish names for cigar wrapper leaf colors

Naming for the colors of cigar wrappers is messy, sometimes in Spanish, sometimes in plain English, and sometimes as a designation of the global region of its popularity. With the exception of Candela wrapper, which is artificially flash-cured to retain its green color, cigar leaf color is the result of a combination of tobacco variety and stalk position. Fermentation —the very same fermentation temperatures and duration— produces lighter leaf from lower on the stalk, and darker leaf from higher up the stalk. There is no need for extra efforts to achieve a specific color. It is intrinsic to the leaf. If all the leaf from an entire plant is fermented together, the lower leaf comes out lighter, the higher leaf darker. It just happens.

With only about a half-dozen wrapper color designations (aimed at cigar consumers), they are always inadequate in describing the continuum of color shades seen in wrappers. Intermediate tones are sometimes designated as, for example, *claro-colorado*. Although one can certainly identify not only wrapper leaf by its color, but also binder and filler, the color designations tend to be reserved for wrapper, while the stalk-position names (*volado, seco, viso, ligero*) are usually applied only to filler grade leaf.

Candela (or Double-Claro): The name (candela) refers to their method of flash-curing, using heat. These bright or dull green, thin wrappers, are usually too delicate for use as binder, and are not used in filler. The leaf retains its chlorophyll, so tastes "green" or "grassy". Sometimes labeled as AMS (for American Market Selection).

Claro: Claro is a light tan color. It presents a mild taste to a cigar, and can be used to somewhat tame a more intense filler blend. Most claro leaf comes from the lower stalk. This is sometimes labeled "Natural", or as EMS. (see below)

Colorado: This is a vague color that encompasses darker claro as well as lighter maduro. In some instances it is literally reddish brown, *rosado*. The flavor is richer. It generally comes from mid-stalk leaf. It also may be designated as EMS (for English Market Selection).

Maduro: The name means, "mature". But its color has nothing to do with leaf maturity. It ranges from a rich chocolate brown to a very dark brown. The flavor is usually full.

Oscuro (or Double-Maduro): This is wrapper that is nearly black. Its flavor is complex and full, sometimes slightly sweet. Only certain varieties of tobacco produce leaf that naturally ferments to oscuro. Some oscuro wrapper burns poorly, and thus requires a binder beneath that burns well.

Determining your preference for nicotine strength

Although many cigar smokers enjoy a range of nicotine strength in their cigars, it is possible to blend cigars to have relatively low nicotine, or by contrast, to have toxic levels that cause you to feel ill. New tobacco users will have a baseline nicotine tolerance lower than that of experienced users.

Nicotine is absorbed from *cigar* smoke into the body almost instantly through the mouth and nasopharynx. Nicotine circulating in the body has a half-life of 1 to 2 hours. That is to say, without additional nicotine absorption, the current level of circulating nicotine will be reduced by half, over a span of 1 to 2 hours.

The earliest indication that you may have taken in more nicotine than you can handle is the sudden onset of hiccoughs or belching. As nicotine absorption continues, an increasing nausea or malaise develops.

In evaluating your own preference for nicotine strength in the cigars that you blend, keep in mind that total cigar consumption per time is a factor. If you smoke two cigars sequentially, within a few hours time, the nicotine of the second cigar is added on top of the remaining nicotine from the first. Thinner cigars release their nicotine more gradually than fatter cigars. Leaf from higher on the plant contains more nicotine that lower leaf. And of course, heavier weight cigars contain more nicotine than lighter weight cigars of the same blend.

Nicotine is cleared from the body more slowly in individuals 65 years and older. Meals and physical activity usually speed the clearance of nicotine by the liver, while consumption of grapefruit juice slows nicotine clearance by the liver.

All of this detail is to highlight that personal nicotine preference can vary in the same individual under differing circumstances, at different times of the day, and at different ages.

> [Benowitz NL, Hukkanen J, Jacob P: **Nicotine Chemistry, Metabolism, Kinetics and Biomarkers.** Handb Exp Pharmacol. 2009; (192): 29–60.]

In trying your own blends of different nicotine strength cigars, your impression from a single cigar at a single moment in time may be misleading. Roll several of each blend, and try those spread over a span of a week.

Cigar filler that is predominantly seco filler is representative of the *low* end of nicotine strength. A very full nicotine strength can be achieved with half the filler as ligero, a quarter viso and a quarter seco. An all ligero cigar (which might have a wonderful aroma) will knock most experienced cigar smokers onto their backsides.

There is no exact science to your preferred range, and only modest rolling experience will give you a feel for your own sweet spot.

Testing leaf

There is more to cigar leaf than nicotine. Each variety has its own unique characteristics. Each grower may ship the same variety, but with subtle differences in character. Each growing region and each growing season add their own nuances to a batch of leaf.

To get a sense of the character of a new batch of leaf, roll a very small cigar (like a petite corona) with filler comprised entirely of that leaf. Use familiar wrapper and binder, or find usable wrapper and binder among the batch of filler leaf, and make a *puro* of that variety. With even the very finest leaf, this may not be the best way to enjoy it in a cigar, but the purpose is rather to identify what is unique about this particular leaf. *Perhaps take notes.*

Blending trials

Keep in mind that the apparent strength of a cigar *using the very same filler blend* increases as the diameter of the cigar increases. A blend that seems too mild in a smaller cigar may be perfect in a fatter cigar. Your impression will also be influenced by other factors beyond the cigar being smoked. Is it the first cigar of the day? Have you eaten? Are you drinking something while smoking it? Are there cooking aromas in the background?

Start with a general combination of seco/viso/ligero ratios that is familiar to you. It will certainly be different with different varieties and batches of leaf, but that minimizes one confounding variable in comparing a new, trial blend to a blend with which you are already familiar.

In making adjustments to a new blend, do so in small increments. *Perhaps take notes.*

Roll the same trial filler blend in different wrapper/binder combinations, and in differing ring gauge cigars. Smoke them thoughtfully, so that you force yourself to analyze the characteristics of each trial cigar.

Your documentation

Even with a great memory, you will find that brief, contemporary notes, taken while thoughtfully smoking a test cigar, can prove helpful in settling on an ideal blend for your tastes. Keeping a tiny writing tablet handy will encourage you to jot down your thoughts as you smoke. Keep it simple, so that the process of documentation doesn't become annoying. There is no advantage to writing elaborate prose, or consulting an "aroma wheel". The notes are for you alone to read. *Retain your notes.*

Resting

There are a lot of opinions surrounding "resting" a newly rolled cigar, prior to smoking it. Most of the resting time suggested by many is indeed required, in order to allow overly moist tobacco, rolled in an overly moist state, to dry-down to an appropriately smokable condition. Melding of aromas, etc. is probably not meaningful for a cigar. If the filler is initially rolled while in *low case*, it will not substantially change over hours or days or weeks (or longer) of resting.

Depending on ambient humidity, the binder and wrapper do need to dry to low case, in order to smoke at their best. This may be a mere 15 minutes or several hours or even longer. But once they are at the same low case as the filler, the cigar is ready to fire up.

If you want to taste cedar, then you will need to rest a cigar inside a cedar chest for a while. But this is more of a flavorant issue, rather than a natural "settling" aspect of tobacco that has been rolled into a cigar.

Cigar rolling problems

Leaf crumbles while stemming: The leaf is too dry—it is *out of case*. Mist it very lightly with non-chlorinated water, place it into a container and wait a bit.

Small holes in the binder: Usually, a few small, random holes in the binder leaf won't matter. If there is a hole that concerns you, lay a small, vein-free segment of leaf (a patch, if you will) onto the hole prior to rolling the bunch, so that it will end up on the interior of the binder.

Binder tears easily: There are two reasons why a binder may tend to tear as you wrap a cigar. Each binder variety, and sometimes each leaf within a batch, depends on its stretch and tensile strength to remain intact as you roll. If you exceed that, usually from expecting it to perform too much compression of the bunch, then any binder will tear. For a novice roller, the most common cause of binder tears is that case of the binder leaf is too low. Mist the binder more, or allow it to hydrate inside a bag for longer, prior to rolling. A soggy binder will also tear easily.

Binder leaf too small for cigar length: If you wish to roll a cigar that is longer than your available binder leaves will permit, then use an additional binder leaf. On the cutting board, lay out the leaf strip that will bind the head end of the cigar, then lay a second binder leaf strip on top of it, but moved toward the foot end. They must overlap for at least one circuit around the bunch, in order to stay wrapped. The "head" segment will trap the "foot" segment. You may need to trim the tip of the "head" segment at a 90 degree angle to its veins, to prevent that tip from dangling from the finished cigar.

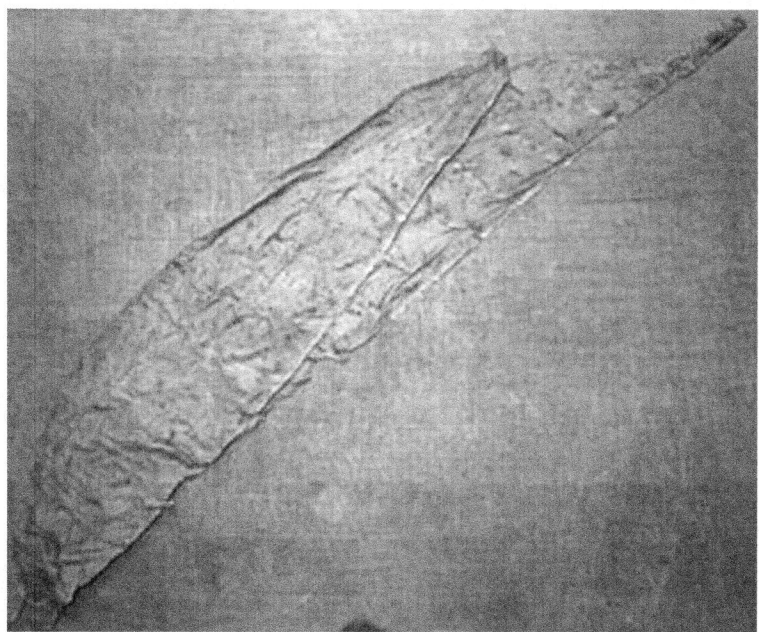

Binder toward the head is laid beneath the binder at the foot.

Bound bunch feels uneven: This is all about your fingers and palms learning to feel a consistent volume in a compressed bunch. With practice, you will sense a softer spot, then simply add a bit of additional filler to the soft spot. It just takes some practice.

Bound bunch has a soft head: Although the head may be simply lacking sufficient filler (see "uneven" above), the head may need to be tapered and compressed more tightly. Consider adding a reinforcement cap to the bound bunch to compress it.

Difficult to lift bound bunch from a cigar mold: Your bound bunch is too fat for the mold. If it requires considerable effort to seat a bound bunch into a mold well, the bunch should probably be taken apart and re-bound to a slightly smaller diameter. It should be a snug fit, but not a tight fit.

Cigar glue won't hold: The glue-water mixture is too wet—too runny. Glue of a proper consistency will prevent sliding of the two contact surfaces as soon as they are pressed together. Allow your glue batch to dry a bit, and try again.

Wrapper frequently splits near the head while rolling: As with the binder, experience using a particular wrapper will provide a sense of how much stretch and tension the leaf can provide, before splitting. Also, a wrapper that is not in high case will tend to split as you approach the head of a tapered cigar.

Small wrapper bursts near the head: Sometimes your chosen wrapper leaf may be too small for the cigar. If you attempt to make do with it, the wrapper is likely to burst near the head (in that last desperate inch of your desire to make it fit).

Remedy for a burst wrapper

wrapper binder

If the cigar is just for yourself, it does not need to resemble any other cigar on the planet. Remove the damaged wrapper, trim it to a reasonable shape, then leave as much of the binder exposed as necessary for the remaining wrapper to easily succeed. You will end up with a wrapper cap, and exposed binder at the foot.

Wrapper outer edge is curled over: Many wrappers can be laid perfectly flat at their outer edge, even without trimming. Some are too wavy at the margin to allow that. The quickest solution (why it is used in cigar factories) is to trim away that outer margin with a chaveta, leaving a flat, flawless edge. Otherwise, care and practice may allow you to maintain a flat, uncurled outer margin without trimming.

Wrapper outer edge does not lay against the cigar: This is due to applying inadequate stretch at the outer margin while wrapping. The wrapper may need additional moisture. It is also possible that the edge needs to have some of its curve trimmed away with a chaveta. Lift the bunch, as needed, to keep it snug.

Wrapper inner edge tends to fold or pleat as I roll a tapered cigar: Wrapper usually needs to overlap only about 3/8 inch. If the wrapper strip is too broad, the inner edge will be unable to lay flat as the cigar curves away. Try a narrower trim to the wrapper strip, while maintaining adequate overlap.

Draw too tight/ too loose in finished cigar: If the cigar appears and feels well rolled, but the draw is too tight or too lose, the adjustment is usually about compression of the filler by the binder. If the filler is in too high a case, it is easy to over-compress it, without applying much pressure while rolling. Stuffing a perfectly compressed bunch into a cigar mold designed for a narrower diameter cigar will lead to a beautiful cigar that will not draw. A "knot" or folded-up chunk of tobacco within otherwise aligned filler can serve as a choke point.

Filler in low case is difficult to over-compress in cigars that are the diameter of a corona or greater (about 5/8 inch). With unusually thin gauge cigars, the very same compression can obstruct flow. You will just have to practice more to acquire a sense of how tightly to compress a *lancero*.

If the draw is too loose, simply increase the compression applied by the binder.

Cigar burns down the side: Bunching using a book or accordion method has a tendency to create air flow channels at the folded corners. If a portion of a "stack" of folded leaf is curved to fit within the bounds of a cigar's sides, the area of filler opposite that curved stack will serve as a low-resistance flow channel for air and combustion, causing channeling down the side, or "canoeing". One remedy is to fold narrower "books" or pleats. Another is to use a different bunching method.

Smoking a cigar in windy conditions may also tend to cause a cigar to burn down one side.

Cigar won't burn: All finished cigar leaves will burn, some better than others. Leaf from lower on the stalk (e.g. seco) usually burns better than leaf from the upper stalk (e.g. viso and ligero). In addition to the intrinsic combustibility of the leaf, some leaf is more hygroscopic (water attracting and holding) than other leaf. With these latter tobaccos, smoking them in very high ambient humidity (where the relative humidity is chronically elevated well above 75%) leads to a cigar that may light easily, but then go out with increasing frequency, and perhaps become "fire-proof" after smoking only about half of it.

There are only two possible solutions. Save these cigars for very dry conditions, or alter the blend. [For home-grown leaf, using fertilizer that contains too much chloride may lead to very poor leaf combustion. Leaf that is not adequately fermented and aged will tend to char, rather than fully burn. Allow it more aging.]

Cigar too mild: Add more viso or ligero, and less seco to the blend. (Ligero is stronger than viso.)

Cigar too strong: Add more seco, and less viso and ligero to the blend. (Ligero is stronger than viso.)

Cigar won't hold an ash: Some wrappers tend to continually shed fine flakes of ash. Tobacco ash is entirely residual minerals, with all the lignin of the leaf fiber consumed in the combustion. What is amazing is that *any* cigars hold a long ash. Of course different leaf ingredients in the filler, binder and wrapper have differing structure to their left over minerals. Cigar ash without a binder or wrapper usually collapses soon after it is formed. So most of the ash retention is due to the layered nature of the wrapper and binder in contrast to the lay of the filler—similar to plywood.   A possible approach to improving ash hold is to increase the overlap of the wrapper, or to just use a double binder.

Cigar won't relight after I set it down for a while: Smoking a cigar increases the moisture content of the filler. Letting the lit cigar go out permits that moisture to be more fully absorbed into the cooling filler leaf, whereas continued smoking keeps the filler warmer, driving the moisture out through the head. If ambient humidity where the cigar sat is higher than your humidor's humidity, it may have absorbed even more moisture.

Some tobacco varieties (and some batches of the same variety) are more hygroscopic than others, and tend to more easily latch on to ambient humidity. Storing in 60 to 65% RH may remedy the problem, except when ambient humidity is quite high.

There may be a lot of factors at play.

Selecting and using cigar blend kits

"These blends are made up of filler, binder, and wrapper parts and include cigar glue so you have everything you need to create your cigars in one package. Each blend contains about 1 lb. Of tobacco which is enough to make approximately twenty 50 x 7 cigars. Cigar kits are a great way to economically sample multiple tobaccos." [Whole Leaf Tobacco]

Unless you are already accustomed to smoking potent cigars, start with one of the milder blend kits, reading the descriptions to determine that. You can always purchase separate viso or ligero leaf of any variety to bolster the strength, if your initial blends seem too mild. Or you can go initially with one of the stronger blends.

The purpose of a blend kit is to allow a novice, who might be unfamiliar with home-rolling cigars, to explore one or more blends of various ingredients, without buying a pound of each.

How Length, Ring Gauge and Pressing Impact the Smoking Experience

It's actually rocket science. A cigar—its length, diameter and cross-section (rectangular or round) and degree of filler compression (obstruction to flow) all influence the flow of air, and with it, the flow of the heat of combustion as the cigar burns. This flow of air and heat determines the combustion temperature of the "cherry", which affects the mix of combustion products (what you smell and taste).

Tobacco combustion

At combustion temperatures that are neither too high or too low, the taste and aroma of a cigar are usually considered to be at their most enjoyable. *A smoking cigar is a dynamic system.* Combustion produces water in the chemical oxidation process. This water is then drawn toward the head of the cigar, where it is partly absorbed by the filler, causing its rate of combustion to slow, and swelling the filler so as to reduce air flow.

Narrower cigars tend to burn at a higher temperature than fatter cigars. So the same blend will seem different when rolled into cigars of different ring gauge.

Square or box-pressed cigars have functional "corners" that channel cooler air around the center of the "cherry". Thus the total air flow drawn through the cigar has a less direct effect on combustion temperature of the "cherry". With this alteration in air flowing into the "cherry", a square-pressed cigar will taste different from the very same cigar left in its natural, round cross-section. Sometimes, harsher filler blends seem smoother when the cigar has been square pressed.

Natural filtering

All cigars filter their smoke through the length of remaining filler —moderating any flavors within the smoke. The longer the cigar, the greater the initial filtering effect. The thinner the cigar, the more these trapped chemicals are concentrated—sometimes to the point that a nearly black, oily and bitter bead of condensate may appear at the cut head.

But with cigars of any size and shape, the flavor and aroma becomes stronger (perhaps harsher) as you smoke toward the head (the cigar butt). Yes, a cigar's head is also its butt. With longer and thinner cigars, you may reach this point with 2 or more inches of cigar remaining. With very fat cigars, you may burn your fingertips before tasting it. How much of an issue this becomes is highly dependent on the filler blend.

Smoke "volume"
A fatter cigar supports a larger cross-section of actively combusting tobacco, which results in more smoke, or denser smoke, per puff (and more nicotine per puff).

Unsmokable butt weight
Although a fatter cigar provides a somewhat lower combustion temperature, a greater volume of smoke per puff, and the opportunity to smoke the cigar to a shorter butt length, when compared to a thinner cigar, the weight of the unsmokable butt (a weight of tobacco that you have paid for, and committed to this particular cigar) is greater than with a thinner cigar.

Cigar Storage
Humidity
Cigars stored above a relative humidity (RH) of 75% or greater will eventually mold. Cigars rolled with overly damp filler may mold, even if the storage RH is below 75%. Below about 60% RH, cigars tend to become too dry, and the foot may split.

Temperature stability
Cigars should be stored in a relatively stable temperature, or at least an ambient temperature that does not swing rapidly. The manner in which rapidly changing temperature affects stored cigars is by its affect on RH. An increase in ambient temperature of 20°F will drop the RH by half. Stored cigars within any container are not uniformly heated or cooled. One part of the

container heats more rapidly than other parts. This creates warm spots and cool spots, creating a heat pump that will drive moisture from the warmer area, and condense it in the cooler areas. Cigars in the cooler area then become subject to mold.

Containers

Cigars can be stored within bags or boxes of various materials. And these may or may not be themselves contained within a humidor or larger box or tub. Wood containers provide better temperature insulation, as well as better stability of the internal humidity. Bags and plastic boxes or tubs do not have those advantages. If a plastic container can be made vapor-proof, with a tight fitting, gasketted lid, or a bag zip-closed or rolled and clamped at the open end, then humidity can be maintained for much longer. Thin polyethylene bags, like sandwich bags, are not vapor-proof. Thicker polyethylene bags, such as freezer bags, are more vapor resistant. Laminated poly-nylon bags are completely vapor proof—the material used for vacuum-sealed foods.

The greater the total mass of cigars (or whole leaf) stored within a container, the more slowly it changes in both humidity and temperature. So a full humidor is more stable than a nearly empty one.

Whole Leaf Storage

Humidity

Whole leaf tobacco should be stored at a relative humidity (RH) of 75% or lower. By keeping filler in low case (RH ~ 60%) and binder or wrapper in medium case (RH ~70%), it will be ready for rolling right out of the container (bag, etc.). Medium case *wrapper* may require some additional humidification prior to use. Leaf that is maintained in high case (RH above 75%) is ready to roll, but may mold if stored in that condition.

Temperature stability

As discussed in detail for storage of cigars, storing whole leaf in a relatively stable ambient temperature is important. If the temperature swings rapidly, moisture will condense in portions of the leaf, and may lead to mold.

Containers

Cigar leaf purchased on-line may be shipped in sealed, vapor-proof bags. Unopened, the leaf can be stored in these bags for at least a few years, provided the ambient temperature is relatively stable.

Once such a bag is opened, it can still serve for excellent storage, so long as care is taken in opening it initially (cut it carefully just below the heat seal using a pair of scissors), and it is promptly re-closed each time that you remove leaf from it. Press out all the excess air. Fold the corners of the open end to a right angle, then tightly roll and flatten the entire open end over itself several times. Follow this with clamping the rolled edge flat, using a chip-bag clamp or two or three clothespins. Simply taping the rolled end may allow it to leak air and vapor.

If you store whole leaf within large, plastic tubs, it will gradually dry. Once completely dry, the tobacco is at zero risk of

developing mold. Tobacco will not age further, so long as it is totally dry (out of "case"). Tobacco that is out of case will instantly crumble to fragments and dust, if handled or dropped in that state. Should the tobacco become completely dry, just mist it lightly with non-chlorinated water, close the container, then recheck it in a day.

Home-rolled figurados by Fair Trade Tobacco Forum member, MarcL.

Home-rolled parejo by Fair Trade Tobacco Forum member, waikikigun.

8. Pipe Tobacco

Ancient glyphs: pipe smokers in Tiahuanaco, Bolivia.

For most of the first 300 years after Europe's discovery of tobacco (already agronomically well developed and widely cultivated by the native peoples of the western hemisphere for thousands of years) Europeans and their colonists consumed tobacco by smoking it in a pipe. ["Snuffing" powdered tobacco into the nose was considered a medicinal use, even though more popular among ladies and in the royal courts of Europe.] Centuries old methods of packing, preserving and transporting tobacco from the New World to Europe by sailing ship resulted in chemical and physical changes in the tobacco that have come to be associated with characteristic classes of pipe tobacco. This is certainly true of Perique and of Cavendish tobacco (the Cavendish process, not "Cavendish cut".)

Styles of Pipe Tobacco

Straight Varietals

For sampling the specific characteristics of a tobacco variety, it can be helpful to smoke a bowl of it unblended with any other tobacco. Sometimes you may just enjoy a particular tobacco all on its own. How enjoyable this is may depend on the acidity (pH) of the smoke it produces.

Flue-cured tobaccos yield relatively acidic smoke. By contrast, Perique produces relatively alkaline smoke. Increased acidity is the primary cause of tip-of-the-tongue bite. Increased alkalinity significantly raises the absorption of nicotine from the mouth and pharynx, and also can cause a bite toward the back of the tongue.

So smoking tobaccos of identical nicotine content will seem stronger or weaker, biting or non-biting, depending on the pH of the smoke it produces. Virginia-perique combinations are popular specifically because these two components can be blended in a proportion (for example, 5 parts Virginia to 3 parts Perique) that is perfectly balanced—eliminating all tongue bite while smoothing the apparent nicotine intensity.

Cavendish processed tobacco (*not* including commercial Cavendish doctored with propyleneglycol—PG—or with glycerin) tends to be relatively neutral in pH, even when made from flue-cured Virginia leaf.

Most *cigar* varieties of leaf tend to be more alkaline, though considerably less so than Perique. Burley and some Maryland varieties start off with higher nicotine, and may also produce smoke as alkaline as that of cigar leaf. Dark-air-cured leaf nearly always creates a somewhat more alkaline smoke, as well as a higher nicotine concentration.

English and Balkan Blends
A hallmark of so-called "English" style pipe tobacco is that it traditionally contained nothing but tobacco—the result of a British law intended to crack down on adulterated tobacco in the market. This is no longer the law, but English-style blends certainly contain no added flavorings. So, in its many variants, all are exclusively non-aromatic pipe tobaccos.

That restriction was accommodated by blending with a number of exotic tobaccos that, in themselves, are distinctly aromatic, such as fire-cured Latakia, and a number of varieties of Oriental (sometimes identified as Turkish) tobacco, each with its own aroma.

A classic Balkan blend may contain flue-cured Virginia, Oriental, Latakia, and perhaps burley, Perique and sometimes Cavendish. These have a pouch aroma of smokiness and roasted nuts.

Other traditional English blends may utilize toasted, steamed, stewed or heavily pressed tobacco (Virginia or burley), and may appear entirely medium brown, rather than the bright and black pieces within a Balkan blend. All of the great tobacco purveyors of Britain (Rattray's, Dunhill, etc.) have now outsourced their production to other European countries, and the blends are no longer the same.

Aromatic Blends, Casings and Flavorings
These are blends of tobacco varieties that are flavored with non-tobacco flavorants, such as vanilla, chocolate, coffee, different fruits, or other natural flavors (e.g. licorice or anise, honey, molasses, Deer Tongue leaf, etc.). They may be flavored with brandy, rum, whiskey or other liquor or distilled spirit. Many of these flavorants evaporate fairly rapidly from tobacco leaf (though Maryland is known for its ability to cling to flavorants), so most commercial aromatic pipe blends include glycerin or propyleneglycol (PG) or both, to retain the flavor.

Forming Pipe Tobacco
Most tobacco takes on a "sweeter" taste and more prune-like aroma when pressed. This is a combination of disruption of cell walls in the leaf lamina (which can happen at as low as 3 to 5 psi), allowing everything that is normally isolated within the cells to be exposed to both air and microbes. If this is done beneath a liquid seal (typically under about 35 psi), then the yeast, *Pichia anomala*, dominates, and turns it into Perique after a few months. With more access to air, that doesn't occur so much, and there is less of a "barnyard" Perique aroma.

So just plain, dry pressing does alter the tobacco, making it somewhat darker in color (nicotine oxidation) as well as more fruity. Since there are infinite variations in the possible applied pressure and moisture content and ambient microbes, there are, like natural cheese, a lot of possible outcomes.

In the nineteenth century (say 170 years ago), several pounds of finished tobacco would be pressed under a screw-press into a thick sheet, to resemble a 1" thick plank of dark wood. These were cut into flat, 1" thick, 1.5" wide bars of relatively dry tobacco, and wrapped that way, to be shipped to general merchants (trading posts and general stores). These rectangular bars were called tobacco "plug". Each merchant had on hand a guillotine-type

Cavendish press cake cut into plug.

cutter (called a *plug cutter*), with a long lever for a handle, that enabled him to cut a plug of tobacco—sold by the inch—into the length desired by a customer. During that epoch, the customer would then take the paper-wrapped chunk of plug home, where it would store well, and later use a common knife to shave off slices for immediate use. This was called "sliced plug". The sliced plug was then either broken into several large pieces, or *rubbed* between both hands, and transformed into shred, for packing into a pipe. Commercial vendors began offering pre-sliced plug (called flake) in small tins, and soon also offered "ready-rubbed" sliced plug, that resembles the typical shredded pipe tobacco sold today.

A commercial alternative to plug tobacco was *twist* tobacco, which is a 1/2 to 1 inch thick *rope* of tobacco, sold as a roughly 1-foot length that had been twisted into a loop. Similar to plug, twist tobacco is first sliced, then the resulting *coins* either just folded and stuffed into a pipe bowl, or sometimes rubbed-out prior to packing the bowl.

A lot of this plug and twist practice really had to do with prolongation of shelf-life, shipping requirements within the commercial supply chain of the 1800s, and the consequent customer expectations at that time. The unique aroma and flavor characteristics that resulted from these processes were not likely the prime consideration for development of the techniques.

Press Cake, Flake and Cavendish Cut

Press cake is a "plank" (1/2 to 1-1/2 inches thick after pressing) of tobacco blend that has been subjected to pressing. This can be accomplished at home by either neatly layering or randomly piling together stemmed *whole leaf* in a ratio that matches the desired blend. This can be done within a specially made, wooden press box, within a sturdy plastic container or tucked into a folded, 1-quart Ziploc bag (unsealed). The tobacco is then subjected to pressure of at least 5 to up to 35 psi. This is fairly

Flake—a slice of a plug cut from a press cake.

high pressure to create at home. *The greater the length and width of the "cake", regardless of its thickness, the greater the total applied weight must be.* If you have a shop press or hydraulic jack, then this is not an issue. Just be aware that such a shop press or jack is capable of applying so much pressure that the pressed cake becomes too hard and dry, and nearly impossible to slice afterwards, without using a band saw.

If you intend to use a simple, lever-arm press with a weight on it, or to just stack a weight on top of the tobacco, then the dimensions of the cake should be kept small. For example, a cake that is 6 inches x 6 inches (typically 2-4 inches thick prior to pressing), has a surface of 36 square inches. So 36 pounds of direct weight (a 5 gallon bucket of water weighs ~40 pounds) would provide 1 pound per square inch (1 psi). The same weight on a lever-arm press that triples the effective weight would get you to 3 psi.

Occasionally, press cake with no added adherents (a casing that will "glue" the layers together) will hold together for slicing to flake or Cavendish cut. But if you want to assure that you will end up with durable slices, then a casing will need to be dispersed into the tobacco prior to pressing.

Depending on the amount of applied pressure, the pressing will need to continue for 1 to 6 weeks or so. The duration determines not only how well pressed the cake becomes, but also the degree of fermentation that occurs during pressing. The longer the press, the more fruity or prune-like the aroma becomes, and the darker the press cake becomes.

For **sliced flake**, cut the finished cake into bars that are about 1.5 to 2 inches wide. Flake is then sliced at your desired flake thickness. **Cavendish cut** is simply well adhered sliced flake that has been *very slightly* rubbed-out.

Roll Cake and Coins

Roll cake is a pipe blend of whole leaf tobacco that has been rolled into the shape of a cigar, as tightly as possible. From among the leaf chosen for the blend, a suitable "wrapper", maybe a contrasting color, is misted with non-chlorinated water, and allowed to reach high case. You may want to double or triple the thickness of the wrapper layer, in order to maximize the roll compression. The remainder of the pipe blend *leaf* is then gathered and cut (or torn) to a cigar length, and tightly rolled within the wrapper layer. You can use cigar glue to hold it wrapped, or just fold the head, and hold it in place with a wooden clothespin.

Coins of perique, sliced from a perique roll cake.

Some commercial producers of roll cake and sliced coins go to great lengths to assure that the cross-section of the coins will exhibit symmetrical patterns of contrasting color, and sometimes strategically located stem (running parallel to the axis of the roll cake), creating "bird's eye" inclusions when sliced. You can give this decorative treatment a try, but it has no impact on the smoking quality of the coins.

The filler for this process should be in low to medium case, and can have a flavored or simply adherent casing dispersed into it prior to rolling, if you wish to produce solid, stable "coins". The roll cake is allowed to age under its own wrapping pressure for 1 to 6 weeks. **Coins** are just thin slices of roll cake.

If you use no casing, the coins will come out somewhat crumbly, which may be just fine for smoking in your pipe.

Simple Shred

A mechanical shredder can quickly produce shredded pipe tobacco directly from *stemmed* whole leaf. The width of the shred is specific to the shredder. Most commonly available tobacco shredders yield a shred that may be ideal for cigarettes, but too fine for your pipe tobacco preferences. A shred width of *at least* 1.5 mm is more suitable for use in a pipe. (Mechanically attempting to shred Latakia to a fine shred will result in a pile of dust and fragments.)

In order to manually shred pipe tobacco with a knife or chaveta, roll a "cigar" from whole leaf of the individual ingredients of the blend, or even of the final blend ratio. The narrower the gauge of the "cigar", the finer the likely shred. A "cigar" diameter of about 3/4 inch produces a nice shred width, when sliced with a chaveta as thinly as is practical—about 2.0 mm.

Select two or three sections of the leaf to rehydrate, for use as a wrapper, then tear or cut the remainder of the *stemmed* leaf to a length that will be wrapped by the chosen wrapper. Once the "cigar" is tightly rolled, attach a wooden clothespin at the head, to hold the wrapper in place, then flatten the cigar beneath your palm. Using a chaveta, rock the blade over the foot of the "cigar", taking a thin slice with each pass. [If you use a traditional chaveta, you may want to cover the back edge with a section of plastic tubing or old garden hose, to serve as a cushion, and allow you to apply more force to the blade comfortably.]

Once the "cigar" is sliced into a row of coins, use the chaveta to cut the entire row down the length of the row. Cut it into halves or thirds, in order to limit shred length.

The sliced, split coins are now gathered into your hands, and rubbed together to rub-out the shred.

Crumble Cake

Crumble cake is similar to press cake in its manufacture and appearance. You end up with a plank of pressed tobacco. The difference is that crumble cake is initially composed of tobacco that has already been shredded and blended. So it looks more like particle board. The purpose of a crumble cake is to prevent a pipe blend that would rapidly settle-out into its individual components from settling at all during storage and handling.

As an example, Cornell & Diehl Pirate Kake is 75% Latakia. Because of the difference in particle size and weight of the Latakia vs the other blend components, even minimal agitation leads to the "Brazil nut effect", in which the larger pieces "float" to the top, with the tinier bits sifting out to the bottom. Pirate Kake is sold as a plank of crumble cake.

To smoke crumble cake, just break off a corner or chunk, rub it out in your hands first, or just directly crumble it into the pipe bowl.

Making Perique

Perique is tobacco that has been pressure-cured beneath a liquid seal, to keep out air completely. Perique can be made using any variety of tobacco, though the nicotine content will vary from one variety to the next. Just be aware that cigar varieties may retain a residual cigar flavor.

It is made by pressing color-cured tobacco inside a liquid-tight container for 3 or more months. It requires the application of about 35 psi, which can be generated either by a shop press / hydraulic jack or using a hand-screwed carpentry clamp. The follower for the pressing container must make a close seal with the sides of the container, and this must be regularly checked to assure that a thin layer of liquid continues to provide a seal at the margins.

The dark color of perique is the result of oxidation of nicotine. The nicotine-rich solution is squeezed from the cells of the tobacco, but will not oxidize fully until the leaf is exposed to air. So development of the very dark brown color of finished perique requires that the pressed leaf be removed from the press a few times, at intervals of weeks, during the months of pressing, and spread out to air for 10 minutes or longer, before being returned to the press, and brought under pressure once again—adding a bit of non-chlorinated water to restore the liquid seal, if needed.

Perique requires moderately cool ambient temperatures (between 50 to 80 degrees F) for the desired microbe (*Pichia anomala*) to dominate the fermentation. Perique will initially produce a stinky aroma which, after the first few weeks, will change into a prune-like, fruity aroma. [Perique fermentation, if allowed to reach higher temperatures (say 100°F+ in a shed or attic) may allow dominance of coliform bacteria, and produce a fecal aroma that might require a year or more to dissipate.]

After 3 or more months of pressing beneath the liquid seal, perique comes out of the pressing container quite soggy. It can be stored in this state in a vacuum-sealed container indefinitely, with little risk of spoilage. Once opened, it is best to refrigerate it.

The alternative storage for perique is to spread the leaf, and allow it to mostly dry out. Then roll it into a "cigar" of perique, slice it into a shred of desired width, and store it as you would any other pipe blending ingredient—in low case.

Cavendish Process
Cavendish tobacco is literally cooked tobacco or stewed tobacco. It's origin is likely in 18th century shipping of massive, sealed

hogsheads of tobacco within the sweltering holds of sailing ships, as they crossed the Atlantic.

Making Cavendish processed tobacco is similar to canning green beans. Damp (not dripping or soggy) whole leaf is packed into a canning jar, capped, then pressure-cooked. It requires 5 to 8 hours of 15 psi pressure cooking (at sea level) to complete the process.

Any tobacco variety can be made into Cavendish. Burley, flue-cured Virginia and Maryland tobacco are good candidates. Which you chose will impact the aroma as well as the nicotine content. Cigar varieties will retain a cigar tobacco quality after Cavendish processing. While the leaf can be processed with the entire stem intact, or stemmed entirely, it is more convenient to frog-leg the leaf first, so that it packs into jars easily, and when it's done, it simply needs to be shredded.

Cavendish tobacco may come out of the process appearing black, but once adequately dried to low case for storage, it will take on a light to deep brown character. (Commercial "black Cavendish" remains black only because of the propyleneglycol [PG] that is added to it to keep it both black and squishy.) If you make Cavendish, then store it moist enough to remain black, it will promptly mold (unless you add propyleneglycol [PG], which will retain the dark color, while acting as an anti-fungal). *Cavendish definitely smokes better without PG.*

Cavendish-cured tobacco is generally smoother and milder than the same leaf prior to processing.

Making Twist
Twist is tobacco leaf that has been twisted into a rope. Depending on the region of the world, twist is made with either air-cured leaf or with well-wilted, green leaf. The overall moisture content should be low to medium case, so that it does not mold in the center. Using either brown or green leaf, the subsequent fermentation within the twist usually requires several

months to run to completion, ultimately turning the tobacco dark brown to black.

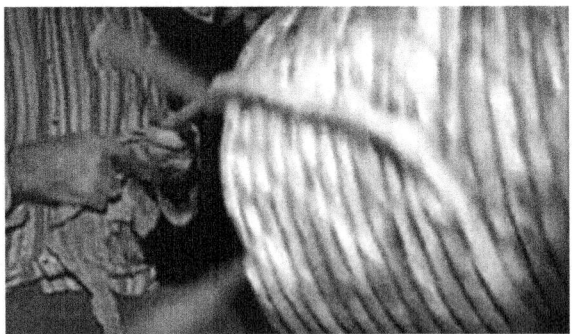

Twisting wilted, green tobacco in Brazil.

The compression and tension of twisting disrupts the cells of the leaf lamina, spilling their contents to the leaf exterior. A combination of intrinsic leaf enzymes (oxidase, peroxidase) together, perhaps with microbes (predominantly yeast like *Pichia anomala*, or even common yeast used for bread or beer making, but ubiquitous in the air) oxidize the proteins and carbohydrates, and ultimately provide a prune-like aroma. As with any open microbial fermentation, it would be subject to unexpected, odd or undesirable outcomes.

Twist is sold in some parts of Brazil by the length the purchaser desires. Its uses include pipe blending (or straight), cigarettes and smokeless. Typically, a pocket knife is used to shave off a slice, which is then rubbed-out to a shred.

Finished tobacco twist rope.

Approaches to Pipe Blending

If you already have an idea of the kinds of pipe tobacco that you like, or the specific ingredients of pipe blends that you enjoy, then making your own blend is a simple matter. Getting is just right, with the right pouch aroma, the right strength and aroma fullness...these are more challenging, though still not difficult.

Where to Start

How you begin will depend on whether you already have specific ingredients that you need to work with, or instead, can obtain any ingredient that you think you might want to use. How you do measurements *and document them* can make the process of blending tedious or a delight—complicated or simple. Some folks use a precision scale (accurate to tenths or hundredths of a gram) to carefully weigh out their blend ingredients. This is admirable, but is far more consistent than the tobaccos that will be blended. The exact character of a tobacco ingredient may change from one purchase to the next. It's an agricultural product. It varies.

If your ingredients are roughly in the same shred size (and degree of "fluffiness"), then you can measure by volume. That is, you can just count tablespoons (level or heaping or whatever, but be consistent) of each ingredient, and document that. An ounce to an ounce and a half (weight) of tobacco blend is about 16 tablespoons of shredded leaf. It is not unreasonable to bend in increments of 1/16 of a batch—1 part per 16. Sometimes, you may recognize the need to be more delicate, and measure using a half-tablespoon (32 of them for a test batch), but that is surprisingly uncommon. [*The late Craig Tarler of Cornell & Diehl recorded many hundreds of pipe blend cards with blend ingredient measurements of 16ths, considering it in terms of ounces (weight) per pound of blend.*]

However you go about measuring the blend proportions, *write it down*, either on the exterior of the Ziploc bag that contains the final blend, using a Sharpie, or on a note pad. You will likely need to refer to it for the next test blend.

Known components: If you can obtain whatever ingredient might be called for, then go to popular websites that sell or review commercial pipe tobacco, and see what information is available on a blend you know you like. While that will probably not provide many meaningful proportions, it may be enough of a clue to get you started. Plan to make very small test batches of about 1 ounce of blend. If you have no clue about relative proportions within the target blend, then begin with equal proportions of each ingredient. Smoke a bowl. If a batch seems close, but not quite there, consider which ingredient seems to be underrepresented, which might be overstated. Make only a tiny adjustment for the next test batch.

Working with the tobacco you already have: Begin your trials by smoking a separate bowl of each available ingredient straight. (You probably don't want to do that with Latakia or perique.) But get to know the characteristics of the potential ingredients. Take notes.
- does it cause tongue bite?
- front or back of the tongue?
- how potent does the nicotine seem to be?
- what is the overall fullness of the flavor and aroma?
- is it sweet? bitter? sour? peppery?
- is it enjoyable straight?

In blending what you have, one approach is to bring together ingredients that compliment one another in their answers to the above questions.   Another is to attempt to amplify certain qualities by combining two or more ingredients that seem to feature it.

This kind of pipe blending is a truly blank slate. You are the only judge as to whether or not a blending test batch is better than one of the individual ingredients alone.

Remember that with any air-cured or flue-cured tobacco you might have, you can turn some of it into Cavendish and some of it into perique, if you don't already have those components.

Blending hints

Burley and **Maryland** will tend to increase the potency of a blend, in both throat hit and nicotine. Burley contributes its distinctive aroma, while Maryland is fairly neutral in aroma.

Oriental leaf usually diminishes the nicotine strength, may add subtle floral notes, and may contribute a bit of sweetness. All of these factors differ by Oriental variety.

Flue-cured Virginia tends to lower the total nicotine, brighten the aroma and feel, and counter some of the throat hit of burley. Darker Virginias are fuller and slightly less acidic. The lower pH (greater acidity) of flue-cured tobacco contributes to tip-of-the-tongue bite.

Dark-air-cured leaf significantly amps up the nicotine and diminishes the bite of flue-cured. In that regard, it can fully replace the need for perique, though it contributes a quite different aroma.

Perique adds a full, rich, deep aroma to a pipe blend. It can completely eliminate flue-cured tongue bite, but if used in excess, can create its own back-of-the-tongue-bite, and dramatically increase nicotine absorption from the blend. A starting point for pH balancing flue-cured with perique is to add perique to the blend in a proportion of about 3 parts perique to every 5 parts of flue-cured. Adjust your preference from there.

Latakia adds a full, smoky aroma, but one that is more like a somber incense, rather than barbecue. By weight, it tends to lower the nicotine concentration of a blend. Typical Latakia proportions range from about 15% up to 50%, though some commercial blends go as high as 75% Latakia. A middle of the road Latakia blend will have between 25% and 35% Latakia. As the proportion of Latakia increases, so does the vague taste of what is described as "soapiness", as well as a sense that your tongue may have been used as a doormat. Very high Latakia concentrations (50% on up) are often reserved for the last bowl of the evening.

Cigar leaf in a pipe blend usually refers to a small proportion of maduro leaf from Pennsylvania Broadleaf, Lancaster Seedleaf, or a similar, American variety. This broadens the flavor profile, and adds a touch of sweetness. Using leaf from most Caribbean (e.g. Habano) cigar types will cause your pipe to smell like a cigar butt.

If your ultimate goal is to create a plug or even an aromatic blend, you should settle on a happy blend *before* the additional processing or flavoring.

Pipe Tobacco Recipes
These are only a few examples of pipe blend recipes. The "Frog" series recipes were created for Whole Leaf Tobacco.

Black Frog–a robust Balkan blend:

Latakia	43.5 %
Virginia Bright	37.5%
Perique	18.75%

Calico Frog–a milder Balkan blend with full Perique

Latakia	18.75%
Virginia Bright	43.75%
Perique	37.50%

Top Frog–English-style Oriental blend

Virginia Bright	50.0%
Perique	30.0%
Stacked Basma	20.0%

Cavendish 43.75%
Red Virginia Flue-Cured 43.75%
Latakia 6.25%
Perique 6.25%

Full-color artwork is much more fun. A printed label can be temporarily taped onto your blend container, then swapped for the next blend.

Curiosity—a rich, American burley blend

Burley	36%
Virginia Red	23%
Fire-cured	23%
Perique	18%

Skree—a basic Virginia / Perique blend

Lemon Virginia	62.5%
Perique	37.5%

Lake Bled—a full blend with both treble and bass

Prilep	37.50%
Burley Red Tip Cavendish	25.00%
Virginia Red	18.75%
Perique	12.50%
Dark Air Cured	6.25%

*

The author's book, **Blend Your Own Pipe Tobacco: 52 recipes with 52 color labels** (Dreamsplice 2019) is available through www.lulu.com and other on-line book vendors.

*

Selecting and using pipe blend kits

These whole leaf blend kits include various tobacco leaf components that can be shredded and blended in the same ratio that is provided, or adjusted in any way you like. Some are shipped with a little spray bottle of casing, specially designed for enhancing the tobacco for cigarette use. You can try the casing on a small batch, to see if you prefer the blend with or without casing. These casings do not render the bend sticky or even what might be considered "aromatic".

Whole Leaf Tobacco's Balkan Tradition kit is surprisingly close in character to the now extinct pipe tobacco blend, Balkan Sobranie Smoking Mixture (Balkan White). Experimenting with it is an excellent way to begin exploring English-style Balkan mixtures.

For pipe blending, you may prefer to shred the leaf to a coarser shred than for cigarette use.

Flavorings and Sauces

There are four general categories of *casings* for pipe tobacco:
- sweeteners
- flavorants
- pH (acidity) modifiers
- humectants

Some of these play multiple roles. For pipe tobacco made from excellent quality whole leaf that has been properly blended, the need for casings may be limited to attempts to create "aromatic" pipe tobacco—sweetening and flavoring.

If you decide to add casing to your whole leaf tobacco blends, be sure to shred the tobacco first. It gets sticky! If you press your cased tobacco blend, purchase some baking parchment from the grocery store, and use it to line the pressing container and follower, again to prevent sticking.

Free Tobacco Flavoring Book: An entire 74 page book on tobacco flavorings (from Leffingwell, Young and Bernasek [R.J. Reynolds], 1972) can be downloaded for free from Leffingwell.com:

http://www.leffingwell.com/download/
TobaccoFlavorBook.pdf

It contains an extensive list of specific chemicals and compounds evaluated for this use, including their smoke taste as well as smoke aroma.

"Materials such as Orange, Lemon, Patchouli, Rose, Neroli, Tonka, Deer Tongue, Vanilla, Valerian, Orris, Bergamot, Cardamon, Cinnamon, Coriander, Cedarwood, Mace, Lavender, Cascarilla, Sandalwood, Lovage, Styrax, Balsam Peru, Balsam Tolu, Foenugreek, Rum, and Geranium are old favorites."

"The use of any given flavoring material is dependent upon several factors:
1. Is the material readily available at reasonable cost?
2. Does it blend well and enhance the smoking flavor of the specific tobacco base to which it is added?
3. What is the optimum use level?
4. What is its effect on package aroma?
5. Is it stable on storage?
6. Is the method of applying the flavoring material to the tobacco base compatible with acceptable manufacturing operations?
7. Is the material safe from a toxicological standpoint?"

Sweetening
Sugar, if burned, tends to caramelize and char, and give off an acrid smoke. There are two types of "sugars" used for casing, reducing sugars and non-reducing Sugars. [Much of this commentary on sweetening is from Fair Trade Tobacco Forum member, *Jitterbugdude*, from Maryland.]

Reducing Sugars: glucose, fructose and invert sugar. These are considered more chemically reactive than non reducing sugars

Non-reducing Sugars: sucrose (white table sugar and brown sugar)

Reducing sugars react with the free amino acids (FAA) in the tobacco leaf as well as with the FAAs from other substances such as cocoa and licorice. These are very pH dependent. The reaction is usually not a complete reaction so a secondary casing is often added. This is where the non reducing sugars come in to play. Brown sugar or regular white sugar are often used.

Non-reducing sugars caramelize more than reducing sugars. Common table sugar can be converted to a mixture of fructose and glucose (both reducing sugars), by heating a sugar solution with lemon juice or citric acid, as is sometimes done while making jellies or jams.

Honey is mostly reducing sugars—a mix of glucose and fructose. The ratio changes depending on the type of honey.

Molasses (known also as treacle) is a residual product from the manufacture of sugar from sugarcane or sugar beets, and is sold in a wide range of consistencies and composition. As a rough average, molasses from the grocery store consists of:
- sucrose   30-35%   non-reducing
- invert (glucose and fructose) 30%   reducing
- other compounds and water 35%

In addition to serving as a sweetener, it adds favors, and also serves to some extent as a humectant.

Maple Syrup is, like molasses, a mixture of several sugars, flavors and water.

Artificial Sweeteners may or may not make sense for oral tobacco (chew, for example), but their addition to tobacco that will be burned is not a good idea. Most artificial sweeteners break down chemically when heated, meaning there is no sweetness contributed to the smoke. Some even produce toxic chemicals when heated.

Flavoring

Flavoring can be derived from all manner of natural products, from foods and beverages to herbs and spices, to oils and liquors. The form in which such flavors are added to a tobacco casing makes a difference. As an example, cocoa or chocolate are a commonly used tobacco flavorant. But if you simply add cocoa powder to tobacco, it inhibits burn, and tastes unpleasant. Instead, chocolate or cocoa *flavoring*, in the form of a specialty liquid, is added.

Liquid concentrates of a host of different flavors are available as essential oils (not water soluble) or as water soluble, in a solution of propyleneglycol (PG). One source for both of these types of flavorants is LorAnn Oils, which offers a huge selection. Generally, oil-based flavors will need to be dissolved into a bit of alcohol (e.g. vodka), which will then allow it to be dissolved into water. PG-based flavorings are readily soluble in water.

Usually, only the tiniest amount of a flavor concentrate is better in casing than so large a quantity that the specific flavor can be immediately identified. Subtle flavoring produces a vague *enhancement* of the smoke aroma, while a strong dose shouts out its name [Some of the "fruit" flavored pipe tobacco blends from Cornell & Diehl, such as "berries", "apricot" or "peaches and cream", while delicious, do not actually taste identifiably like the named flavors.]

Modifying pH (acidity)

Modification of tobacco pH (a lower number means more acidic, while a higher number means more alkaline) causes changes that can be grouped into two general categories: chemically altering amino acids and other compounds within the tobacco or tobacco casing, and directly altering the acidity of the smoke of combustion. Citric acid solution, for example, is commonly used as a casing on flue-cured tobacco to "smooth" away the "harshness", though what exactly this means is unclear.

In contrast to using the more alkaline nature (higher pH) of perique smoke to neutralize the relative acidity (lower pH) of flue-cured tobacco smoke, directly adding acid or alkali chemically removes (or alters) some offending compounds.

Humectants

The character of a humectant is that it tends to attract and hold on to water. Humectants are used in skin moisturizers. Similarly, a humectant may hold onto a flavoring ingredient which might otherwise promptly waft away. Honey and molasses (and other syrups) serve to some extent as tobacco humectants.

Glycerin and propyleneglycol (PG) are the most common humectants used in commercial pipe tobacco. Not only do they (alone or in combination) hold onto moisture, keeping tobacco eternally soft and "consumer-friendly", they also do the same with flavorants. Consumers are reluctant to buy dry tobacco.

In addition, PG exerts a mild, anti-fungal effect, decreasing the risk of mold developing. For this latter reason, PG is added to every commercial pipe tobacco on the market today. Even brands noted for being initially on the "dry" side contain some PG. Glycerin is mildly anti-bacterial.

Unfortunately, some pipe smokers can easily taste PG. Regardless, PG compromises the burn properties of a tobacco blend, and is the primary cause of a gooey, tar-like mess created in a pipe stem and at the bottom of a pipe bowl. Natural, PG-free pipe tobacco simply doesn't do that.

For a pipe blend that contains no humectant, storage within a vapor-proof container (not a common, pipe tobacco tin) will maintain its current moisture for weeks or months. If it becomes too dry, flicking in a few drops of water from your fingertips, then re-closing the container will restore the tobacco to a higher state of case, and restore its pouch aroma.

Forum Members' Casing Recipes for Pipe Tobacco
Earl Grey: a casing with a drop each of bergamot and lavender (LorAnn Oils) into a 1/4 teaspoon of glycerin and a 1/4 cup of vodka and 1/2 teaspoon of invert sugar and added that to 100 grams of my Cavendish and put in a press for 3 weeks. I tried some after cutting and drying it and what an awesome flavor. It truly tastes like Earl Grey. It is rather strong in flavor and will benefit being blended.
[Fair Trade Tobacco Forum member, *chillardbee*, Canada]

Below are two recipes for casing *during* the pressure cooker Cavendish procedure.

Unflavored Black Cavendish: Glycerin at a 1:20 to 1:40 ratio by weight of glycerin to tobacco, before pressure cooking. This is not a precise procedure to begin with, but for the sake of making it simple, this involves about 20 parts tobacco, 19 parts water, and 1 part glycerin. Then *pressure cooked in a sealed jar* at 15lbs for 3 to 4 hours. If this is done with a flue cured bright tobacco, dried, and aged a month, it makes a sweet but tobacco flavored black Cavendish.
[Fair Trade Tobacco Forum member, *ChinaVoodoo*, Canada]

Vanilla Black Cavendish: Follow the black Cavendish procedure (above) but use vanilla extract. This means 20 parts tobacco, 10 to 15 parts water, 5 to 10 parts vanilla extract. It must be an alcohol based vanilla extract.
[Fair Trade Tobacco Forum member, *ChinaVoodoo*, Canada]

Berry-infused tobacco: Roll tobacco into a rope. Pack into a jar. Fill jar with dried elderberries or dried currents. Put some water in. Bake at 220°F for a couple hours.

[Fair Trade Tobacco Forum member, *ChinaVoodoo*, Canada]

Toasted Burley:

1. Combine 1 Tbsp Hershey's syrup (may also use molasses if preferred or a combo of both) per 1 ounce of water (distilled preferred but not necessary)
2. Spread your Burley out onto a cookie sheet and preheat oven to approximately 180°F.
3. Toast the tobacco until almost dry (not crispy) and remove from the oven.
4. Spritz the Burley with casing solution, mixing well, until covered but not dripping wet.
5. Place the tobacco back in the oven and dry again.
6. Repeat these steps 3 or 4 times.

[Fair Trade Tobacco Forum member, *Cobguy* (Darin), Arizona]

"Coffee House" Red Flue-cured Virginia (FCV):

1. Combine 1 Tbsp Apple Cider Vinegar (Bragg's) per 1 ounce water (distilled preferred but not necessary) and add 1/8 tsp cinnamon.
2. Spritz whole Red FCV leaf while in low case until it's brought to high case.
3. Allow the leaf to dry back down to medium case and make a stack.
4. Press the stack into a plug using your home-press of choice for at least 3 days.
5. Slice into flakes and jar for at least 3 months.   9-12 months is better.

[Fair Trade Tobacco Forum member, *Cobguy* (Darin), Arizona]

Storing Pipe Tobacco

Once you have prepared a pipe tobacco blend, and brought it to your desired case (degree of humidity), an ideal container is one that is transparent (so you can see what's in there), relatively vapor-proof, and informatively labeled. These requirements can be met by a number of kinds of containers. And if you disregard transparency, even more kinds. The classic tobacco tins in which small and large quantities of pipe tobacco are sold are not transparent, not vapor-proof (once opened), and simply provide a known name of the blend, but not its composition.

If, on your chosen container, you clearly identify the recipe, either by writing directly on a bag, or taping a paper label onto other containers, then multiple variations of a blend you may be experimenting with will be easy to keep straight. A colorful, printed label taped onto a container, can also add the inviting aspect of graphic art to your your blend.

Ziploc bags are commonly available. A "freezer" Ziploc provides a more effective vapor barrier than a sandwich bag. Depending on ambient conditions, a sandwich bag may be adequate for storage for a week or two, whereas a freezer bag may keep the tobacco from drying for a month or two. The difference may be meaningless for tiny test batches.

Ziploc brand tubs, and similar, small food containers are available with tightly-fitting, snap-on lids. They come in a dozen different sizes and shapes, and work fairly well for pipe tobacco.

Tobacco bag pouch: If you happen to receive some whole leaf that is contained within a 7-inch wide poly-nylon bag, you can trim the empty bag with scissors to make a handy, effective and attractive pipe tobacco pouch.

If the pouch apron is long enough, the pouch will remain well closed without using tape. And the apron serves as a convenient spot to pack your pipe, allowing any fallen tobacco to glide back into the pouch.

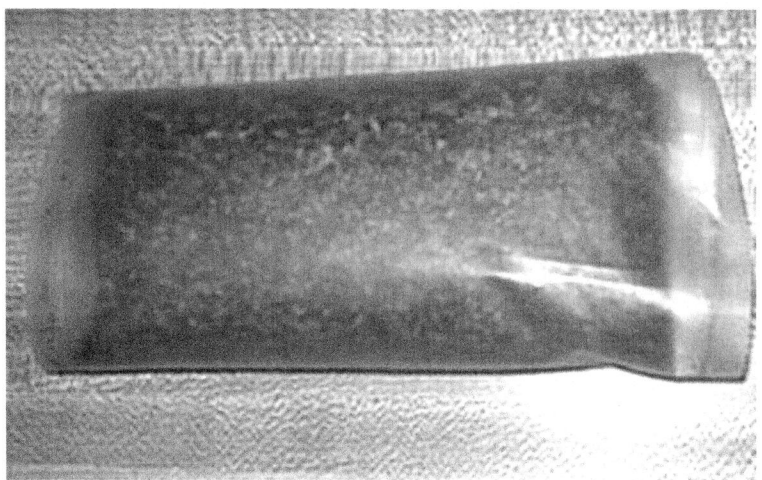

This home-made pouch will hold a 2 oz. tin worth of shred.

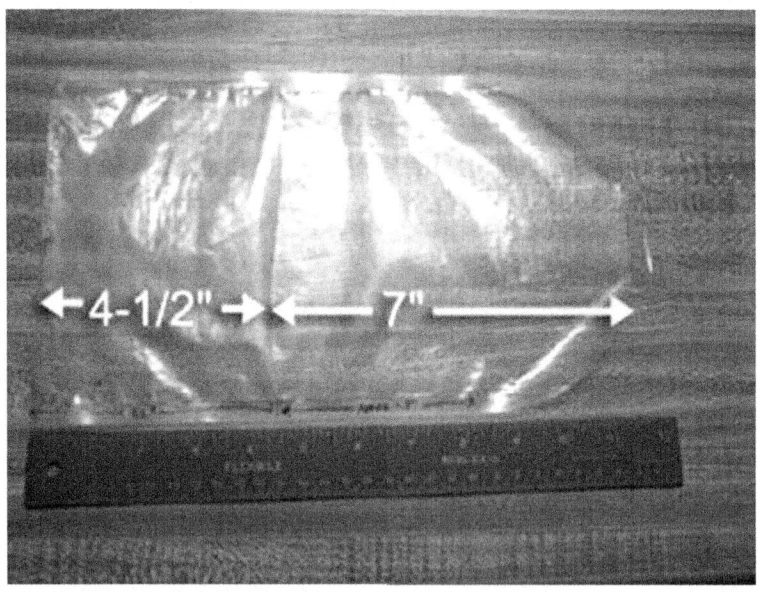

Cutting the pouch from a 7" wide whole leaf bag.

Plastic jars with a good lid seal are wonderful for holding a medium-size batch or larger, and allow a graphic label to be

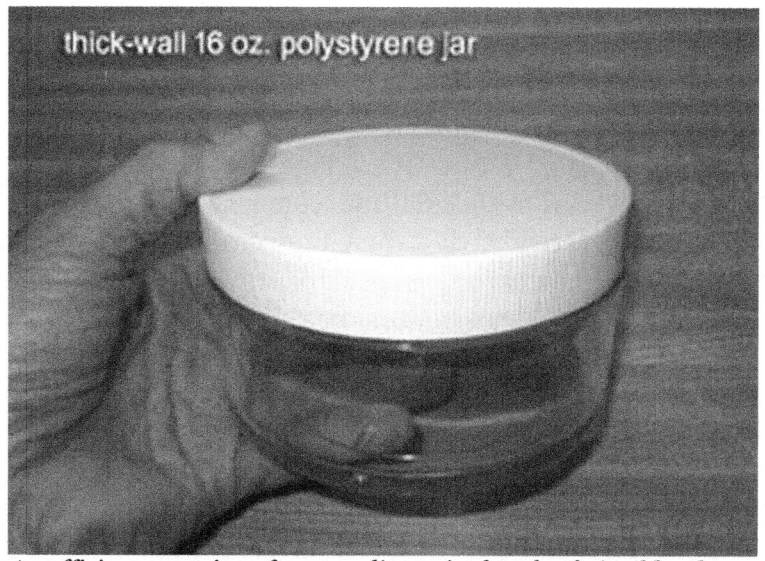

thick-wall 16 oz. polystyrene jar

An efficient container for a medium-size batch of pipe blend.

A huge, free jar for large batches.

temporarily taped to the lid. The wider the lid of a jar, the easier it is to pack a pipe from the jar.

Pipes in General

A pipe is just an object with a big hole into which to stuff pipe tobacco, and a smaller hole from which to draw out the smoke from the bottom of the big hole. Pipes have been made of any material that can withstand the combustion temperature of tobacco: glass, ceramic, clay, mined mineral (like Meerschaum), stone of various sorts (e.g. soapstone), many varieties of wood, some plastics (Dr. Grabow "Brylon" pipe bowls are made with nylon that has been blended with briar dust.), and of course, corncobs. Wood pipes, made from nearly any non-toxic hardwood, are available with and without the tree bark still on. The stems can be made of acrylic, hard rubber, bamboo or any other suitable material that can provide an enclosed, stiff tube.

Most pipes found at a tobacconist will be made of briar root. This is the extremely hard root of a Mediterranean heather shrub.

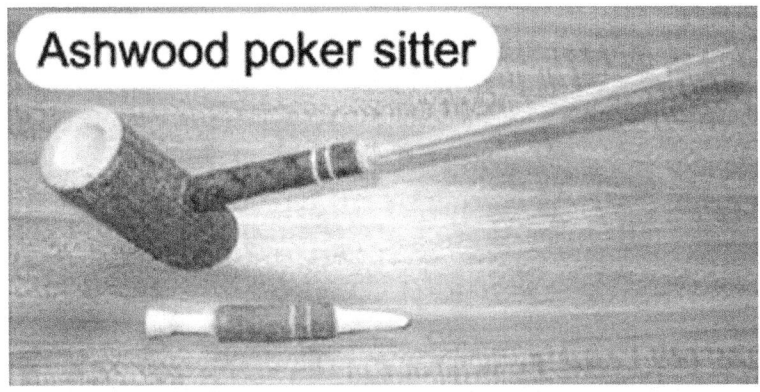

Bowl and shank are ashwood. Stem is bamboo, with a plastic tubing bit. The matching tamper is also from ashwood.

Ash is unique in that the pith of the branches, both large and small ones, is soft and spongy. This can be cleanly removed by passing a hot wire or rod through it. This also means that the bottom of the bowl should be lined with a spackle of 50% plaster of Paris: 50% fine sand, to seal and fire-proof the pith there.

Corncob Pipes

The center of a corncob is hard and woody, when fully dried. Nearly every cob can be made into a pipe, though a nice internal diameter bowl requires a particularly broad cob. Some of the varieties of corn with the largest ears do not provide the fattest cobs. The cob shown below is from an ear of Boone County Kentucky field corn.

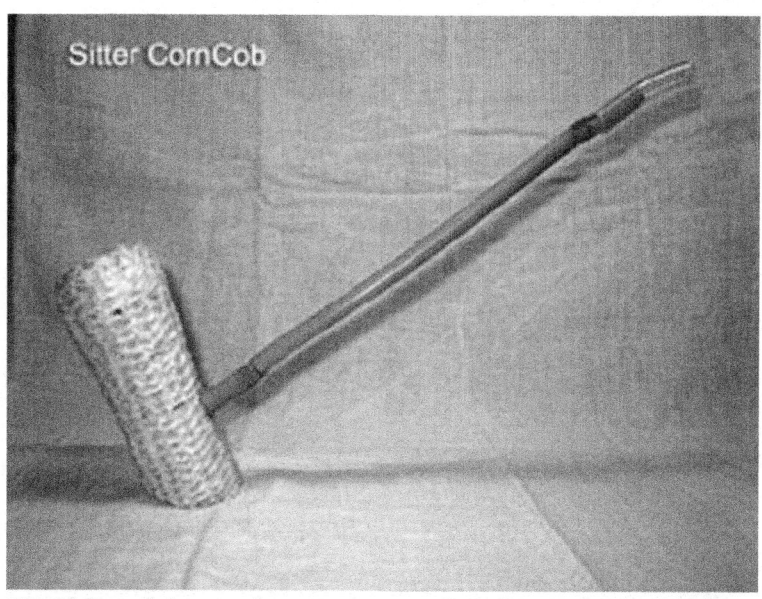

Hand bored from a home-grown cob. The stem is a bamboo garden stake (undyed). The soft bit is a section of Tygon plastic tubing.

Corncob pipes are easy smokers, requiring no break-in period, and are available ready-made at very low prices. Some pipe smokers contend that they smoke better than briar pipes, though their lifespan in shorter.

Of course, a variety of ready-made corncob pipes are available for purchase from Missouri Meerschaum as well as other manufacturers, typically at 1/4 to 1/10 the price of a common briar pipe.

Pipe Tools

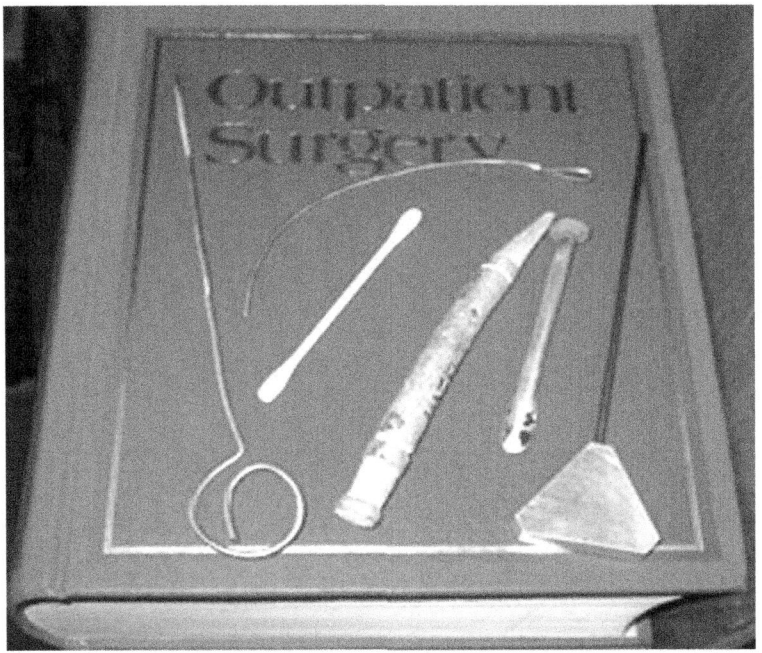

Pipe tools: *(left to right) home-made 14 gauge steel smoke hole ream, 17 gauge aluminum bit ream, Q-Tip, whittled tamper with a wedge, pipe nail tamper, machined steel smoke hole ream.*

There are several tools that are useful while packing a pipe, smoking the pipe, and maintaining and cleaning a pipe. Some are easy to improvise at home, while others may need to be purchased.

Tamper
You can pack a pipe with your fingertip, but you can't tamp the tobacco without some sort of tool, once it is burning. The simple, whittled end of a twig from the lawn does a fair job. Inexpensive pipe nails (from a tobacconist) are excellent. An ideal tamper

head is flat and circular, but created with a narrower neck, so that the tamping can be slightly angled if needed.

Spoon or wedge
This is used to adjust the bottom of the packed tobacco inside the bowl, in the event that the draw becomes too tight while smoking, and also for scraping out the bowl. The simple, sharpened wedge of a twig does the job, as does the flattened end of a pipe nail.

Bowl ream
After months to years of smoking the same pipe, the layer of char that builds up on the interior of the bowl needs to be scraped

Reaming the bowl requires a relatively blunt edge, and the absence of a sharp point that might easily gouge the bowl. Only certain knife blade types in certain sizes provide that.

away. There are specialized pipe bowl reams to accomplish this safely, and are the safest option when reaming a relatively soft bowl material, such as a softer wood or meerschaum bowl. For the much harder, briar bowls, a knife blade with the right shape will work well. The objective in reaming is, for a meerschaum bowl, to remove *all* of the char, but for all other materials, to remove only *most* of the char.

Smoke hole ream

With continued use, and especially with smoking aromatic tobaccos, the smoke hole in the pipe shank accumulates a thick,

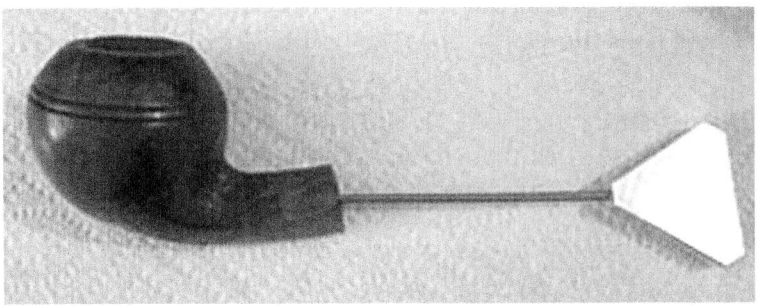

sometimes hardened coating of tarry combustion products that, little by little, narrow the opening, and reduce its air flow. A typical smoke hole will accommodate a rod or wire of about 14 gauge. The tip of this smoke hole ream should ideally be flat—cut at a right angle to the rod. The crud within the hole is forced into the bowl, for removal.

Bit Ream

Pipe bits need love too. But they tend to be made from fragile material. Both acrylic and hard rubber (Vulcanite) bits can endure significant *compression*, but easily fracture when an outward force is applied from inside the smoke hole. A flexible probe made from aluminum wire, 17 gauge or smaller, can be curved to match the bit's curvature, and used to gently remove materials too adherent to come clean with just a pipe cleaner.

Pipe cleaners

These are fine, twisted wire with fuzz entrapped into them. They are manufactured with cotton or synthetic fibers. Some are startlingly expensive, while others are dirt cheap. *Either will clean equally well.* Although burning an occasional cotton fiber is less noticeable than burning acrylic fiber, this is not a problem if you blow through the pipe after using a pipe cleaner.

The most economical *and efficient* pipe cleaners are 12-inch long synthetic ones sold in the craft section of big-box stores, and labeled as something like "fuzzy sticks".

Q-Tips
Keep a small container (e.g. a shot glass) filled with Q-Tips near where you smoke or clean your pipes. After each bowl of tobacco, forcefully blow through though the bit (with a paper towel in front of the bowl, since stuff may come flying out), to force any retained liquid out of the bit and shank, then clean the bottom of the bowl with a Q-Tip. This allows the pipe to dry, ready for the next smoke much more quickly than waiting for evaporation. (An alternative would be to insert a pipe cleaner into the stem, down to the bowl, and leave it there while the pipe rests.)

After using a pipe cleaner or smoke-hole ream in the shank, clean the goo from the bottom of the bowl with a Q-Tip. Consider them as important as pipe cleaners.

Pipe rack
A pipe rack, while it may or may not be decorative, is useful in allowing a pipe to adequately dry between use. Keep space efficiency in mind when purchasing a pipe rack, since the number of pipes in your collection may creep upward over the years. Racks with a closed hole in the upper rail (into which the pipe stem is inserted) are more secure and stable than those with just a slot in the upper rail, but some pipe shapes and bits can be difficult or impossible to insert through a closed hole, or with other pipes in adjacent positions.

A one-pipe "rack" that simply allows a pipe to be set upon it while smoking is usually called a pipe stand or pipe rest. Sitter pipes won't work with a pipe rest, but most other styles of pipes are more conveniently set in them, allowing a pipe smoker to put down a pipe that contains burning tobacco. Sitters acquire their name, because they are shaped and balanced to sit all on their own.

Folding, pocket pipe rest and other tools. [Fair Trade Tobacco Forum member, Sid.Stavros, from Athens]

A handy, pocket pipe rest can be made from a stiff loop of leather (e.g. a piece of an old leather belt) or thick vinyl, that is joined face-to-face. It can lie flat within a pocket, yet be forced into an open loop at a table. Pipe rests are manufactured in various woods, ceramics, plastics or even glass, and are available from most tobacconists.

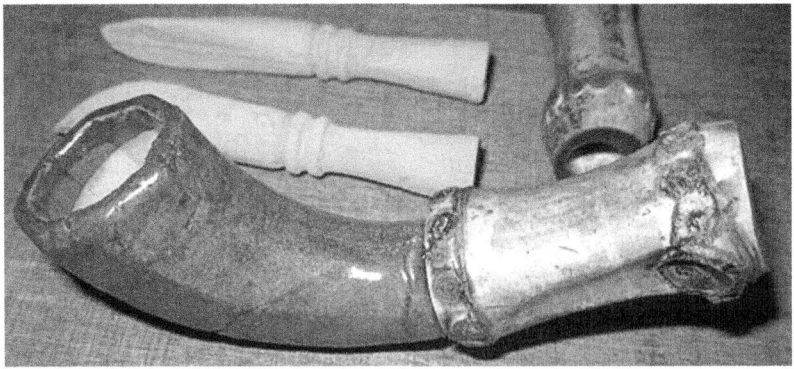

A clay pipe with a bamboo shank, created by Fair Trade Tobacco Forum member, Akias, from Japan. A common bit is shared by this and two other clay pipes. The clay pipe tampers were also cast by Akias. Despite the diminutive appearance of the pipe bowl, its thin walls allow it to hold as much tobacco as a medium-size briar pipe.

9. Cigarettes

A cigarette is usually defined as smokable tobacco wrapped within a paper wrapper. At one time, every cigarette smoker knew the skill of hand-rolling shredded tobacco into a slip of paper, using his or her fingertips. Cigarettes were as thick as desired, often tapered, and as long as the available scrap of paper might allow.

With the invention of industrial, automated cigarette rolling machines during the mid-to-late nineteenth century, cigarettes acquired a set of specific dimensions. As the need to hand-roll a cigarette vanished, the notion that a cigarette should be instantly available to light became the norm.

Today, home rollers of cigarettes generally use an injection device to stuff the tobacco into a ready-made tube that is already tipped with a cigarette filter. And the tubes themselves are offered in milder or stronger versions, as well as in menthol.

Cigarette Tobaccos

There are only a handful of general types of tobacco that are used in most cigarettes, even though a cigarette can be made from any of the 3000 varieties of smoking tobacco, as well as *Nicotiana rustica* varieties.

Flue-cured or Bright Tobacco: The generic term, "bright tobacco" refers to any flue-cured tobacco. Flue-cured Virginia tobacco is usually the primary component of a cigarette blend. Since leaf harvested off different stalk positions flue-cures from brighter (at the base of the plant stalk) to darker and redder going up the stalk, flue-cured leaf is available in a range of shades. Typical ranges are from a light lemon yellow color to "red" Virginia. While the brighter (lower) leaf presents a lighter though sweeter edge, the redder leaf offers a richer aroma and a higher nicotine content. Flue-cured leaf from Canada is generally milder and lighter in color, though not as flavorful, as that from the US. This difference is mostly due to the use of milder strains of Virginia tobacco that were specifically developed in Canada.

Burley: This is a specific class of tobacco with a relatively high nicotine content, and a more alkaline smoke than flue-cured. Burley is always air-cured. It lacks the sugars of flue-cured tobacco. It is known for increasing the "throat impact" of a cigarette blend, as well as for being able to better absorb any casing solution applied to the tobacco. Burley is often the second ingredient, by weight, in an American cigarette blend, though some Canadian brands have no burley. There are nonetheless Canadian varieties of burley (e.g. Harrow Velvet) that are generally milder and lighter in color than most US burley varieties.

Maryland: Maryland class tobacco (for example, MD 609) may be substituted for some or all of the burley in a blend recipe, providing a similar nicotine concentration (higher than that of flue-cured Virginia), while not contributing a distinctive burley taste. For cased cigarette blends, Maryland tobacco has a greater tendency to hold on to the casing than does burley.

Oriental: This is a large group of milder, sun-cured tobaccos from the regions of the former Ottoman Empire. These are sometimes referred to simply as "Turkish". As a group, they are low in nicotine, relatively sweet, and sometimes mildly floral in aroma. In typical American cigarette blends, an Oriental makes up around 10% of the tobacco. Camel cigarettes traditionally contained Samsun as their Oriental component, while others use or used the milder, Basma types. including Xanthi and Izmir. Prilep is a unique, sweet, Basma-like leaf developed in Prilep, North Macedonia.

Perique: A small portion of deep brown, pressure-cured perique will nudge up the apparent strength of a cigarette. It does this by raising the pH (reducing the acidity) of the smoke.

At least one commercial cigarette brand adds perique to their blend.

Rustica: *Nicotiana rustica* is a different species than common smoking tobacco (*Nicotiana tabacum*). It tends to be harsher and generally a lot higher in nicotine. Commercial cigarette blends with *rustica* are not uncommon in Russia and Eastern Europe.

Cigarette Types

American Cigarettes: All American type cigarettes contain flue-cured tobacco as their primary tobacco ingredient. Flue-cured Virginias range from 30% to about 80%. Most also contain burley at about a third or less, with the strongest cigarettes containing the most burley. Forty or higher percent is not unusual. The burley may be subjected to toasting, a process that lightly caramelizes some of the scant sugars of burley, but decreases its harshness. The third ingredient frequently found in American cigarettes is one of the Orientals.

> A typical recipe might be:
>
> | | |
> |---|---|
> | flue-cured Virginia | 60% |
> | burley | 30% |
> | Oriental | 10% |

It's worth noting that American *brand* cigarettes have swept away many traditional, regional and national brands of cigarettes throughout the world. But often, these "American brands" are manufactured outside of the US, using ingredients from other sources, and in some cases, scarcely resemble their American prototypes. (Over 50% of cigarette smokers in Mexico say that they regularly smoke American *brands*.)

Canadian Cigarettes: Traditionally, Canadian cigarettes are mostly, if not entirely composed of flue-cured Virginia tobacco, grown in Canada. Orientals may also appear, but burley is not as common in the blends.

Western European Cigarettes: Many western European cigarettes are notably stronger than American cigarettes. Some may contain fire-cured tobacco. Dunhill's most popular cigarette is 100% Virginia, while the now extinct Balkan Sobranie cigarettes contained a portion of Latakia.

Eastern European Cigarettes: Some of these are quite potent, due to their content of *rustica* tobacco. They may contain stronger Orientals, as well as one of the imponderable variety of so-called Hungarian tobaccos. Most contain some burley, and may be predominantly flue-cured Virginia.

Turkish Cigarettes: Pure Turkish cigarette may contain high proportions of Oriental tobacco. Some of their famous brands would use 100% of a single Turkish varietal.

Shredding

Most home-rollers of cigarettes tend to make up 20 or more cigarettes at a time. This places a time demand on tobacco shredding tasks. In addition, most prefer a fine or very fine tobacco shred, which is not practical using scissors, a knife or a chaveta. So some form of mechanical shredder is helpful. Given the demand that will be placed on a shredder, purchasing a purpose designed shredder is more cost effective than attempting to get by with a pasta shredder or paper shredder, neither of which are designed for the unique challenge of shredding whole leaf tobacco. One can certainly just allow tobacco leaf to go out of case, then shatter it into "flakes" with a food processor or similar kitchen tool, but you end up with random flake size, and an awful lot of dust (which used to be the fine quality tobacco leaf that you paid for or grew and cured).

Mechanical tobacco shredders come in two general categories: electric and hand-cranked. The latter can sometimes be fitted to a variable speed, hand-held drill to power it.

Electric shredders are the least hassle, though their switches etc. do eventually require replacement, either at the factory, or at home, with components purchased from the factory. Repair at home requires some skill with managing shaft bearings of different kinds, as well as relatively simple wiring and other electrical matters. These shredders typically produce a shred of 0.8 mm width or somewhat finer. They typically shred faster than the user can stem leaf to feed into it.

The crank shredders come in "budget" and "heavy duty" models, with a shred width of 0.8 mm or a wide shred of 1.5 mm. They

Heavy-duty manual shredder.

are designed to be clamped onto the edge of a table, counter or shelf for use. The heavy duty may be more cost-effective.

With all shredders, *the leaf fed into them needs to be stemmed—* the hard, central vein removed to within a couple of inches of the leaf tip. For Oriental leaf, their diminutive stems *do not* need to be removed prior to shredding. While the shredders can eat stems on occasion, it deposits sharpened chunks of stem into your shred, and significantly shortens the lifespan of the shredder (both blades and bearings).

Ideally, leaf to be stemmed and shredded is in low case (somewhat noisy, but does not crumble when handled). Drier leaf (out of case) will shatter while being stemmed, and while being shredded. Moister leaf may shred beautifully, but will more rapidly gum up the cutting blades.

For all shredders, the mechanism should be turned in reverse after a shredding session, to remove some of the particulates that have adhered to the blades. Some users regularly finish up with a dose of vodka or beer into the cutters, to clean them. Instead, **use hot water to clean the shredder cutters followed immediately by thoroughly drying the shredder using a hair dryer.** An additional approach is to follow the tobacco shredding session with shredding some stiff, bright white paper— the color being useful in making sure all the paper is cleaned from the cutters prior to next use. [Heavily finished copy paper contains a coating of rolled clay that may come off in the cutters.]

Stuffing or Rolling

Hand rolling with individual cigarette papers is the same as it has been for the last 150 years or longer. The paper is held lengthwise between the fingers of both hands, with the gum up on the more distant side. A 'U' shaped trough is created, and held by the fingers of one hand, while the tobacco shred is piled and distributed along the trough. The gum edge should now be at the top, inside surface of the trough, facing you. It is licked, and the trough gently closed into a tight cylinder. This takes a bit of practice, though not much, If you are not concerned about having a perfectly cylindrical cigarette, one or both ends can be tapered, and glued that way with the gummed edge. Search the Web for "hand roll cigarette" for videos.

Although it is possible to hand-roll a cigarette with a separately inserted filter at the head, filter cigarettes are usually made using

PowerMatic 1-plus injector.

pre-manufactured "tubes" that already include a filter. A cigarette stuffer (entirely mechanical or an electrified one) pushes a pre-measured quantity of your shred into the foot end of the tube, and against the interior surface of the filter.

A third option is a sliding-mat or rolling mat type of manual cigarette roller (based on the Lieberman cigar rolling device). These can easily accommodate a separate filter, and use standard cigarette papers. They come in simple, cheap, plastic, all the way to elaborate, hand-crafted devices suitable for displaying on a coffee table.

Approaches to Cigarette Blending

The exact blend of any particular cigarette brand is truly a moving target. Well recognized brands subtly alter their blends intentionally, from time to time. In addition, the crop years, sourcing of the leaf, location of the factory and other factors contribute to considerable variation geographically as well as over time. And similar variations will likewise influence your own blending results. While the massive scale of tobacco acquisition and use by a factory provides something of a buffer to noticeable change, the same is not the case for a home-roller, given the relatively minuscule scale of production by an individual roller.

Traditional European Style Cigarette blend from *FmGrowit*, of the Fair Trade Tobacco Forum and Whole Leaf Tobacco:

> 120 grams Bright Virginia
> 40 grams Red Virginia
> 40 grams Lemon Virginia
> 90 grams Fire cured
> 160 gams Maryland 609
> *A casing spray is often added.*

Traditional American Style Cigarette blend from *FmGrowit*, of the Fair Trade Tobacco Forum and Whole Leaf Tobacco.

> 115 gams Bright Virginia
> 115 gams Red Virginia
> 160 grams Maryland
> 90 grams Turkish
> *A casing spray is often added.*

Strength

The apparent "strength" of a cigarette blend can be increased by a larger proportion of burley (or Maryland) leaf, and decreased by a larger proportion of flue-cured. Increasing the flue-cured component will increase tip-of-the-tongue bite. An Oriental component may also be used to decrease the apparent strength, while not having as much impact on tongue bite as flue-cured. Increasing the burley component will increase what is described as "throat hit". Adding a bit of perique to the blend will notably increase nicotine absorption by the body, but might make the smoke harsher in the throat and trachea. Fire-cured tobacco will contribute both strength and a smokiness. These are factors that a home-roller can adjust while attempting to identify an "ideal" blend for his or her taste.

Casings (or flavors)

Online vendors offer a variety of different tobacco casings, shipped in a small spray bottle, for application to leaf *after* shredding. Some are crafted for use on particular categories of tobacco, such as air-cured, flue-cured and more general blends of leaf, or as a named flavor. After stemming and shredding leaf, casing is misted onto the shred, then allowed to dry-down to a moisture level suitable for use, prior to storing or rolling it.

Tubes

Tobacco stuffing tubes, usually with a filter already attached, typically come in boxes of 200 tubes, some with menthol added, each with differing tip color and decoration.

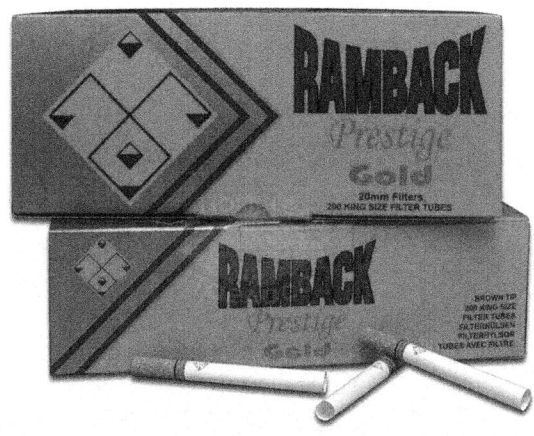

An example of empty cigarette tubes, with a filter, for stuffing at home.

Selecting and using cigarette blend kits

On-line vendors offer a variety of whole leaf blend kits for cigarettes. They range from very full-bodied American cigarette styles, to milder ones, as well as pure Virginia blends. There are also Turkish-style blends, some of which mirror varietal blends manufactured in Turkey. A Balkan blend is also available.

If you want to see just how fine whole leaf tobacco can be, when made into home-rolled cigarettes, one or several of these blend kits will be a revelation. A 1 to 5 pound kit of a blend should be stemmed, shredded, then thoroughly mixed, prior to rolling. If casing is included, try it first on a small portion of the blended tobacco, to help you decide whether or not to use it on the remainder. **One pound of a cigarette blend kit will yield approximately 2 cartons of cigarettes.**

Storing Cigarette Tobacco

If you shred more cigarette tobacco than you plan to use immediately, it should be stored in a food-safe, vapor-proof container. Although polyethylene bags are not vapor-proof, using a "freezer" bag inside another "freezer" bag is reasonably effective. Single plastic bags can also be stored within a plastic tub with a good seal, or even in 5-gallon plastic buckets, with the lid snapped on.

Storing the tobacco in the bags in which it was received may be a very good option, shredded or otherwise.

Shredded tobacco should not be stored in high case (anything near damp), or it will mold. If it is stored very dry, then mist it with non-chlorinated water, and allow it to relax, prior to use.

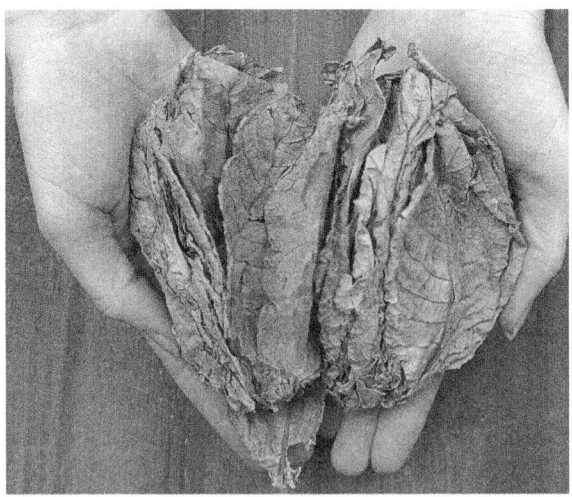

The delicate leaves of Oriental Stacked Basma, from Whole Leaf Tobacco.

10. Smokeless

Smokeless Tobaccos

This broad category of tobacco product includes any oral or nasal tobacco preparation that is used without burning it. The names for them are confusing. Below is a delightful, historical perspective on snuff, snus and dip, provided by *squeezyjohn*, a member of the Fair Trade Tobacco Forum, from Great Britain.

The confusion is an historical one connected with the spread around the globe of different tobacco types, which took them through several languages as well!
WARNING: LONG ETYMOLOGICAL ESSAY FOLLOWS

Snuff is an old English term for anything powdered you took medicinally through the nostrils, related to the word sniff. It was one of the many techniques used to get old herbal remedies into the body, and we still use related words like snuffling or snuffly to describe the sound of a person with a cold (or an animal that sounds similar).

Around the year 1500 the first travelers to the new world of the Americas discovered tobacco being used by the native elders in a snuff format, via types of tubes, and brought the plant back with them to Spain and Portugal, where it was touted as a new medicine to be used as a powdered form taken in to the nostrils.

In the 1560s a Frenchman called Jean Nicot was ambassador in Lisbon. He sent some tobacco back to Paris, where Queen Catherine had been suffering from chronic headaches, and advised her to use it to relieve the pain. It worked very well, and became fashionable amongst upper class and courtly circles throughout France and wider Europe. Jean Nicot's name lives in history as the Latin name of the plant family Nicotiana...and by association, the chemical nicotine is also named after him.

Snuff gained it's English name when it arrived in the English courts of the early 1600s, as this was already the name for a medicine taken nasally. Over time, the word snuff became almost exclusively associated with this form of tobacco. Meanwhile, this nasal tobacco spread to Sweden via the courts as well. The word Snus is of a similar Germanic origin to the English word snuff, and is first documented in Swedish in 1637. At that time it still referred to nasal snuff. By the 1700s, nasal "snus" was very popular in Sweden, and tobacco farming had become a common thing throughout the country (unlike in England, which relied on it's American colonies to provide tobacco).

By the early 1800s, tobacco use had filtered down to all levels of Swedish Society, however the farmers and workers had taken to using their ground up tobacco by wetting it a little, and placing it in their upper lips, instead of using their noses. Presumably this was an easier way to use the product while actively working. This method became the default way of using snus, while nasal snuff was rapidly going out of fashion amongst the upper classes. Certain brands and recipes were set up in this period, including Ljunglof's Ettan (Ettan means number one in Swedish) which is still available today, made by Swedish Match. Many other brands followed including Generalsnus (regular snus) and Röda Lacket (Red Seal).

In the late 1800s, more than a million Swedes crossed the Atlantic to set up new lives in the USA, and brought their snus habit with them. Brands were set up to serve the demand, and some used old Swedish names like Copenhagen and Red Seal. Throughout the 1900s the styles of recipe used in this oral tobacco diverged in it's Swedish homeland and in the USA, so the products now are very distinct from each other. The word snus was still in common use as an alternative to dip as late as the 1950s in some parts of the USA. Nowadays, "dip" or "snuff" is the normal word used in the states to describe American moist oral tobacco [even though dry, nasal snuff is still its own distinct product in the US].

But the term dip has yet another nasal-snuff related origin from much earlier in history. During the British colonial period, the French-inspired upper-class snuff habit had also made the journey across the Atlantic. Whereas cigars became the favourite form of tobacco use amongst gentlemen, ladies took to dipping a moistened stick in nasal snuff and rubbing it in to their gums, which was considered more discrete and ladylike than either snorting it or smoking cigars! Dipping became the term for this, and at some point in the 1900s the term became confused with the recently imported Swedish form of using snus in the upper lip. The American preference for dipping in the lower lip also happened at some point in time near this.

So there you have it. Snuff, snus, dip. It's all really the same thing, separated by cultural evolution over time, and several language changes.

Dry Snuff

At its most basic, nasal snuff is simply fully cured and aged tobacco leaf, pulverized to a fine or coarse dust. A screen can be used to remove any larger bits or pieces. Some have used a burr mill coffee grinder to pulverize the leaf, after stemming it. The variety of leaf used is your choice.

It can be used unflavored (or unscented), or essential oil can be added to modify its character. This is usually dissolved in water or plain alcohol (e.g. vodka), then mixed into the powder. For nasal use, it needs to first be fully dried.

An Example of an American-style loose dry snuff

Component	% (wet weight)
Dark-fired tobacco	22.75
Fire Cured Virginia Tobacco	19.66
Air Cured Tobacco Stem	33.03
Flue Cured Tobacco Stem	15.20
Sodium Chloride	0.36
Water	9.00
Total	100

[North Carolina State University, CORESTA reference product.]

Moist Snus

Moist snus is intended for oral use, either loose, or enclosed within a permeable packet.

A recipe for **Swedish snus** from *jojjas*, a member of the Fair Trade Tobacco Forum from Sweden:

> You could use any kind of tobacco leaf you want, even stems could be used (I prefer burley and or Virginia), but they must be very dry or it becomes too heavy to grind them. You could even use unfermented leaves, but only if they are dry.

> **Grind** tobacco leaf to a fine powder, something between fine sawdust and oatmeal flour. When that is done, **add** equal weight of **tobacco flour** with **boiling water**, with approx 50-70g **salt** (2-2.75 oz weight). You could use more salt if you prefer.

> example: 0.5kg tobacco you should mix with 0.5 liters water (1 pound tobacco: 1/2 quart of water).

> Then mix tobacco and salty water together, so everything is well mixed, and then put it in the plastic container and **press** it hard with the end of a wooden plank or

something similar, to remove excess water. Put on the lid and make sure its tight.

Place the container in a 90°C (~194°F) **oven** for 24 hours (Here is where the fermentation occurs.)
After 24 hours, take out the container and **mix** the tobacco so there are no lumps.

Next step is a little bit critical. **Do this out side**. If its hot direct from oven, it can irritate your eyes and nose when you mix it together.

[Editor's note: Sodium carbonate is a relatively strong alkali, and will react with iron, aluminum and other metals. The mixing and heating with sodium carbonate should be performed in a non-reactive container— stainless steel, ceramic, glass, a well-enameled pot without interior scratches, or an oven-safe plastic container, in order to avoid dissolving some metal into the snus. The oven temperature is below the boiling point of water.

Sodium carbonate can be made from sodium-bicarbonate—common baking soda (not baking powder) by heating it in the oven at ~ 93° C (200°F) for about an hour.]

Boil 0.25 liters (1 cup) water with 40-70 g of **sodium carbonate**, and add to the tobacco. (I prefer 45-50g.) If you want stronger (more nicotine, stronger) snus use, the high dosage. Put it in the plastic container and press it hard with the end of a wooden plank or something similar. Put on the lid, and make sure it's tight. Place it in the **oven** for 12 hours at 90°C (~194°F).

After 12 hours, take out the snus from the oven, let it cool down, and mix it well so there are no lumps. Now is the time to add **flavor** if you want, and perhaps some

substance to keep it moist (glycerin or PG). **Store** it in the refrigerator to keep it moist and fresh.
*****

A recipe for **Swedish snus** from *POGreen*, a member of the Fair Trade Tobacco Forum from Sweden.
This is how I make 5.5 lbs of "Swedish Snus ":

2.2 lbs tobacco powder (I use a meat grinder to grind my leaves.)
1.75oz to 3.50z of Salt
1.2 liters or 2.5 pints of water

Heat the water in a saucepan to lukewarm, take the pan off the burner, and pour the salt into the water to dissolve it by stirring it until the water is clear.

Have the tobacco powder in a bucket, and pour the lukewarm saltwater over the powder. Mix them with your hands, or a spoon, if it's too hot. MIX VERY WELL.

You should have 2 plastic boxes with lids to put the mixed, wet tobacco powder into.

Take a little at a time. Give the powder a light packing all the way to the top. There should be no holes in the lids.

Preheat the oven to 194°F.

Make sure the boxes can take 200°F in the oven. [Microwave-safe food containers should be fine, other than in a toaster-oven.] Heat for 24 hours.

Warm 1.5 pints of water in a non-reactive saucepan [stainless, ceramic, glass, or well-enameled] to lukewarm. Take the pan OUTSIDE, then add 1.75 ounces to 3.5 ounces (weight) of sodium carbonate. Dissolve it by stirring until it is clear.

Remove the box of heated tobacco from the oven. Pour the tobacco into a clean bucket, together with the sodium carbonate solution, and mix it very thoroughly with a spoon.

Transfer the mixture back into the boxes, and cover it. Return them to the oven at 194° F for another 12 hours.

Allow the heated boxes to cool with THE LID ON. When it's cooled to about room temperature, store it in the fridge.

The longer you keep it in the fridge, the better.

The sodium carbonate raises the pH (makes it more alkaline), and increases nicotine absorption. For increasing the apparent strength of the snus, consider using a stronger tobacco instead of using too much sodium carbonate, which can irritate the mouth.

I have used both a Swedish type of Virginia called Alida, together with *rustica*. *Rustica* is great for snuff, in my opinion.

*****

A recipe for **snus** from *Nic*, a member of the Fair Trade Tobacco Forum from Finland.

We need:

--An oven

--A meat thermometer to monitor oven temperature

--Roasting bags (that are designed for oven use) and a baking dish to support the bag

--Something to grind the tobacco with, like a meat grinder

--Mixer

--Big bowl or bucket

--Tobacco leaves

Remove the midrib of each leaf. Allow the leaf to dry for a few days at room temperature. You can add some of the midrib, so long as it's not moldy, to the leaf for grinding. A hand-cranked meat grinder that is connected to a power drill is one way to grind.

Ingredients:
--100 grams of salt
--100 grams of sodium carbonate or potash. If you do not have access to this, painting soda or soda ash can be bought from the local hardware store and serves as a good substitute
--1 kg of tobacco flour.
--1-1.5 liters of water.

Step 1: Mix the boiling water with salt, stirring until the salt is dissolved. Mix the saltwater with the tobacco flour in a bowl. Stir well until all the tobacco flour is "wet". Set the oven at 90°C (~194°F) and let snuff bake in the sealed roasting bag for at least 24 hours.
Step 2: OUTDOORS, mix the sodium carbonate with about 3-5 cups hot water and mix with the baked tobacco flour. Stir well!
Step 3: Bake the snus for 12h in 90°C (~194°F) oven, in a sealed roasting bag.
Step 4: Pack the snus in buckets or boxes and leave in a cool place for about 2 weeks.

An alternative method is to extend the cooking time in step 1, to 3-5 days and skip step 3. This results in a true black and delicious snus but unfortunately this method increases the risk of the snus getting burned. The process requires some monitoring. Flip the roasting bag every day, and make sure it is tightly closed. If you think your snus looks dry after some time in the oven, you can add more water.

Choosing tobacco variety:

The choice of tobacco variety affects the flavor of the end product to some degree. The traditional types used in snus production are Burley, flue-cured, dark air and fire-cured.

--Burley gives a good tobacco taste, and is perfect for making snus. Usually rich in nicotine, a personal favorite!

--Flue-cured usually gives less taste, and contains less nicotine. Suitable to mix with other varieties.

--Dark Air usually contains more nicotine but, according to me, it is less flavorful than the burley.

--Fire-cured varieties provide a strong, smoky flavor, and are perfect as a complement to the other variants.

*****

A snus recipe from British member of the Fair Trade Tobacco Forum, *squeezyjohn.*

There are many different reasons why people might like to try making their own snus at home. If their country has restrictions on importing snus, because they want to experiment with flavours, or for sheer cheapness! It is as simple as cooking... really!

There are many recipes, including my own, on SnusOn.com, and you will find many more on the wider internet. Much of the knowledge I used to get myself started have to be credited to JustinTempler who used to frequent this forum and whose posts are still some of the most informative on tobacco growing and snus making available on the internet.

This blog post is simply trying to put together all the basics you will need to get started in one neat place.

INGREDIENTS

Snus is essentially made from 4 basic ingredients: tobacco, water, salt, alkali.

TOBACCO FLOUR
This is simply tobacco leaf that has been ground up to a fine powder. You can buy it from Sweden or make it yourself. The kind of tobacco used in most every brand of snus today is Air Cured or Sun Cured. This is because the alternative methods of fire-curing or flue-curing can lead to higher TSNA levels which can in turn increase the risk of mouth cancer. Bearing this in mind, you can create some kind of snus out of every imaginable variety of tobacco if you wish to. The variety or blend used is very influential on the final taste of the snus:

(i) Virginia - normally flue cured - medium strength - light, sweet and aromatic
(ii) Burley - normally air cured - strong - dark bitter and chocolaty
(iii) Dark Air Cured - mainly for cigars - very strong, pungent and bitter
(iv) Oriental (Turkish) - sun cured or air cured - very little nicotine but aromatic - of little value to snus making
(v) Rustica - a wild tobacco type - very high nicotine, but light flavoured and useful. Hard to source, but very easy to grow yourself.

To create flour from your [*cured*] tobacco you will need to first dry it completely in a low oven (or in the full sun of a dry summers day). Then you will need to grind it. Coffee grinders with a very fine setting can work, but I do mine in a food blender followed by sieving. Once converted to flour, the tobacco can be kept indefinitely in an airtight jar.

WATER
The only thing to watch out for here is chlorine in tap water which can develop off tastes in the finished snus.

You can use bottled spring water or simply leave a jug of water [open] in the fridge overnight to allow the chlorine to evaporate off naturally.

SALT
Simple salt is an important ingredient in snus, but avoid standard table salt as it can contain iodine and other additives to make it pour better. Sea salt or Kosher salt are best.

ALKALI
After cooking the snus, you need to raise it's pH by adding an alkali to the recipe. This free-bases the nicotine and also develops the characteristic snus taste. The two ones used are Sodium Carbonate or Potassium Carbonate. Potassium carbonate solution can be bought from oriental supermarkets under the name Lye Water. It's food grade and perfect. To make your own sodium carbonate, take some regular baking soda (sodium bicarbonate) and bake it in the oven for at least one hour at above the boiling point of water (100°C or 212°F) - when it comes out of the oven it is perfect Sodium Carbonate for making snus with.

FLAVOURINGS (OPTIONAL)
There are two ways to flavour your snus, the most common being to add essences or essential oils after the cooking process. The other type of flavouring is to add spices such as pepper or cinnamon or sweetening agents such as powdered liquorice root. This type of additive is best mixed with the tobacco flour at the beginning.

ADDITIVES (OPTIONAL)
While it is a common aim with home-made stuff to drop the additives in search of a more 'organic' product, several are commonly included in home snus recipes:
(i) Glycerol (Glycerine) - this is only for loose snus recipes and holds the snus together for longer

(ii) Propylene Glycol (PG) - a humectant. It keeps the snus from drying out

(iii) Salmiak (Ammonium Chloride) - more of a flavouring chemical, popular in Scandinavia - an ammonium salt. It is an acquired taste!

EQUIPMENT

Heat control
You need to be able to maintain your snus mix at constant high temperatures (up to 85°C/185°F) for long periods of time (longer than 24 hours). Many different approaches have been tried:

1) The Swedish snus oven... basically an insulated cardboard box with an old fashioned light-bulb inside it! With a little care and attention it can maintain a fairly constant temperature but you need to keep an eye on it.
2) A regular oven... a standard kitchen oven can happily be used to keep temperatures fairly consistent, provided you are not worried about the high energy bills and no-one else in your house wants to cook for a couple of days! The important thing here is to realize that it's the temperature of the snus that is important - not the temperature the oven is set at, so you need to check with a manual thermometer occasionally to see how close you are.
3) The "sous-vide" method... also known as the crock pot water bath because commercial sous-vide machines are prohibitively expensive, and the much cheaper option is to buy a PID device designed to convert a crock-pot (slow cooker) in to a constant temperature controlled water bath. This method has by far the most control over temperature and needs the least monitoring.

... other useful items:

Water-tight glass storage jars for the snus (use with the
   crock pot)
Weighing scales
Measuring jug
Mixing bowl
Fork
Coffee Grinder
Food processor
Fridge

THE BASIC METHOD

1 - Add the water and salt to the tobacco flour and mix
thoroughly.
Firstly I dissolve the salt in the water, and then I mix with
the tobacco. I find that doing this in a large mixing bowl
with a fork is the best way to ensure the water and tobacco
are thoroughly mixed together to form a light brown
paste. Transfer back to the glass jar and compress down
before the next step. A general rule of thumb is using
between 100 and 150ml water and 6-9g salt per 100g of
tobacco flour. The amount of water depends on how
absorbent your particular tobacco flour is. My standard
recipe is 120ml water and 8g salt per 100g of tobacco
flour. In imperial measures that works out at just over
half a cup of water and a level teaspoon of coarse ground
salt per ¼ lb of tobacco flour.

2 - The first cook
The snus then needs to be brought to a high temperature
and maintained there. You can go between 55 and 85°C
(130 - 185°F) - but the lower the temperature the longer
you need. A rough rule of thumb is that the upper
temperature of 85°C (185°F) needs to be maintained for
at least 24 hours whereas with the lower temperature of
55°C (130°F) you need at least 6 days! The temperature
does have an effect on the taste of the finished product
with lower temperatures keeping far more of the aromas

of the original tobacco intact, and higher temperatures tasting dark and more cooked.

The best test of whether your snus is fully cooked is to note the colour. When it hits a dark chocolate brown it is ready for the next step.

3 - Freebasing the nicotine with an alkali
This step is simply to take the snus from it's heat source and adding either sodium carbonate or potassium carbonate, mixing thoroughly and returning to the heat for a further 8 hours. If using dry powdered carbonate then 5-10g per 100g of tobacco flour can be added. The more carbonate you use the stronger your snus will be - but if it is very high then the alkalinity can make it hurt your lips so use common sense. If using potassium carbonate in the form of lye water add 1.5-3 tsps of the solution. Given a normal tobacco strength - 7g of powder or 2 tsps of lye water is sufficient for a normal strength snus.

You can try your snus at this point, but be warned, it will taste horrible! The reaction with the alkali causes a lot of ammonia to be given off and the pH will be far too high for your lip too. It will not be good to use until it has had further weeks aging to allow the ammonia to gas off.

4 - Flavouring
This is where you can let your creativity run wild! In addition to the classic essential oils, you can also add just about anything you can eat provided it can be mixed with the snus properly. Espresso coffee, booze of any description, spices, minced anchovies ... the only rule I follow here is that it must not make the snus too wet to use. The other thing to note is that it is VERY easy to over flavour your snus at this point, especially with essential oils. A nice subtle taste might be achieved with only 1/10th of a drop of essential oil - so experiment with your

oils diluted in a little vodka otherwise your project might be ruined.

5 - Aging

What we're doing here is not really aging. It's allowing the reaction started in step 3 to completely finish. In the pursuit of freshness it's best done in the fridge or other cold place, and you need to make sure the ammonia gas can escape from the container your snus is sitting in. Meanwhile all the flavour compounds you have added will mingle with the snus. Let this happen for about a week and then test it.

This is the first time you will really know what your snus tastes like. If you followed a good recipe then hopefully it will be pretty good stuff!

And that's all there is to it. I know this guide looks like a long drawn out technical thing, but hopefully it should be all the reference you need to have a go at doing this yourself. It's definitely a lot easier than home brewing (with a lot less equipment) - and you could save yourself a fortune.

*****

Chew

Twist

Making a twist for chew begins with whole leaf tobacco (variety of your choice, or any blend) in high case, from which the thickest portion of each stem has been removed. Several leaves are bound together at the tip, and twisted tightly, gradually adding additional leaves to increase the length to about 2 feet of twisted tobacco. Continue twisting until the length begins to coil upon itself, leaving an open loop in the middle, with the two ends twisted together. The ends are twisted out to a point, tied together in a knot, or wrapped with the end of a leaf or some string. (Sometimes a wrapper is added to the entire length. This is done by wrapping the first wrapper for as far as it will wrap, then beginning the next wrapper leaf so that it overlaps the previous wrapper leaf for at least an inch or two.) Hang the twist to dry. For use, a disc of tobacco is sliced off with a sharp knife.

Old fashion twist, from the southern US. [civilwartalk.com]

A **Sugar-free twist** recipe from *squeezyjohn,* a member of the Fair Trade Tobacco Forum from Great Britain:

> I make a sugar free twist by this method. It's a northern European salted chew but if you don't want it you can leave the salt out!

> I take a 4 inch liquorice root and hammer it into fragments, then place in a saucepan with a little water (about 200ml) and 1 teaspoon of salt. I boil it down until the liquid has reduced by half, and then strain and cool the liquid. The liquorice doesn't have a lot of flavour but it adds a natural tooth-friendly sweetness. I then take that cooled liquid, add one teaspoon of propylene glycol (stops it from drying out too much) and a few drops of bergamot essential oil as a nice flavouring. You could use any flavouring if you like as long as it's food-safe. I then brush this mixture on the de-stemmed tobacco leaf and when pliable enough I roll it up into twists and hang the twists to dry.

> With all these kinds of recipes, there's a bit of trial and error needed. You could use a booze of your choice, substitute the liquorice for xylitol, even add brewed coffee as a flavouring. I find that without sugar the propylene

glycol is pretty essential, as it dries up rock hard otherwise.

*****

Loose

A recipe for **loose dip** from *Jitterbugdude*, a member of the Fair Trade Tobacco Forum from Maryland.

1. Pack a mason jar with *shredded* tobacco to which I have added a salt/water mixture to get it nice and moist (not sopping wet).

2. Cook for 8 hours at 185°F (The time is not that critical so don't get wrapped around "exactly 8 hours"). I'm not sure why you would want to do a double cook (like they do for snus making) but for dip it would be a waste of time.

3. Pour hot tobacco into a large stainless or ceramic bowl, and add glycerin/sweetener.

4. Let cool/age for about a week. (I keep the bowl on a counter top with a lid partially covering the bowl. I fluff up the dip once per day.)

5. After about a week or two, I will separate the dip into smaller batches and add my various flavorings.

Detail:

Into a large mixing bowl:

Add 3 cups of packed tobacco

Mix 1/2 tsp of salt to 60 cc (1/4 cup) of water (You can double the water if you like. It's an art more than a science.) Add the salt/water solution to the tobacco. Stir well and let it set for about 20-30 minutes. It will seem very dry at first but after about 20 minutes the tobacco will absorb all of the water.

Place in a small pint mason jar (the flat squat kind), and seal. Place in a crock pot. Fill completely with water. You will need to add a weight to the top of the jar otherwise it will float. *Make sure your jar is short enough to fit in your crock pot and completely covered in water.*

Place in Crockpot, slip in a temperature probe from your Thermostat. Set for 185°F and cook for 8 hrs. I use hot tap water. It'll take about 2 hours to reach 185° but that's ok. 8 hrs, for the overall process is fine.

After 8 hours, use canning tongues (or a thick glove) and remove the jar. Pour contents into a big bowl.

Add:
Xylitol 2 tsp
pure sucralose 2 tsp
glycerin 2 Tbsp
Stir with your hands or a fork. Place partially covered on a counter top for 1 to 2 weeks. You want it to dry out some because if it is too wet it will mold. It'll initially stink. For a cover I use a fine mesh screen. This allows good air circulation and prevents bugs etc. from getting in the container.

After the waiting period, try some. Then add a flavor of your choice. The amount of flavoring to add is very personal. Start light, and add till you like the taste.
I store large amounts [*of loose dip*] in the freezer.

Notes: 2 Tbsp of glycerin makes a somewhat dry mix while 4 Tbsp makes a wet mix. I like things sweet, so 2 tsp of pure sucralose might be too sweet for you. You just need to make small batches to find something you like.

Flavorings I like: Wintergreen, Anise, Orange, Maple and apple-cinnamon.

For a sweetener I use Xylitol and pure Sucralose. Since I am going to have dip in my mouth I do not want to use sugar. Xylitol has excellent anti-tooth cavity properties as well as anti-microbial properties (the two being related). You can use any sweetener you want (sugar, honey) but I prefer to make mine sugar-free.

The effect of glycerin is two fold. It has good anti-microbial properties, and it adds "mouth feel" to the tobacco. This means that when you put dip in your mouth, all the flavor will not be sucked out in 30 seconds.

*****

Chimó

Chimó has been used as an oral tobacco product in the Andean portions of Venezuela and Colombia for eons—likely thousands of years before Columbus. It's essentially a thick paste or formed gum, produced from the strained juice of cooked tobacco, and may or may not be flavored or sweetened in various ways. It is still commonly used in those same geographic regions, and available in most markets there—sometimes packaged like Tootsie-Rolls, with branded, wax paper wrappings.

With thinner preparations, a smear of it is rubbed in the cheek. The pellet of the thicker version is used in the same manner as a Skoal Bandit. It increases salivation, and requires occasional spitting.

A Chimó recipe from Fair Trade Tobacco Forum member *CobGuy* (Darin) from Arizona:

> The basics involve boiling your green leaves, straining them, adding a little sweetener and cocoa and cooking down to a paste.
>
> The flavor of this batch is a little too sweet but not too bad for the first try ... think bitter, yet sweetened, chocolate. Also, it will require further dehydration to be able to roll it into a ball as it's still somewhat of a paste.
>
> The starting amounts are approximate.
> About a pound of green leaves in about a quart of water.
> My ending paste was approximately 1/4 cup or so from this starting amount.

I have a feeling these folks weren't pulling out the measuring spoons, and just learned from experience how much to toss in. My initial trial definitely confirms that the amount of sweeteners added were too much.

Not that it's bad. It's like a sweet nicotine paste for your gums.

1. Chop your green tobacco leaves and place into a pot with just enough water to almost cover them.
NOTE: Next time I will start with less water as the leaves themselves expel their water as they heat.

2. Bring to nearly a boil but do not let the temperature get above 100°C. Hold this simmer for about 90 minutes.

3. Strain the leaves out using a cheese cloth or other method to remove most of the vegetative matter.

4. Add your desired alkalizers, sweetener and / or cocoa. I used 1/4 tsp Slaked Lime with 1/2 tsp honey, 1/2 tsp molasses and 1/2 tsp cocoa
NOTE: Next time I'll cut those additives by half and use 1/4 tsp's and also increase the alkali amount.

5. Bring the remaining solution back to a simmer and keep the temp under 100°C again.

6. As the solution starts to thicken it will become much easier for the temperature to rise too high, so be diligent.
NOTE: Taking the pot off and back on the low burner is an easy way to continue safely. *[or use a double-boiler]*

7. Once it's reached a paste-like consistency it can be removed and refrigerated.

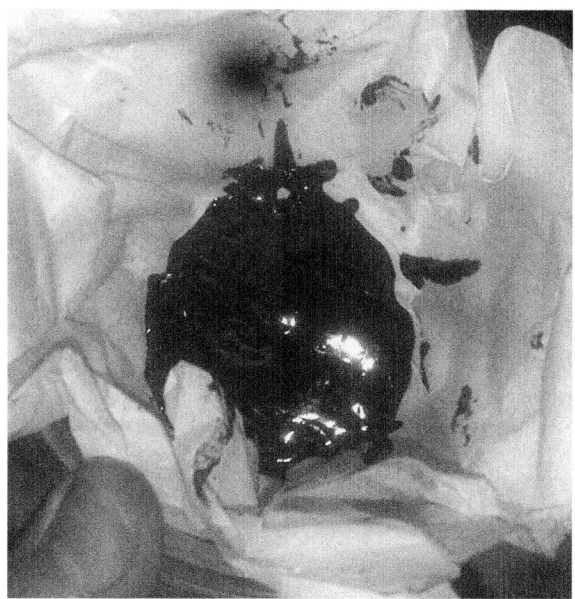

Chimó, after straining and thickening. [CobGuy (Darin)]

NOTE: Next time I will scrape it out onto parchment paper and continue the dehydration process in the oven at 90-95°C.

8. When it's ready to sample, roll up a very small ball and place it under the tongue.
NOTE: Use caution and a small portion at first, as this stuff kicks like a mule.

Hope someone can use this information and keep these ancient methods alive!

*****

Reproduction of a Mayan priest smoking tobacco (as rendered in the 19th century), at the "Temple of the Cross" in Palenque.

Appendix 1.
Tobacco Glossary

Over the centuries, terminology used by tobacco growers and the tobacco industry has accumulated into a set of words that make perfect sense to insiders, but can be vague, ambiguous and even misleading to those not a part of it. While cigars, pipes, pipe tobacco, cigarettes and smokeless tobacco also have their unique terms (discussed in their sections), only general tobacco terms are covered here. Keep in mind that nearly every variety of *Nicotiana tabacum* (so-called smoking tobacco) can and probably has been used for nearly every kind of tobacco use or product.

class (or market class): These semi-official USDA ARS-GRIN classes are vaguely useful in deciding what tobacco leaf variety to grow or obtain for a specific purpose. Those classes that are use-based, are indications of the predominant use (or their similarity to it), *in the late 19th century*, of specific varieties by the manufacturers of various tobacco products or by exporters. They do not indicate the exclusive or even most suitable applications for a particular variety of tobacco. The geographic classes are *mostly of historic interest*, since nearly all varieties of tobacco can be (and are) grown in most regions of the world.

BURLEY

Burley, as a group of tobacco varieties, is predominantly derived from Ohio White Burley, which in 1864 was an accidental genetic variant discovered in a seedbed of a now lost "Red Burley." Burleys tend to have lighter or cream-colored stalks and veins while growing, and produce a large, relatively smooth leaf that quickly color-cures to a bright yellow, then dries to a light brown. Burley seedlings are sometimes fragile, and transplants are more tender and slow to establish. For most of its growth, the leaves are held upright, near the stalk, with a close distance between the leaf nodes. In contrast to this, once well established, it lengthens rapidly, and may mature earlier than other varieties. It is often stalk harvested when fully ripe, though primed leaf can make excellent cigar wrappers and binders. Burley is historically air-cured, and can be cured by any of the other curing methods, though flue-curing produces unimpressive results. Burley leaf tends to be low in sugars, and relatively high in nicotine. Burley tobacco, when smoked, offers a distinctive and recognizable aroma.

Uses: Cigarettes, pipe blending, smokeless. Most commercial Burley is used in blending cigarette tobacco (together with flue-cured, sometimes a small percentage of Oriental, and occasionally with Perique). Primed lower leaves make fine, light-colored cigar wrappers, and most Burley leaf is sufficiently sturdy to serve as cigar binder.

CIGAR BINDER

Binder is a diverse class of tobacco varieties that tend to produce a leaf with sufficient elasticity and tensile strength to withstand the stress of compressing a bunch of cigar filler. Some of these varieties are nearly identical to varieties classified as Cigar Filler. Their flavors, aromas and burn qualities are not a consideration in classification.

Uses: Cigar wrapper, cigar binder, cigar filler, pipe blending, chew. When air-cured or flue-cured, cigarette blending.

CIGAR FILLER

Since most tobaccos can be used as cigar filler, this formal class includes only those that found a major market as filler with cigar manufacturers, either in the U.S., or in its primary growing regions elsewhere. Varieties that regularly produce leaves which are thick or corrugated or intensely rippled are unsuitable for use as wrapper or binder, since they can not be flattened. Some of these varieties are nearly identical to varieties classified as Cigar Binder.

Uses: Cigar filler, pipe blending, chew. Finer leaves can be used as cigar binder or even cigar wrapper. Wrapper and Binder varieties that are damaged are frequently *graded* as filler. When air-cured or flue-cured, cigarette blending.

CIGAR WRAPPER

Wrappers for cigars require a leaf (or portion of a leaf) that is without flaws, both for reasons of air flow as well as aesthetics. While some are preferred to be thin, such as Connecticut Shade leaf and Indonesian Sumatra, others are noticeably thicker, such as Ecuador Sumatra, Connecticut Broadleaf, and most wrapper leaf that is grown in full sun. Some varieties naturally attract fewer insects (or more effectively repel them) that make pinholes in the lamina. Shade-grown wrappers (grown beneath a canopy of shade cloth—40% shade) are larger, thinner, more fragile and less intensely flavored than sun-grown wrappers. Ideally, wrapper leaf burns to a white ash. Some traditionally shade-grown tobacco varieties can be successfully grown without shade.

Uses: Cigar wrapper, cigar binder, cigar filler, pipe blending, chew. When air-cured or flue-cured, cigarette blending.

DARK/AIR CURED

These typically have very dark green, thick, sticky leaves. They air-cure to a strong, intensely flavored leaf.
Uses: Chew, snuff, cigarette and pipe blending.

FLUE-CURED

This is the primary tobacco used in manufactured cigarettes. Often generically called, "Virginia," these tobaccos were selected to be effectively and rapidly flue-cured (by heat alone, in the absence of smoke) to a bright yellow or deep gold color. That curing process results in a leaf that produces acidic smoke, and ages very little, thereby maintaining the bright color. All flue-cured varieties can be successfully cured using any available curing method.

Uses: Cigarette blending, pipe blending. When air-cured and fully finished, can be used for cigar wrapper, cigar binder or cigar filler.

FIRE-CURED

Fire-cured varieties tend to produce dark, heavy, sometimes sticky leaves that can cure well during a multi-week exposure to the smoke of open curing fires. The resulting leaf is tough, darkened, and gives off a distinct smoky aroma and taste. The fire-curing process yields a leaf that is high in nicotine, and sometimes does not burn well.

Uses: Chew, snuff, cigarette blending. Blended in some Appalachian-style cigars and stogies. Sometimes used as a minor component in pipe blending.

Fire-curing barn. *[Workman Tobacco Seed Company]*

HUNGARIAN

This wide-ranging collection of tobaccos has its origins in the tobaccos grown within the many Eastern European member states of the Austro-Hungarian Empire. There is no distinctive characteristic of the class. [It would be similar grouping the numerous varieties of tobacco grown in the U.S. to an "American" tobacco class.] Some are strong, some are mild.

Uses: Any tobacco applications, depending on the specific variety.

MARYLAND

These tobaccos resemble the large, seedleaf varieties, from which they were derived. Though they tend to be mild in flavor and aroma, the nicotine concentration may or may not be high. They are traditionally stalk-harvested and air cured, and often used to increase the flavor-holding capacity of a cased blend.

Uses: Pipe blending, cigarette blending. Can be used as mild tasting cigar wrapper / binder / filler.

NO TYPE

This class was applied by USDA ARS-GRIN personnel to indicate "unidentified" class. These are generally GRIN accessions received from undeveloped geographic regions, and received without adequate documentation, yet never classified by GRIN.

ORIENTAL

"Oriental" is a term for tobaccos that, in the early twentieth century, were often labeled as "Turkish." These initially reached the Middle-East, Iran, India and Indonesia via Dutch and Portuguese traders soon after the first arrival of tobacco in Europe (~1500). Many derivatives were cultivated in wide-ranging areas within the Ottoman Empire. Today, these are frequently grown in Albania, North Macedonia, Greece, Bulgaria, Cyprus, Syria, Turkey and the Republic of Georgia. Oriental tobaccos have a reputation for being small-leafed, delicate, aromatic and low in nicotine. This is true of some, though not all. Oriental tobaccos are traditionally sun-cured, though they are successfully cured by any of the available curing methods. Latakia, grown in Syria and Cyprus, is an indeterminate Basma-like variety that is intensely fire-cured in the smoke of aromatic herbs and scrub wood typical of the Mediterranean basin.

Uses: Cigarette blending, pipe blending. The larger leaf Oriental varieties can be used as cigar wrapper, cigar binder, cigar filler.

OTHER

This ARS-GRIN class may be considered, like NO TYPE, as "no information available."

PRIMITIVE

These are varieties that, according to the classifier at ARS-GRIN, appeared to definitely be *Nicotiana tabacum*, but to have been subjected to little or no agricultural improvement effort, in comparison to the hypothetical "wild" type. Their splayed venation patterns may make it difficult to utilize as cigar wrapper or cigar binder. Some have distinctive, sometimes odd, aromas and flavors. Some make excellent and rich cigar filler and cigarette blending leaf.

leaf grade: This is an indication of how intact an individual leaf is found to be, following curing and any additional finishing processes. It also takes into account the general size of the leaf (as relates to suitability for a particular use), the overall color of the leaf, and the consistency of that color over the entire leaf surface. Usually, the "higher" the grade, the greater the market value (cost) of the leaf. But this does not limit its use for purposes not indicated by its "grade".

wrapper

Regardless of "class", wrapper grade leaf is larger leaf that is almost entirely free of small holes or tears. The various wrapper leaf grades (there are well over a dozen) assess the color, tensile strength, stretch and the thickness of secondary veins, since their intended use is for the visible, exterior of a cigar or plug.

binder

A binder *grade* requires a greater tensile strength than does wrapper *grade*, since it must contain most of the compression force surrounding a cigar's filler bunch. Binders may have occasional, small holes and non-critical tears. Binders are often, though not always, thicker than wrappers.

filler
The leaves of most types of tobacco that are not intact enough to be used as wrapper or binder are graded as "filler". Leaf graded as filler may contain the entire stem (central vein), or be frog-legged, by removal of only the thicker portion of the stem.

broken leaf and pieces
This is exactly what it says. Some is used in applications of shredded tobacco, while other is used for chemical extraction of the nicotine in industrial applications.

tobacco variety:
There are over 3000 documented varieties of *Nicotiana tabacum*. They are all the same species, like domesticated dogs, but show a continuum of characteristics, depending on their genetic heritage. While "Virginia tobacco" may refer to a host of different varieties of tobacco intended to be flue-cured, *Virginia Bright Leaf* for example, is the name of a specific variety. While "burley" is a market class of tobacco, *Tennessee 89* (or TN 89) is a specific variety of burley, and different from TN 90. Varieties are being continually developed to alter various characteristics, such as specific disease resistance or dominance of nicotine production over that of nornicotine.

species:
smoking tobacco
Common smoking tobacco, and the general tobacco of world commerce is exclusively *Nicotiana tabacum*, which originated along the eastern slopes of the Andes mountains, and spread into all of South and Central America and the Caribbean. Different varieties of *N. tabacum* are now successfully grown throughout the world, including Nepal, Scandinavia, the Alps, and on every continent except Antarctica. With the ability to start seed indoors, and then transplant outdoors after about 8 weeks, and to cure green-harvested tobacco indoors as well, tobacco can be successfully grown in any location that experiences a vegetable growing season of at least 70 to 80 days. Shorter season varieties also exist. *N. tabacum* cannot easily propagate itself.

rustica

The cultivated, Native American tobacco of the regions stretching from Mexico north-eastward, into the Mississippi valley, and as far as southeastern and south-central Canada was *Nicotiana rustica*. *N. rustica* will propagate itself to a very limited extent, but it is not wild, and will not persist after more than a few years. Its millennia of intentional, human cultivation and selection limited its ability to adequately disperse its own seed spontaneously, though it does so more efficiently than *N. tabacum*.

Sacred Cornplanter (Nicotiana rustica) tobacco. The blossoms are bright yellow.

wild tobacco species

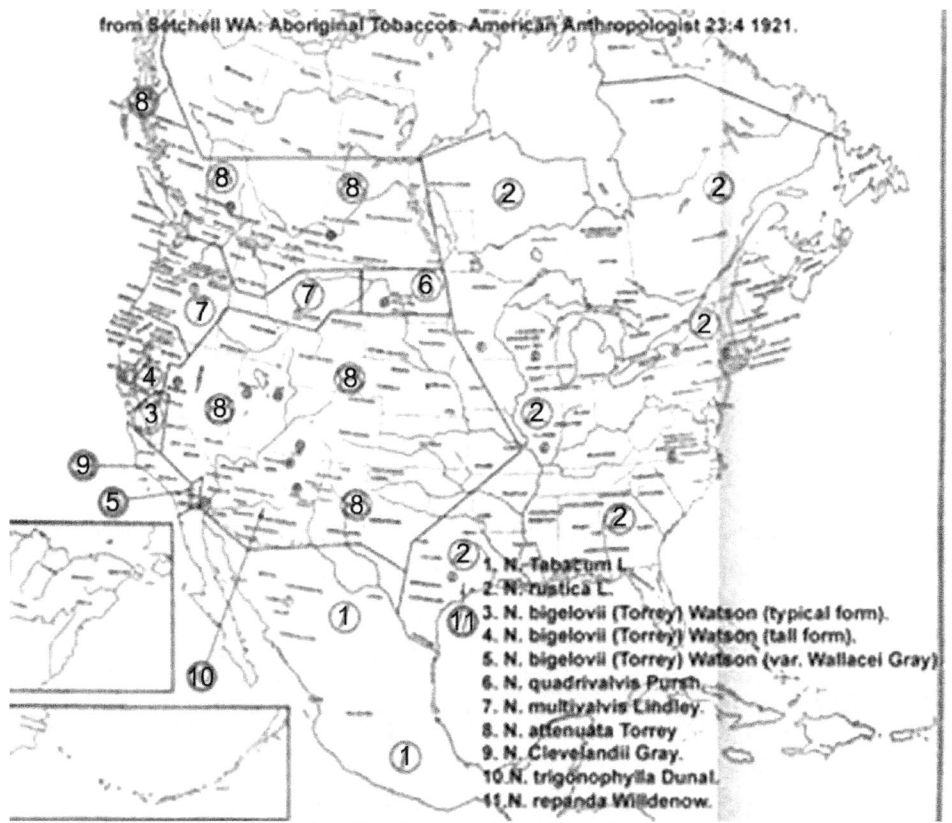

The general ranges of native North American Nicotiana *species.*

In the upper mid-west of the US, the west coast, and up into western Canada, several other species were used and sometimes traded, but these were and continue to be wild species (e.g. *N. quadrivalvis*, *N. bigelovii*, *N. attenuata*) that generally propagate themselves without human intervention—though they were sometimes intentionally cultivated. Blending with a portion of *N. rustica* is used today in cigarette manufacture in some countries in Eastern Europe and elsewhere, to increase nicotine concentrations. Continued consumption of wild species is generally limited to ceremonial uses by Native Americans.

case: This is a quite old tobacco term that vexes most people unfamiliar with its use. With regard to tobacco, it is a statement of its moisture content. *Out of case* describes tobacco that is so dry that it crumbles to fragments and dust when handled in any way. *In case* describes tobacco that contains a high enough moisture content that it can be easily handled, without damaging the leaf. With regard to *users* of whole leaf tobacco, there are four general levels of case:

> **out of case**: very noisy, like dried autumn leaves, and crumbles when handled
>
> **low case**: much quieter, is mostly flexible, though it may crack slightly
>
> **medium case**: sounds like thick vinyl, is entirely flexible, and has a moderate stretch
>
> **high case**: silent, feels somewhat moist, though not wet, is flexible and fully stretchy

casing: This is different from *case*. Casing is a liquid preparation that is added to tobacco to alter its taste or aroma, or to improve its ability to retain moisture and hold flavorings. Some may contain simple chemicals, such as citric acid. Flavor casings may include essential oils, which are either alcohol-based or propyleneglycol (PG) based. They may also be common food flavorings, such as honey or syrup or brandy or other commercial alcohol product. Casings that are not intended to alter the flavor or aroma, but rather to increase the hygroscopic (water holding) nature of the tobacco include PG or glycerin, or both. PG also acts as a mold inhibitor, while glycerin is mildly bacteriostatic. These latter casings are what allow commercially distributed cigarettes or especially pipe tobacco to retain their soft look and feel for months or years on the shelf. Essential oils alone tend to rapidly lose their aroma, in the absence of PG. It is PG that permits so-called *black Cavendish* to remain black in appearance, instead of its natural deep brown. PG does not impact aroma, but it does affect the taste and burn of tobacco.

fermentation: Living tobacco leaf contains several enzymes that continue to function after the leaf has dried and died. These oxidize carbohydrates and proteins, and are a primary cause of what we identify as *aging* in finished tobacco. The speed at which these chemical changes occur is dependent on temperature and the presence of moisture. Many different methods can be used to increase the speed of this process, though it still may require as long as several years to run to near completion. This is why "aged" leaf usually seems "better" than leaf with less age. Basic tobacco fermentation—aging—does not depend on the action of microbes, though they may influence subtle characteristics late in the aging process.

hand:

In the distant as well as the recent past, all whole leaf tobacco of commerce was tied into bundles of 20 or 30 similar leaves, using an additional leaf as the "tie" or wrap at the stem end of the bundle. These so-called *hands* of tobacco could be more efficiently handled, packed into bales or wooden hogsheads (huge, squat barrels) for transport by wagon or ship, and subsequently handled after unpacking.

Video: How to Tie a Hand of Tobacco
https://www.youtube.com/watch?v=UvhmJ7RTNEc

Tied hands of tobacco.

Perique pressing.

perique process vs *a perique:*

perique meaning 1

The perique process and the unique tobacco that it produces go by the same name, p*erique.* It is produced by applying pressure (~35 psi) to leaf that is sealed beneath liquid, rendering it mostly oxygen free. This is continued for several months, allowing anaerobic microbes (namely the yeast, *Pichia anomala*) to dominate the microbial culture. Perique tobacco is dark in color, relatively strong, and creates a more alkaline smoke when burned. This is the Perique that is commonly blended with flue-cured Virginia tobacco to make Virginia—perique pipe blends.

perique meaning 2

By contrast, *a perique* of tobacco (in the same sense as *a plug* of tobacco), and also known as a carrotte of tobacco, is a cylinder of tobacco that has been tightly wrapped within a coil of rope to compress it and preserve it. These were popular with sailors during the early nineteenth century, as a way to keep tobacco smokable during long ship voyages. The character of the tobacco resembles twist-rope or pressed plug, more than pressure-processed perique tobacco.

A perique or carrotte of tobacco, tightly wrapped in rope. [Killebrew, 1884]

ring size or ring gauge: Cigar thickness is often stated as a ring gauge, because, over the centuries, cigar factories would sort their hand-rolled cigars by thickness (diameter), using a wooden plank with smooth, carefully calibrated holes into which the end of a cigar could be passed. *Ring gauge is a measure of 64ths of*

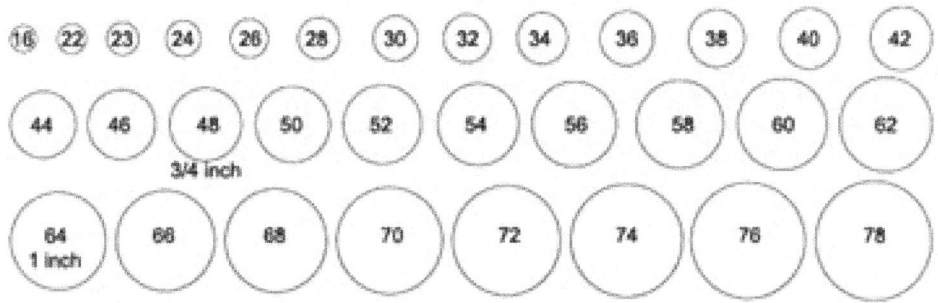

Example of a ring gauge tool, not shown actual size.

an inch. So a 64 ring cigar has a 1 inch thickness or 1 inch diameter. A 32 ring cigar is 1/2 inch thick. Likewise a 48 ring is 3/4 inch.

stemming:
Stemming is the process of removing the central vein from individual tobacco leaves

stripping:

Stripping is the process of removing the leaves that have cured from stalks that have been hanging in the shed (or have sun-cured) after stalk-harvesting.

Stripping Burley
A vignette provided by Larry Butcher.

I'm going way back to when I was a young kid and stripped tobacco for market that was entirely hand tied. The tobacco was stripped into three grades. A pile of tobacco on the stalk was placed on one end of a stripping room table. The table was 12 to 16 ft long and 4 ft wide. One person would pull off the bottom leaves, (Flyings or trash), then the stalk was laid over to a second person, who pulled off the Middle leaves (Lugs) to the red tip. You would see a color change easily. Then the stalks were laid over for the last person, who removed the rest of the leaves (Red) on the top of the stalk. These names are for burley and may not apply to other areas as some call the bottom leave sand lugs.

Now in each leaf position the hands were tied, and placed on a tobacco stick—12 hands per stick. The stick that was used was the same stick used to cure the tobacco on hanging in the barn. Each person's hands would be of different size, and wrapped a little different. Women's hands were small, and most men's hands was larger. Learning to strip into hands, you would get to making your hands all match without thinking about it. You could look at a finished stick of tobacco and tell which worker stripped that stick of tobacco. The sticks would range from 10 pounds red tips, while the lugs would range from average of 12 to 18 lbs per stick with 12 hands on them.

Appendix 2.
Plastics Safe for Storing Tobacco

Plastics for Food-Contact

A plastic that has been approved for direct contact with food is safe for direct contact with tobacco.

FDA Compliance
Within the FDA, there is no government-operated process of inspection of plastics produced for food contact use. Rather, the FDA in their regulations provides certain specifications regarding composition, additives, and properties. A material which meets these standards can then be stated as FDA COMPLIANT. This is based exclusively on material composition.

USDA Compliance
For a product to be USDA COMPLIANT, components used in direct food contact must be documented as to their compliance with the Federal Food, Drug and Cosmetic Act ("FDA compliance"). Therefore, USDA requirements for material approval are satisfied by a certification of FDA compliance. This is approved only for individual manufactured products, on a product by product basis, and only for products falling under the purview of the USDA (in the agricultural food industry).

http://www.usplastic.com/knowledgebase/article.aspx? contentkey=683

The information below is specific for sheet and slab plastics available from US Plastics, but may be useful in some tobacco applications that are heated to various temperatures.

ACETAL (Delrin®)

White Acetal-150 has excellent load-bearing qualities in both tension and compression. Acetal does not absorb a large amount of moisture and are resistant to a wide range of solvents. Acetals are attacked by both strong acids and oxidizing agents. The service temp range is -20 to 185 deg F, intermittent 200 deg F. High yield strength at elevated temperatures. It is an excellent material for bearings, gears, cams, and other small parts. Properties include low friction, high wear resistance, and ease of fabrication. Meets FDA standards and is USDA approved. It is not UV stabilized.

ACRYLIC

This plastic sheet is completely transparent, flexible, and exhibits great resistance to breakage. Acrylic is excellent material to use in place of glass for windows, skylights, doors, partitions, etc. It is lightweight, half the weight of glass, and it is virtually unaffected by nature. Acrylics transparency, gloss and dimensional shape are virtually unaffected by years of exposure to the elements, salt spray or corrosive atmospheres. These materials withstand exposure to light from fluorescent lamps without darkening or deteriorating. They ultimately discolor, however, when exposed to high-intensity UV light below 265 nm. It can take temperatures from -40 deg F to 180 deg F (intermittent to 200 deg F). Fabrication is easy, as it can be sawed with fine tooth blades, drilled with plastic drills, sanded and polished. Also, it can be cemented with Acrylic cement. It meets FDA standards, is UV stabilized, and has a UL 95 Flammability rating. The forming temp is 350 deg F. Applications include inspection windows, sight gauges, windshields, meter faces, protective covers, safety shields, tanks, desk tops, displays, trays, and chair pads.

NYLON

With ease of fabrication and many superior properties, Nylon has found wide application for bearings, bushings, washers, seals, gears, guides, rollers, wear plates, fasteners, insulators, forming dies, sleeves, liners, cooling fans, and many other parts. Properties include high wear and abrasion resistance, with low coefficient of friction, high strength to weight ratio. It has corrosion resistance to alkali and organic chemicals. It is non-abrasive to other material, with noise dampening characteristics, also good electrical insulator. It is not UV stabilized, but it is USDA and FDA compliant. The temp range is -40 deg F to 225 deg F.

POLYETHYLENE LDPE

These sheets can be heat formed, shaped and welded to fabricate ducts, hoods, and much more. They have excellent corrosion resistance to a wide range of items. Polyethylene is susceptible to stress cracking when exposed to ultraviolet and some chemicals. Wetting agents such as detergents accelerate stress cracking. It cannot be cemented but easily welded with a plastic welder. LDPE can be cut with a wood saw and drilled with regular metal bits. Not UV stabilized but does meet FDA standards. The Low Density Polyethylene has a .92 density. Semi-rigid with good impact resistance and abrasion resistance. It is white translucent with working temps of 0-140 deg F. and a forming temp of 245 deg F.

POLYETHYLENE HDPE

Rigidity and tensile strength of the HDPE resins are considerably higher than those of LDPE & MDPE materials. Impact strength is slightly lower, as is to be expected in a stiffer material. These sheets can be heat formed, shaped and welded to fabricate ducts, hoods, and much more. They have excellent corrosion resistance to a wide range of items. HDPE cannot be cemented, but are easily welded with a plastic welder. It can be cut with a wood saw and drilled with regular metal bits. Not UV stabilized but meets FDA standards. The High Density Polyethylene has a density .95. Rigid, good impact and abrasion resistance. It is white translucent with a working temp of -60-180 deg F and a forming temp of 295 deg F.

POLYPROPYLENE

Offers a good balance of thermal, chemical and electrical properties with moderate strength. It possesses a good strength to weight ratio. Due to its hard, high gloss surface, PP is ideally suited to environments where there is concern for bacteria build up that can interfere with flow. These sheets can be heat formed, shaped and welded to fabricate ducts, hoods, and much more. They have excellent corrosion resistance to a wide range of items. Cannot be cemented but are easily welded with a plastic welder. PP can be cut with a wood saw and drilled with regular metal bits. Not UV stabilized but is USDA approved and meets FDA standards. Polypropylene has a .90 density, rigid with fair impact resistance and very good abrasion resistance. It is white-tan, translucent with working temperatures of 32 deg F to 210 deg F and a forming temp of 310-325 deg F.

PVC EXPANDED SHEET
Sintra PVC sheet is a moderately expanded high density, polyvinyl chloride (PVC) sheet. As a lightweight plastic material, it can be easily cut, sawed, drilled, and fabricated. The sheet is an excellent material for model exhibits and displays. For interior signage only. Can be painted and silk-screened. Its characteristics include: foamed PVC sheet material that is approx half the weight of solid PVC; durable and hard wearing under many adverse conditions and resists most chemicals and water, with its porous interior and hard smooth surface; it can be painted, printed, silk-screened, laminated, etc; easy to clean and has an attractive surface, and is fire retardant. Good sound dampening-UL 94 flammability class 94 V-O-945; USDA approved. Colors available: white, black, gray, and beige.

STYRENE
Use this high impact styrene sheet for models, prototypes, signs, displays, enclosures, and more. It can be drilled, threaded, sawed, sheared, punched and machined. It can also be painted and has excellent forming properties (vacuum pressure). It is non-toxic and odorless, dimensionally stable, has low water absorption, and is heat and electronically sealable. Maximum heat resistance is 180 deg F and the forming temp is 325 deg F to 350 deg F. Styrene meets FDA standards, but is not UV stabilized.

UHMW

This Ultra High Molecular Weight (UHMW) Polyethylene bar has exceptionally high abrasion and impact resistance properties. It will outwear all other materials, including metals, nylons, urethanes, and fluoroplastics. In corrosion resistance, it has the same qualities of other polyethylene plastics. The working temperature range is from -60 to 200 deg F. Because it resists wear, friction and corrosion, it cuts maintenance costs, energy consumption, and extends equipment life. Applications include guide rails, wear plates, rollers, conveyor augers, bin and hopper lines, chutes, bearings, bushings and gears. Its properties include: low coefficient of friction, self-lubrication, non-adherent surface, FDA and USDA concurrence for contact with foods, drugs, etc.

Maximum hot fill temperatures for plastic bottles and jars

PET (polyethylene terephthalate)	120°F
PS (polystyrene)	150°F
HDPE (high density polyethylene)	145°F
LDPE (low density polyethylene)	120°F
PP (polypropylene)	165°F

Plastics used in bottles and rigid containers:

Polyethylene Terephthalate: Soda bottles, water bottles, vinegar bottles, medicine containers, backing for photography film.

High-density Polyethylene: Containers for: laundry/dish detergent, fabric softeners, bleach, milk, shampoo, conditioner, motor oil. Newer bullet proof vests, various toys.

Vinyl/Polyvinyl Chloride: Pipes, shower curtains, meat wraps, cooking oil bottles, baby bottle nipples, shrink wrap, clear medical tubing, vinyl dashboards and seat covers, coffee containers.

Low-density Polyethylene: Wrapping films, grocery bags, sandwich bags.

Polypropylene: Tupperware®, syrup bottles, yogurt tubs, diapers, outdoor carpet.

Polystyrene: Coffee cups, disposable cutlery and cups (clear and colored), bakery shells, meat trays, "cheap" hubcaps, packing peanuts, styrofoam insulation.

Search U.S. Plastics Technical Knowledgebase:
https://www.usplastic.com/knowledgebase/default.aspx

Appendix 3.
Kiln / Flue-Cure Chamber Plans

The purpose of a tobacco kiln is to raise the ambient temperature of previously color-cured leaf to above 122°F (and below 130°F), while maintaining adequate humidity (greater than 60% RH). These conditions need to be sustained over a period of 4 to 6 weeks. The effect is similar to that achieved within only the *center* of a giant pile (pilon) of tobacco. It dramatically accelerates the "fermentation", or oxidation of carbohydrates and proteins within the leaf lamina, utilizing the plant's own oxidase and peroxidase enzymes. All enzymatic reactions are highly temperature sensitive.

If the temperature ever reaches 149°F, then the most active of the oxidizing enzymes is permanently destroyed. Above about 191°F, the other remaining enzyme (the much slower-acting peroxidase) is also destroyed. So kiln temperature needs to be controlled by a thermostat of some kind.

I initially used a water heater "thermodisc" thermostat on my first, small kiln. This works, but is troublesome to install, since it is intended to be firmly attached to the exterior surface of a metal container, and not exposed to high moisture.

Far safer and easier to both install and manage is a digital controller. These are essentially an electrical relay (switch) that is turned on or off according to the temperature registered by a temp probe that is inserted into the interior of the kiln. The digital controller itself remains outside the kiln. They are widely available on-line for $15 to $20, and come with their own specific wiring instructions. I simply used the digital controller to switch on or off an extension cord that provides power to my heat source. A circulation fan significantly improves the performance of a kiln, by helping to equalize the conditions throughout the kiln space. Since the fan is inside the kiln, and is exposed to high humidity conditions, it should be one designed for such a setting.

The poplar framework for my kiln. The hinge is a "piano" hinge that runs the length of the door frame. The angled component simply serves to prevent the rectangle from racking. XPS foam provides rigidity to the entire frame.

I selected a basic, bathroom ventilation fan (cost ~$20) for this purpose. Although I also purchased and installed a "ceiling fan speed controller" (a dimmer specifically designed to handle the stress of switching on an electric motor), I found that I usually left it turned to its max speed setting. So the fan controller really needs to be only a simple on/off switch.

For insulation, which is critical for an efficient kiln, I chose 2-inch thick, extruded polystyrene (XPS) foam board, which has an R rating of 10. The foam for this entire kiln, including the bottom, was cut from two 4' x 8' XPS boards. The layout diagram of the foam panels shown allowed me to cut the boards in half at the home-improvement store, so that I could fit them into the trunk of my car.

XPS foam board is rigid, and can be easily cut with a thin-bladed, sharp kitchen knife. Its two inches of thickness prevented me

For latching the kiln door, I used 3 pairs of hook-and-eye, screen door hooks. After a gasket is attached around the door opening, the hooks make a very tight seal.

from extending the sides of the kiln insulation beyond the seam of the door opening (since it would block the swing at the equally insulated hinge edge of the door, and interfere with its radius of swing at the closure. This leaves that portion of the kiln without insulation.

I attached the foam to the wood frame using 2-1/2" and 3" galvanized exterior wood screws, each fitted with a fender washer where it presses against the foam board. These are the same screws that I used to assemble the wood frame itself. Theoretically, the kiln can be disassembled for storage, though I have never found the need to try that.

The *exterior* of the XPS foam floor is reinforced by a panel of 1/8" plywood. I added large casters to the bottom (attached directly to the frame) for both mobility and to create an air gap between the kiln bottom and the floor on which it rests.

Insulation above and below the door closure is from the extension of both the top XPS panel and the floor XPS panel. For the two sides of the door (hinge edge and opening edge) I needed columns of XPS that could swing out of the way, whenever I opened the kiln. These two long sections of foam were hinged to the foam side boards using Tyvek tape on both the inside and outside of the hinging area. These Tyvek tape hinges have held up without any sign of wear or fatigue for over five years. The foam hinging blocks are held in a closed position by long rubber bands (2 for each edge) that are attached to an extended screw on the side, and a matched screw on the door. I usually need to replace the rubber bands every one to two years. Each is tied to its side screw (with a larks head knot), and is free to be hooked or unhooked from the matching door screw.

The temperature probe of the digital controller comes with a 36" wire. A small hole was punctured through the foam of the kiln top, and the probe inserted so that it hangs several inches below the top of the interior. The opening for the probe was then sealed with bits of Tyvek tape.

The interior of the kiln is fitted with enameled wire (closet) shelving, cut to fit. The top one is fixed, and allows things to be hung from the top of the kiln, while the lower one is removable, to accommodate very long hands of tobacco. The ventilation fan is also suspended from the wire shelving.

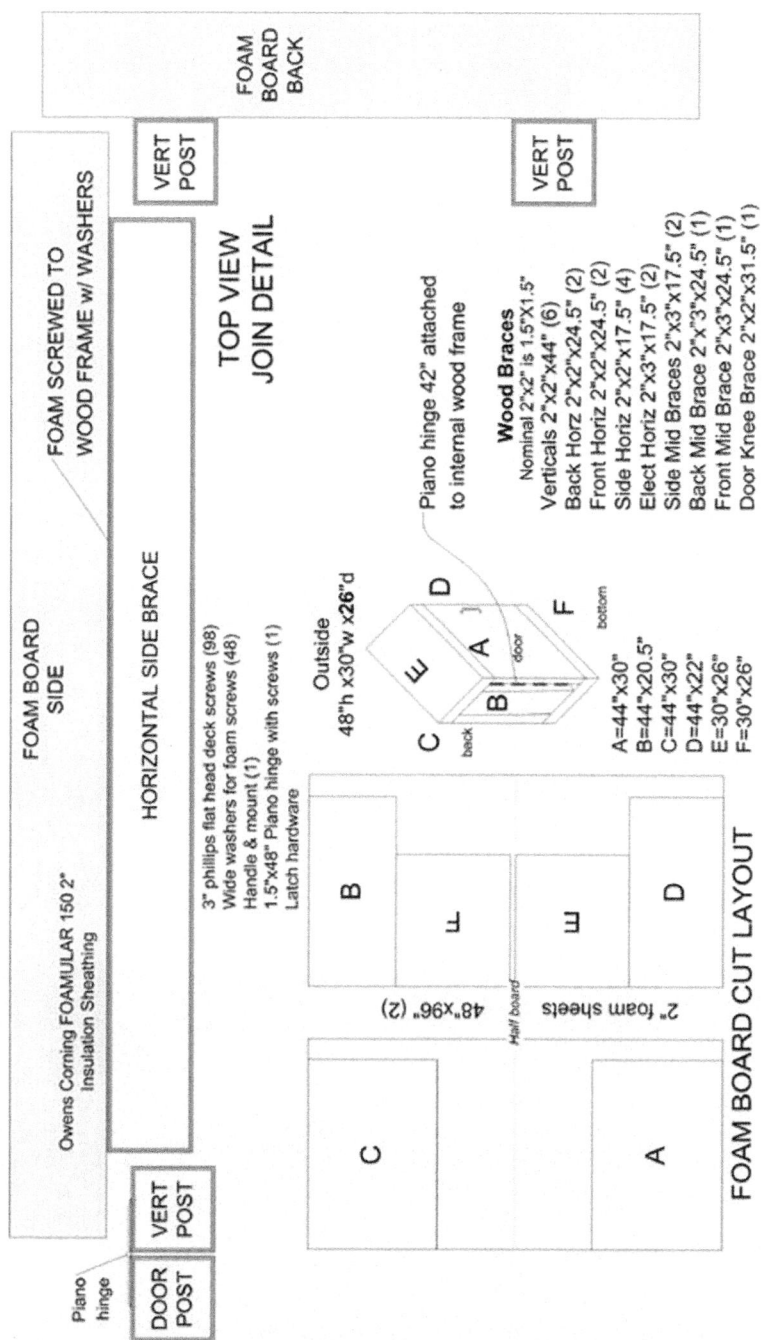

Every seam inside the kiln was sealed with Tyvek tape, to minimize vapor loss. This Tyvek tape has also held up well, even during the kiln's use for flue-curing (up to 165°F).

Coving of the side XPS foam to accommodate the hook latches.

I chose a silicone fire door gasket, though plain rubber is okay.

Tyvek hinges of the front corner blocks.

Most strip-style gasket materials will do just fine. What is important is to make sure that the gasket surrounding the door opening has no gaps, and that it matches against the framing of the door itself. Any gaps or mismatches will lead to substantial loss of both humidity and heat, and increase the power consumed for maintaining the kiln temperature.

temp probe

The seal of the door gasket is not as important for flue-curing—if that is the only purpose you plan for your kiln. During flue-curing, the temperatures above about 120°F are reached in extremely low-humidity conditions.

My initial heat source, which also served as my humidity source, was a 2-1/2 quart Crockpot. With it set to its "low" setting, the kilning process worked well. At this setting, it was consuming about 70 watts of power—similar to that of a single incandescent light bulb. When flue-curing, and set on "high", the power was still only 100 watts, but 165°F was a challenge to reach. (I had to drape fleece blankets over the chamber to reach 165°F.)

Subsequently, I replaced the small Crockpot with a 6 quart Crockpot, having a max power consumption of 300 watts. When using it for either kilning or flue-curing, I leave it set on its "high" setting. This now reaches the set temperature more quickly, reduces the temperature swings, and maintains a more stable temperature environment. The larger Crockpot also requires less frequent refilling with water—averaging about once every 5 days in a warm environment, and every 3 to 4 days in a cooler environment.

The Tyvek tape, used extensively in this project, is not made of Tyvek material, even though it says, "Tyvek", all over it. Rather,

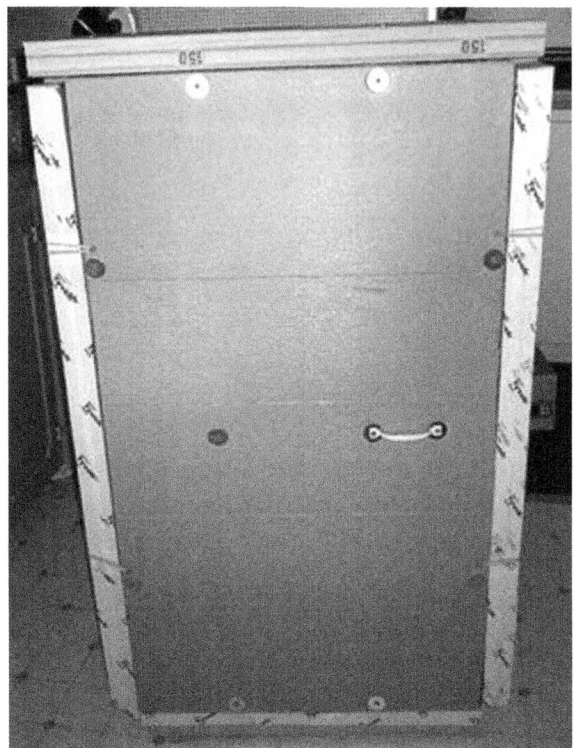

The front of the completed kiln. Note the swing-away corner insulation, and the extension of the top and bottom to the full thickness of the door.

it is tape that is designed for use on Tyvek exterior, vapor-proof sheeting, in housing construction. It is weather-proof, oriented polypropylene tape with weather-proof, acrylic adhesive.

There are two electrical appliances within the kiln: the Crockpot and the ventilation fan. To allow their electric cords (and their end plugs) to pass through the XPS foam, a somewhat tapered rectangular block, large enough to pass one electric plug, is cut into the wall. A carefully measured slot, deep enough to hold both flat electric cords is cut from the block. The cords are passed through, one at a time, positioned into the slot, and the block of XPS foam replaced. Both the outer and inner seams of this are taped with Tyvek tape. The tape and foam block are removable, should one of the appliances need to be changed.

Looking into the open kiln. Note that all interior seams are taped with Tyvek tape. The center, wire shelf is removable. The front corner insulation sections swing away.

I whittled an opening into a wooden cigar box, to hold my digital controller, and drilled holes for the various wires. The bottom of the box was screwed into the side of the kiln. Its sliding lid allows me access to the controller's wiring, should that be necessary. An electrical box holds the fan speed control dimmer. These two boxes and their wiring are entirely separate. (Again, just a simple on/off switch is adequate for the ventilation fan.)

The bathroom ventilation fan is suspended from the wire shelf. A "duct" of plastic is taped on, to divert the air flow upward.

Rather than directly wire the fan and the Crockpot into their respective controllers, I left the appliance cords intact, and used the controllers to control extension cord outlets. These are clearly labeled as to their functions.

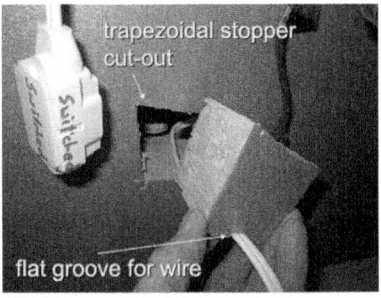

Because the digital controller is so inexpensive, I have always kept a spare duplicate of it on hand. The controller failed once in five years, and had to be replaced. The middle of a kiln run or worse, a flue-cure run, is not the time to wait for an ordered replacement to be shipped and received.

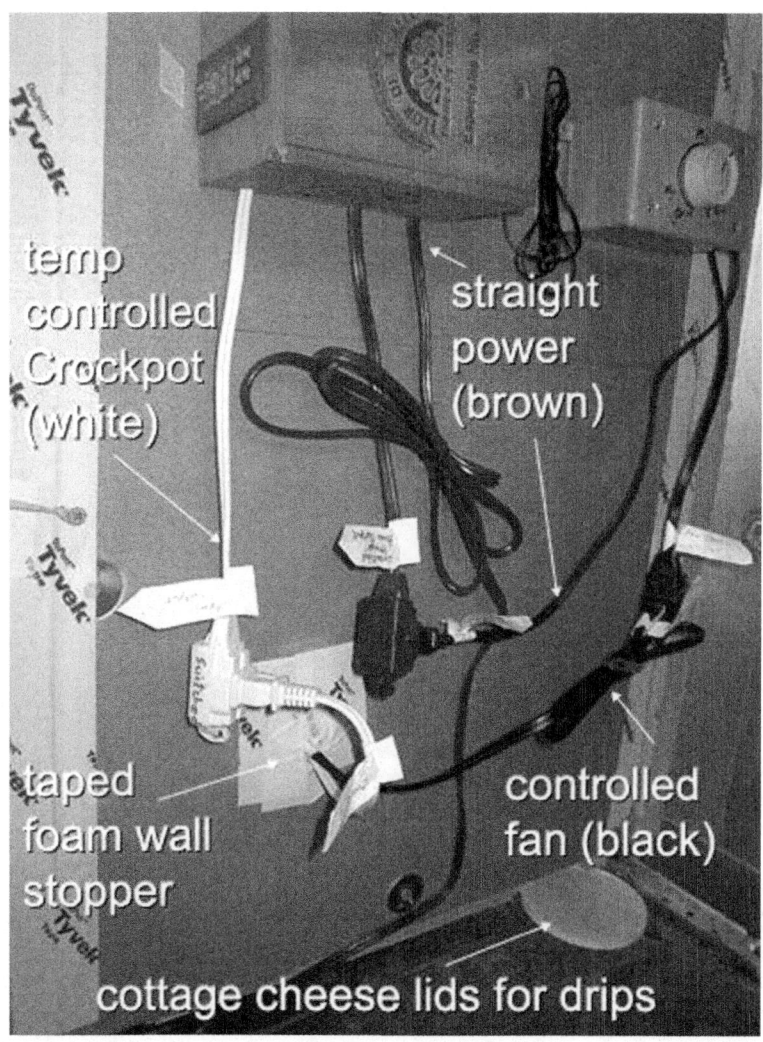

For flue-curing, the leaf must be hung in strings, in order to adequately ventilate and consistently yellow and dry. For kilning, leaf can be strung up, or just stuffed into large plastic bags (left open).

The Crockpot is resting on two small planks of poplar, rather than directly on the XPS foam floor of the kiln. Whenever I have very small items to kiln, I suspend a wire basket beneath the middle shelf to hold them.

The kiln loaded for my first batch. I have since replaced the small Crockpot with an oval-shaped 6 quart Crockpot.

To kiln with large, open bags of leaf, rather than strings of hanging leaf, disposable aluminum grill pans are taped to the portions of the door, walls and floor that might make contact with the bags. This permits better temperature equalization around all sides of the bags.

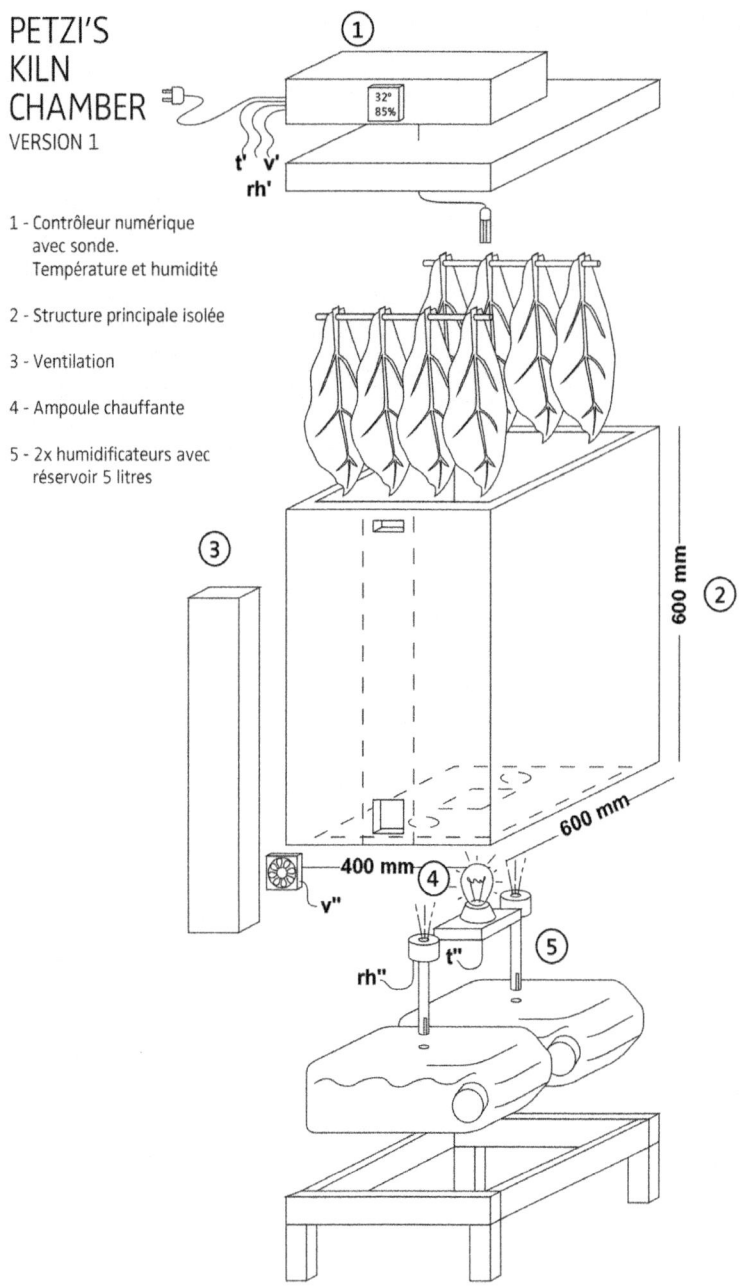

PETZI'S KILN CHAMBER
VERSION 1

1 - Contrôleur numérique avec sonde. Température et humidité

2 - Structure principale isolée

3 - Ventilation

4 - Ampoule chauffante

5 - 2x humidificateurs avec réservoir 5 litres

Fair Trade Tobacco Forum member, Petzi, from Switzerland, designed and built this flue-curing chamber. It uses a digital temp and humidity controller. The container is made from two foam boxes. Ventilation is provided by a computer fan. The USB-powered humidifier heads are inserted into plastic jug reservoirs.

Appendix 4.
Tobacco Pests

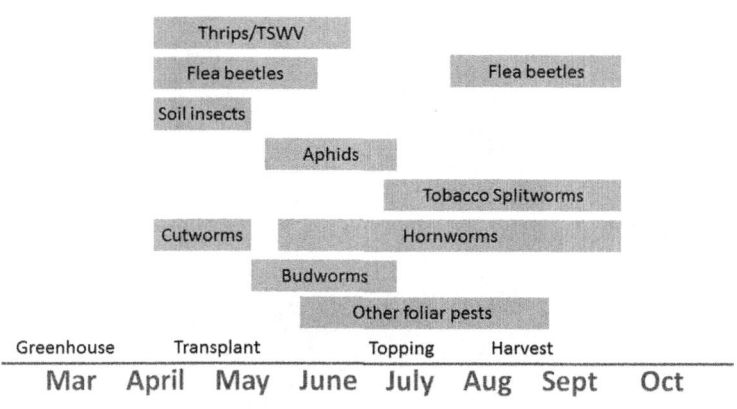

Tobacco pest insect timeline. [CES NCSU]

Different insects become active at different times of the growing season. The graphic above is for North Carolina. Your own season and local insects may, of course, be different. But it provides a reasonable pattern of what to look out for during which parts of the season.

Insects, slugs and worms

Cutworms are larvae that dwell individually, often 8 or more inches beneath the soil surface. They typically attack new transplants, and will lop them off near the surface. Cutworm damage is more common near the edges of fields with a weed border. Since cutworm larvae are active only at night, you will not see them actively feeding except late in the evening or during the night. In the morning, you may see one or more small transplants that have been clipped off near the surface of the ground. Tilling the garden bed at least 4 weeks before transplanting reduces cutworm infestations. Established sod may harbor cutworms, so be alert for these in a freshly tilled area of sod.

Cutworm on a seedling. [R.J. Reynolds Tobacco]

Wireworms, the larvae of click beetles, cause wilting and growth failure of plants, by damaging the roots and the stalks. Wireworms burrow into the stalk just above the ground, leaving a small hole. They cause stunting of the plant. They can be

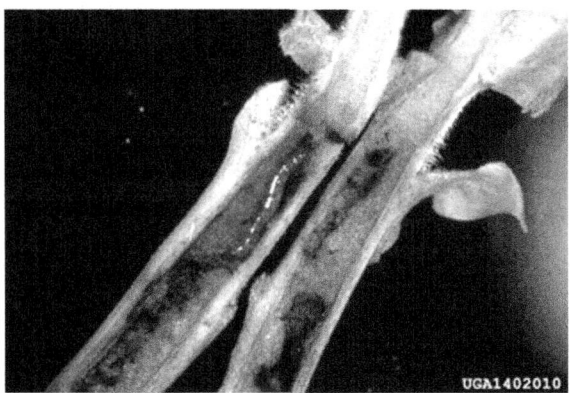

Wireworm in a cut stalk. [R.J. Reynolds Tobacco]

identified by spotting the hole in the base of the stalk, then splitting the stalk to visualize the worm.

Flea Beetles produce a pattern of small leaf holes sometimes described as "buck-shot holes". They seem to strongly prefer certain varieties of tobacco, and not others, if you grow multiple varieties. The holes not only make the affected leaves worthless as binder or wrapper, but also compromise the orderly process of color-curing. A sure identification is a dark, flea-sized beetle that springs away from your fingers. Since these insects jump, you will need to be quick to crush them against the leaf. Watching for them early on will minimize the flea beetle burden throughout the growing season. They can be prevented (up until shortly before harvest) by adding imidacloprid to the transplant water. Flea beetles seem more attracted to early-planted tobacco.

Budworms are indicated by limited damage to multiple small leaves near or at the growth tip, and by their dark droppings—which look like coarsely ground black pepper—on those leaves. They can only be located by delicately separating the tiny leaves of the growth tip to expose the inside of the bud, and inspecting both the top and bottom surfaces of these leaves. The larva may be less than a third of an inch long. If you see the typical damage, but do not see a worm, then keep looking. Later, as the damaged leaves grow, you will see smooth-edged, large divots in the leaf—well after the budworm is gone. Tobacco planted early is more inviting to budworms.

Hornworms (the caterpillar of the huge, hawk moth) are voracious consumers of tobacco leaf. When a hornworm emerges from its egg (several days after laying), it immediately eats a tiny hole through the full thickness of the leaf lamina. Hornworm eggs can be spotted as a translucent green, single egg the size of Lincoln's chin on a cent: 1 mm. They appear anywhere on a leaf, and on either surface. The easiest thing to do with a hornworm egg is to remove it from the leaf, then crush it between thumb and forefinger. They can appear in several waves, about 3 or 4 weeks apart, during each season. Tiny hornworms will leave a BB size hole with a smooth margin in the leaf, and can usually be found on the undersurface. These tiny ones can be crushed directly on the leaf. Once they grow larger (up to 3 inches in length, and as thick as your thumb), the damage they cause increases rapidly. Their nearly black droppings are barrel-shaped, and the diameter of the worm—tiny hornworms have tiny droppings; huge ones leave huge pellets of droppings. The larger hornworms should be removed, and crushed between two small stones. Regular spraying with BT (*Bacillus thuringiensis*) can prevent them. Tobacco that is planted early may suffer less damage from hornworms, whereas late-planted tobacco may see greater damage.

A parasite of hornworms is the braconid wasp, which lays eggs on the hornworms. These will appear as numerous, white cocoons

A hornworm covered with parasitic cocoons.

protruding from a hornworm's back. The parasite larvae will eventually kill the hornworm, then increase the population of braconid wasps. Since parasitized hornworms feed at a rate only

1/5 that of a healthy hornworm, it is usually to your advantage to not kill these.

Japanese beetles can feed on tobacco, but usually will not, if other preferred plants are in the area. Their damage is usually minimal, requiring no action on your part. Occasionally they may assemble in larger number on a small number of leaves, and severely damage those leaves.

Stink bugs may cause minimal damage to tobacco, sometimes resulting in a single wilted leaf per affected plant. This wilting often recovers, unless it is further complicated by sun scald. No action is usually required.

Tobacco thrips are tiny insects (requiring a hand lens to see) that feed on tobacco during the first few weeks after transplant. They cause no significant damage. But they serve as a vector for viruses. The feeding time required to infect a plant is shorter than the time it takes for an insecticide to kill the thrips. Tomato Spotted Wilt Virus (TSWV) can be transmitted. There is no effective preventive measure, and no treatment that is effective after infection. TSWV, if it becomes systemic, will lead to bilateral wilting of the plant. Seriously affected plants should be removed.

Aphids exist in a flying form, that lays eggs on leaf, and a flightless form that sucks on plant juices. It is these latter aphids that present a problem. Aphids transmit a number of virus pathogens to tobacco. They can, with a heavy infestation, reduce leaf growth. But the greatest problem they present is that they foul the leaf with not only their dead bodies (when the leaf color-cures), but with their excrement, which is called "honeydew". Honeydew is colorless, sticky and hygroscopic. Honeydew does not go away during curing (or even with kilning). This results in sticky patches on the cured leaves. These patches also retain more moisture than the surrounding leaf, and may lead to focal areas of mold on the lamina. Aphids prefer young or new leaf over more mature leaf. The sucking aphids, once they attach their mouth parts into the leaf tissue, are no longer mobile, and are unable to return to the leaf if washed away—as with a garden hose. For home-growers, aphids can be minimized by removing all suckers as soon as they are large enough to snap off without injuring the adjacent leaf. Soapy water, if sprayed (in the early morning or the evening, not in the hot sun) directly onto aphids, will kill them by dehydration within a day or two. This kind of treatment usually needs to be repeated on several consecutive days, and works best if an infestation is caught early. Aphids can be prevented for most of the growing season by using imidacloprid in the transplant water. If aphids are carried into the curing shed, they may proliferate there. Tobacco that is planted early is sometimes a less favorable target for aphids. Aphid infestations are most troublesome on tobacco planted around the middle of the usual transplanting time.

Grasshoppers and Crickets create random, jagged-edged holes in tobacco leaf. Although they cannot be easily controlled, damage is usually only an issue if tall grass or weeds are close to the growing tobacco. Prevention is pretty much limited to keeping nearby weeds or grass cut short.

Slugs are mostly a risk to young transplants, and will eat ragged holes or may top the plant. They usually leave visible slime trails. They seek shelter during the day beneath bricks, flat rocks and large wood chips, so clearing these away from the tobacco bed can reduce the risk. Sprinkling granules of slug bait (bran and iron phosphate), such as Sluggo, will fairly promptly halt their feeding and kill them. Using slug bait preventively, a week prior to transplant adjacent to a house foundation or wall can be useful. The bait may need to be reapplied following a heavy rain.

Tobacco insecticides by group and mode of action for resistance management.

Goup #	Mode of action	Chemical sub-group or active ingredient	Product name
1A	Acetylcholine esterase inhibitors	Carbamates	Lannate
1B	Acetylcholine esterase inhibitors	Organophosphates	Orthene
3	Sodium channel modulators	Pyrethroids, Pyrethrins	Brigade/Capture Karate/Warrior
4	Nicotinic Acetylcholine receptor agonists / antagonists	Neoicothinoids	Actara, Admire Pro, Assail, Platinum, Provado
5	Nicotinic Acetylcholine receptor agonists	Spinosyns	Tracer
6	Chloride channel activators	Avermectins	Denim
9	Selective feeding blockers	Pymetrozine	Fulfill
11	Microbial disruptors of insect midgut membranes	*Bacillus thuringiensis* var. *kurstaki Bacillus thuringiensis* var. *tenebrionenses*	Dipel, etc.
28	Ryanodine receptor inhibitor	Chlorantraniliprole Flubendiamide	Belt, Coragen

Insecticide groups. *To manage resistance, repeat treatments should be chosen from a different group. [Virginia Tech 2011]*

Bacterial, fungal and viral infections

There are numerous microbial pests of tobacco. Generally, many of the same microbes that can affect other members of the *solanaceae* family (tomatoes, potatoes, peppers, eggplant, and many solanaceous weeds) can affect tobacco as well. For most of these, their precise diagnosis depends on laboratory examination or, in some cases, just a microscope. The gross changes that they cause in tobacco plants can sometimes be recognized by its pattern of chlorosis (loss of chlorophyll), as well as the symmetry or lack thereof. Some diseases may cause unilateral wilting, whereas others may cause bilateral wilting. Subtle color changes are helpful. Some of the best color images of many tobacco diseases can be found on-line at:

https://www.ipmimages.org/browse/AreaSubs.cfm?area=62

The same image database is also available through the websites of a number of agricultural extension services supported by individual, tobacco producing states. One approach to identifying an apparent abnormality of your tobacco is to click each of the links in the image database, one by one, to compare the photos to the appearance of your tobacco. Though a slow process initially, looking through the images can, with repetition, become less tedious and, in fact, educational. Some of those images (particularly those supplied by R.J. Reynolds Tobacco) will provide, on the "image detail" page, a textual discussion of the disease, its processes, vectors, and impacts.

Another source of excellent, detailed information on diseases can sometimes be found on the websites of extension services (though the political environment has caused some of these sites to either hide or even remove this valuable science).

As for what actions you should take, there is often no treatment, but sometimes preventive approaches. During the season in which you discover a microbial infection, the decision then comes down to removing the affected leaves or entire plants vs. simply living with reduced yield and damaged leaves. The pathogens that infect living tobacco leaf can not infect humans or other mammals.

Some of these pathogens require solanaceous plants (tobacco, tomato, peppers, eggplant, potato, and a large list of weeds) in order to persist in the soil. So a helpful habit is to practice crop rotation of your growing area for one to three years with some non-solanaceous plant, before once again planting tobacco there.

Aphid-transmitted viruses can be minimized by the preventive use of a systemic insecticide, such as imidacloprid in the transplant water. Those viruses transmitted by tobacco thrips are transferred to the plant too rapidly for insecticides to make a large difference (estimated at 25 to 30% reduction in infection rate with imidacloprid use).

Alfalfa mosaic virus (AMV) is usually limited to flue-cured varieties, and causes a characteristic yellow mosaic pattern and eventually chlorosis (blanching) of the affected leaf areas. The virus overwinters in legumes, and is transmitted to tobacco by aphids.

Bacterial barn rot (*Erwinia spp.*) affects leaf that has been harvested wet. The common soil organisms cause darkening and rotting of the leaf stem and veins, even though the lamina have not colored.

Bacterial hollow stalk (*Erwinia aroideae*) and bacterial soft rot (*Pectobacterium carotovorum*) is caused by common soil organisms, and often starts at the site of topping or sucker removal. It rots the pith of the stalk, and eventually leads to leaves wilting and dropping off.

Bacterial wilt of tobacco (*Ralstonia solanacearum*) [see Granville wilt]

Black root rot (*Thielaviopsis basicola*) is a fungal disease that results in some plants being more stunted than their neighbors. It is more common in cool wet conditions. If the season dries and warms later on, then the plants may outgrow the effects. Diagnosis is by pulling the plant and examining the roots, which may show black tips, and black spots on thicker roots. There is usually nothing that can affect its course meaningfully.

Black shank (*Phytothora spp.*) most commonly appears as a root and crown rot. Flue-cured varieties are most vulnerable, though there are varieties of these that have been bred to provide some resistance to at least one of the three races of the pathogen.

It may present a minor problem, or may cause 100% plant mortality. Black shank is of most concern for home-growers who live in traditional flue-cured tobacco growing counties.

Blue mold (*Peronospora tabacina*) of tobacco is a fungal infection that begins as a coin-sized yellow lesion in the lamina of younger leaf, and progresses to a purple discoloration. A fuzzy fungal growth can be seen on the underside of the lesion. The disease is favored during wet, cloudy and cool weather. When it is hot and humid, blue mold can appear if nights are cool. There is no treatment (other than removing the affected leaves or plants). Certain varieties of tobacco (e.g. CT Broadleaf) seem to be notably more sensitive to this mold.

Brown spot (*Alternaria alternata*) shows up as dark, concentric circles on older leaf, lower on the plant. It results is dead patches on the leaf. Some varieties are particularly susceptible. It spreads most during moist conditions, though it may affect only a few leaves.

Frog-eye leafspot (*Cercospora nicotianae*) appears as small, circular beige spots with a reddish margin. Usually seen in the lower leaves, but may appear higher during the later season. It can not easily be differentiated from brown spot, wildfire, weather fleck and physiologic spotting, without a microscope.

Fusarium wilt (*Fusarium oxysporum*) causes leaves on one side of the plant to yellow and wilt prematurely. The stalk may curve toward the affected side. The inside of the stalk on the affected side appears deep brown. This may be confused with Granville wilt.

Granville wilt (*Ralstonia solanacearum*) [also called Bacterial wilt of tobacco] is endemic to the southeastern United States. It shows wilting of a small number (1 or 2) leaves, on one side of the plant, with the other side of the plant appearing normal. The leaf color of affected leaves turns a yellowish green. Though it initially causes wilting on one side of the plant, it eventually kills the entire plant. The base of the stalk may blacken (resembling black stalk), and dark streaks extend up the stalk. The bacterium is harbored by infected soil, and is transmitted by contact with soil, splashed mud, dirty tools or dirty hands, and can be transferred from one area to another on the wheels of a tiller, lawn mower or tractor. Disease is increased in hot, moist soil, and in warm wet growing seasons. Poor soil drainage may also be a factor. Wilt-resistant varieties may be available, but can still become infected if nematodes damage the roots.

"A simple diagnostic test for Granville wilt can be done on-farm. When an infected stem segment is suspended in a glass of clear water for a few minutes, bacterial streaming occurs. The bacterial streaming appears as white ooze or a smokey stream, which originates from the cut end of the stem, where the dark streaks are observed under the bark, and slowly moves out into the water." [The North Carolina Plant Disease and Insect Clinic: Bacterial wilt of Tobacco]

The most significant action that a home-grower of tobacco can take with regard to Granville wilt is crop rotation of at least one year to any non-solanaceous crop. So, no tobacco, tomato, peppers, eggplant or potatoes in that bed for a year or more.

Phoma blight (*Phoma exigua*) is seldom a significant problem, tending to appear on lower leaves during the late season. It causes beige laminar spots that can be confused with brown spot. The spot may disintegrate, leaving a ragged edge.

Potato virus Y (PVY) is a common problem of tobacco in some European countries. It causes a yellow mottling of affected leaf, and blackening of the mid-rib. Leaves may die and drop off. More severe infections may lead to plant death. Rather than being inherent in the soil, PVY is transmitted by aphids. It can persist in seed potatoes, and be perpetuated from there.

Pythium stem rot (*Pythium aphanidermatum*) of tobacco in the field resembles signs of black shank, and requires laboratory tests to distinguish them. There is no effective treatment, and no resistant tobacco varieties have been developed.

Sore shin (*Rhizoctonia solani*) starts as a brown discoloration of the stalk, near or below ground level. The lower leaves may yellow prematurely, and the plant may be stunted. Affected plants tend to wilt during the day. With minimal infection, tobacco yield may be normal. Signs are similar to those of black shank and Pythium stem rot. It can be specifically identified by a laboratory.

Southern bacterial wilt [see Granville wilt]

Southern blight (*Sclerotium rolfsii*) is a fungal disease that grows little, white balls on the stalk of tobacco, eventually turning brown like a mustard seed. Leaves hang down, and die. Affected plants tend to be widely scattered in the field.

Tobacco etch virus (TEV) (Potyvirus TEV) shows light green mottling of affected leaf, though less noticeable than the mottling of TMV. In addition, what appear to be chlorotic scribbles (etching) appear in the lamina. The virus overwinters in solanaceous weeds and is transmitted to tobacco by aphids.

Tobacco mosaic virus (TMV) causes crinkled, puckered or elongated leaves which show light and dark green mottling. The yield may be reduced. It can be transmitted from solanaceous vegetable transplants (e.g. tomatoes, peppers, eggplant), as well as commercial tobacco products like cigarettes. Avoiding smoking while handling tobacco, and keeping hands and tools clean can reduce its spread.

Tobacco ringspot virus (TRSV) (Nepovirus TRSV) causes chlorotic "rings" to appear on the leaf lamina. These may become necrotic. This tends to be seen early in the season, and is often outgrown.

Tobacco streak virus (TSV) (Ilarvirus TSV) causes necrotic streaks in budding leaves along the mid-rib, and on the adjacent stalk. The leaves curl. Later, the plants often recover, though the affected leaves are lost.

Tobacco vein mottling virus (TVMV) (Potyvirus TVMV) creates mottled chlorosis, damaging leaves and leaf stems. It is transmitted (like TEV) from solanaceous weeds by aphids.

Tomato Spotted Wilt Virus (TSWV) can infect over 174 (to date) different plant species, including tobacco and all its relatives. Alternate hosts include a huge range of common weeds. The virus is transmitted by tobacco thrips, which themselves cause no significant damage to tobacco. Thrips are quite tiny insects, and difficult to spot. The infected plants may show wilting of a single leaf, or more classically, bilateral wilting.

Wildfire / Angular leaf spot (*Pseudomonas syringae pv. tabaci*) "most commonly occurs in the field in mid-summer during periods of cloudy, wet weather. Leaf spots develop, which are 1/4 to 1/2 inch in diameter and dark brown to black in color. They are limited by leaf veins making spots angular in shape. Concentric rings may be evident within the spots. Spots may coalesce, forming large irregular dead areas. The center of the spots may fall out, giving the leaf a ragged appearance. Leaves will turn yellow when numerous spots are present. Angular leafspot is most severe on lower leaves. Generally worse on the windward side of plants where water soaking from driving rains increases infection." [R.J. Reynolds Tobacco]

Environmental Factors
Frost, sandblast, air pollution, herbicide use, some bird droppings, and the time of day when liquids are applied to leaves can all affect tobacco in ways that may resemble the effects of bacteria, fungus and root worm damage.

Canvas burn is the term applied to physical damage to small plants by contact with row cover material during foul weather conditions. It can be recognized by yellowing or other signs of damage limited to the outermost edges of leaves, and sometimes the growth tip.

Drowning: Tobacco subject to flooding suffers root damage in less than a day. The submerged roots initially lose some of their root hairs—from lack of oxygen, and may, if they remain submerged for a day or more begin to die. This is more likely in low lying areas and in soil with poor drainage. While the plants may recover, if the water drains within a couple of days, their growth will be retarded.

Hail: As one might expect, hail physically damages tobacco leaf. But a severe hailstorm may completely strip tobacco down to its skeleton of stalk, leaf stems and veins. There is little that can be done in advance for fully grown tobacco. For recent transplants or young plants, it may be possible to cover them with row cover or a tarp when a hailstorm threatens.

Herbicide drift: If any herbicide is sprayed near tobacco, then expect it to damage or kill the tobacco. If you or a neighbor spray herbicide on a breezy day, even one with a light breeze, any tobacco that happens to be downwind of the spraying may be affected. Keep in mind that tobacco *is* a broadleaf weed, and its large surface area makes it particularly prone to catch drifting herbicide. Many herbicides are systemic, meaning that exposure of even a single leaf to herbicide may initially appear to affect only that one leaf, but may go on to kill the entire plant, once it reaches the roots.

Lightning: "Damage is usually in a circular pattern in the field. Plants nearest the strike will suddenly wilt and may die. Whole plants or individual leaves on plants in the surrounding area may also wilt. Some leaves will have black or shriveled midribs and veins. Areas of lamina may pucker because growth of the midribs or veins is reduced. The stalk may be hollow, or the pith may be disced with irregular separations. The pith remains white, which differentiates lightning damage from black shank and hollow stalk." [R.J. Reynolds Tobacco]

Ozone: "The spots usually start as small dark green water-soaked areas. Within 48 hours, the lesions change to a brown color then to a gray or white and appear as sunken necrotic areas bordered by chlorotic tissue (on dark tobacco you usually do not see any yellow halo). The spots are often concentrated along the side of the midrib and large secondary veins but can be found anywhere on the leaf. On expanding leaves the spots appear near the tip. Lower leaf surfaces may show no evidence of damage in the early stages. Lesions may run together causing the leaf surface to become necrotic and fall out. Symptoms may occur at any growth stage, but most commonly occur during periods of rapid growth. Older leaves are more susceptible. Dark tobacco types usually show less injury than burley types when at the same growth stage and exposed to the same level of ozone." [U. KY Research and Education Center]

Sand blast: "Windblown sand may cause physical damage to young transplants on the side of the plant toward the prevailing wind. Mild symptoms include some death of tissue between lateral veins of the lower leaves. More severe damage results in entire leaves being killed and stalks being destroyed down to the woody layer. Some plants may be killed and others may be covered by sand. Soil texture and moisture, wind intensity and duration, presence of plant residue on the soil surface, and windbreaks will determine the extent of the damage." [R.J. Reynolds Tobacco]

Sun scald: When water that pools within depressions of a leaf surface is exposed to full sun, the laminar tissue may suffer heat damage. This can happen when bright sunshine follows a brief shower. It can also happen if any liquid is sprayed onto leaves during mid-day. It is recognizable by the pattern of injury being limited to dependent puckers in the leaf surface.

Weather fleck [see Ozone]

Generalized wilting and growth failure, following exposure to herbicide. Note the failed budding.

Appendix 5.
Fertilizers

Fertilizer commercial availability

If you live in a traditional tobacco growing region that continues to produce tobacco commercially, then most farmer supply stores or fertilizer suppliers in the area will know what fertilizer to recommend for your home plot, and will have purpose-blended fertilizers for tobacco. Elsewhere (that is, for most home-growers), you will not readily find tobacco-specific fertilizer.

As a general recommendation, you can simply purchase a low-chloride fertilizer specifically marketed for growing tomatoes or similar vegetables. A 10:10:10 (N:P:K) blend will usually work well with tobacco, when applied at the rate recommended for growing tomatoes.

The shorthand notation means literally 10% nitrogen: 10% phosphorus: 10% potassium by weight. 10 pounds of 10:10:10 fertilizer would contain 1 pound of nitrogen, 1 pound of phosphorus and 1 pound of potassium. The remaining weight is made up of the minerals from which those specified elements are derived. Since recommendations are based on, for example, pounds of nitrogen per acre, this is irrespective of which mineral is providing the nitrogen. 10:10:10 is known as a "balanced" fertilizer.

The least expensive "garden" fertilizers contain more chloride (listed as "CL" or "muriate" or "muriatic") than is recommended for growing tobacco. Excess chloride can dramatically reduce the burning characteristics of finished tobacco. Don't do all the work of producing and finishing tobacco that will not burn. So look specifically for low-chloride fertilizer.

Fertilizer costs as an issue

Commercial tobacco growers are under economic pressure to minimize the cost of their fertilizer program. Their scale of production means that shaving a few percent off the total cost makes a significant difference in their profit at the end of the season. Also when considering run-off from acres of soil treated with fertilizer, caution and attention to typical rain patterns can make a significant difference in downstream fertilizer content.

Home-growers produce tobacco at a tiny scale, by comparison. A home-grower's fertilizer decisions are more likely to be driven by what fertilizer can be obtained with relative ease in her or his locality. There is little benefit to spending a lot of money to transport tobacco-specific fertilizer over a long distance, only to apply it to 1000 square feet of dirt. Unless you plan to plow up your entire yard, run-off is not often a meaningful consideration.

You should also keep in mind that the "Tobacco Production Guides" that are published annually by the extension services of Kentucky, North Carolina, Tennessee and elsewhere are focused on the traditional varieties of tobacco grown in their specific regions, as well as the soil types in their traditional tobacco growing locales. While these documents contain a lot of useful information, there is seldom specific information for varieties not usually grown in the US tobacco belt, such as Orientals, cigar varieties, Hungarian varieties and others.

Pounds per acre on a small plot:

1 acre = 43560 square feet = 0.4 hectare = 4000 sq. m.
1 hectare = 10000 square meters = 2.47 acres = 107639 sq. ft.

The size of your tobacco plot, if a single bed, is the length times width. For example, it it were 20' x 50', then the bed is 1000 square feet. So a recommendation of Z pounds per acre would be $(Z * (1000/43560))$ pounds, or $Z * 0.023$ pounds per 1000 square feet. If you have multiple beds, then calculate the application rate for each bed separately. My own 5' x 12' beds are 60 square feet each, so my arithmetic is (Z * (60/43560)) pounds, or Z * 0.0014 pounds.

With standard 10:10:10 low-chloride fertilizer for tomatoes, the rate may be stated on the label as both pounds per acre as well as pounds per 1000 square feet, making the math a bit simpler. But once you do the calculation, write it on the bag with a Sharpie marker. If you will be applying the fertilizer from a cup (which is what I do for my separated beds), then use a scale to measure the proper weight into your container or cup, then write down the cup volume required, for future reference.

Timing of fertilizer

Early application of chemical fertilizer, such as more than a month prior to transplanting, only becomes an issue with coarse soil textures, low potassium or excessive rainfall. And this is mostly with regard to potassium. If you have concerns that your fertilizer may leach away too quickly, then apply half of it just prior to transplant, and then the remainder 3 to 4 weeks after transplant. Applying fertilizer later in the growing season may prolong the time needed for leaf maturation, delaying harvest.

For organic fertilizer timing, compost or composted manure may require more time to become available to the plants, and is best be applied in the late fall of the previous season.

Organic fertilizers

If you decide to use manure, be sure that it has composted over the winter, both to break it down and to hopefully heat enough to kill viable grass and weed seeds that may be present. Mixing the fertilizer with straw will help loosen its texture.

Horse manure is notorious for containing persistent weed seeds. It also is prone to remaining as hard, dried spheres (road apples). These should be crushed and mixed, if you decide to use it.

Applying *fresh* manure to a transplant bed may burn the plants, so it's best to apply it the previous fall, and till it into the soil of the bed. Better yet, avoid using fresh manure.

Home improvement stores and garden shops sell 50 pound bags of "compost" or "composted manure". (The best of the latter category is Black Kow.) Be sure to read the chemical analysis on the bag, if this will be your only source of fertilizer. The most useful compost for fertilizer usually has an analysis of 0.5:0.5:0.5, so the weight of this compost needed to supply the same nutrients as a 10:10:10 fertilizer is 20 times as much weight.

If you purchase the more common, 0.05:0.05:0.05 compost, then consider it as only a supplement for improving the texture of the soil. It's use as a fertilizer would require 10 times as much as with, for example, Black Kow, with its 0.5:0.5:0.5 analysis.

The chemically organic nitrogen in many manure fertilizers needs to undergo mineralization within the soil to become available to the plants. This is delayed by cold soil as well as by excessively dry soil. If you apply compost or manure fertilizer, then you may wish to water the area during dry spells that occur prior to transplant.

Tilling in any compost will definitely demonstrate an improved soil texture, by an increase in the number of earthworms present during the season. Go out after dark, with a flashlight. Earthworms will be above the surface of the bed. The presence of earthworms can be taken as a sign of enhanced soil aeration.

Soil Testing

A home-grower can probably get by without a soil analysis for a first time grow in newly tilled sod. Other than that circumstance, you won't have any idea of the pH, phosphorus or potassium needs of your soil without a soil analysis. These can usually be performed by a local agricultural extension service at a relatively low cost (free in some locations). A box of dirt from your field or growing bed is sent to the lab, accompanied by a form that indicates what you intend to grow. Within a few weeks, a report will be provided which includes not only the analysis, but recommendations for fertilizer application.

A soil test is only as representative of your soil as the sample you send. You should submit a box of dirt that includes several well mixed samples from random areas of the bed or field. If you have several growing areas that differ in any way (slope, drainage, soil type, etc.), then you submit separate boxes of dirt from each of these.

For a home-grower, soil testing performed in one year is probably sufficient for guidance for multiple years after that, unless there are serious deficiencies shown in that initial sample. Of all the information provided in the soil analysis, pay most attention to the soil pH. It should be in the range of 5.8 to 6.2. Soil outside that pH range may cause nutritional deficiencies in the tobacco, even when the specific nutrients are present in adequate amounts, or may cause nutrient toxicities. While a formal soil analysis will make a remediation recommendation (lime, sulfur, etc.), once you know the general pH of your soil, you can correct it with dolomitic lime or with sulfur compounds from the local garden store.

An alternative for determining the soil pH is to purchase a hand-held meter designed to measure soil pH. These are subject to various errors, but may provide general guidance.

Lime: Soils in some areas are too acidic for tobacco to grow well. The most common remediation is the application of dolomitic lime. This is finely ground limestone bits, which may require several months to begin to adjust the pH. These are ideally applied and tilled into the soil a month or more prior to transplant. While many tobacco growing guides from extension services assume that your soil is too acidic, this is mostly true of commercial land that has been fertilized and planted with tobacco over many years. So determine your soil pH before just applying lime.

From the NCSU: 2019 Flue-cured Information
Quick Reference Guide to Fertilization

1. Have a soil sample tested to determine nutrient and lime needs. Use dolomitic lime, if needed, to adjust pH and supply magnesium as well as calcium. Do not overlime!

2. Use a base nitrogen rate of 50 to 80 pounds per acre. Your portion of the rate range will depend on topsoil depth and texture, previous crop grown, and personal experience.

3. Apply 20 to 30 pounds of sulfur per acre on deep, sandy soils. Sulfur application recommendations are now provided in soil test reports. Read the label to be sure that the complete (N-P-K) fertilizer contains sulfur. If the complete fertilizer does not provide this nutrient, then apply a sidedresser containing sulfur.

4. Determine and make leaching adjustments for nitrogen losses with caution, only after leaching occurs. Do not assume that leaching will occur and apply extra nitrogen up front in the growing season.

5. Use a method of fertilizer application that maximizes nutrient uptake efficiency but minimizes fertilizer salts injury and early season leaching losses. Examples include the bands at transplanting and bands within 10 days after transplanting methods. The latter method is more risky than the first on poorly drained soils because frequent rains after transplanting could delay fertilizer application for more than 10 days. Fertilizers should be incorporated into the soil to reduce nutrient losses through runoff and/or volatility. Liquid nitrogen materials can be injected through a sidedress application or applied to the side(s) of the bed and incorporated with cultivation.

Table 5-6. Nitrogen adjustments for leaching

Topsoil Depth	Estimated Water Percolated through Soil	Percentage of Applied Nitrogen to Replace after Transplanting[a]		
		1–3 Weeks	4–5 Weeks	6–7 Weeks
Less than 10 inches to clay	1 inch	0	0	0
	2 inches	20	10	0
	3 or more inches	30	20	0
10 to 16 inches to clay	1 inch	30	20	0
	2 inches	45	30	10
	3 or more inches	60	40	15
17 or more inches to clay	1 inch	50	25	15
	2 inches	75	35	20
	3 or more inches	100	45	25

[a] Apply about one pound of potassium (K_2O) for each pound of nitrogen used as a leaching adjustment if the topsoil is deeper than 10 inches.

Leaching of nutrients from heavy rains is worse when the clay layer is farther below the surface. In shallow soils, nutrients tend to stay put, while in deep topsoils, nutrients may be leached by heavy rains to below the tobacco root zone. This may not be significant for most home-growers.

For larger grows, it may be reasonable to make an adjustment application of fertilizer following very heavy rain. The NCSU 2019 Flue-cured Information adjustment table (previous page) suggests application rates for nitrogen, based on a percentage of your your initial rate, and an equivalent poundage of potassium. Phosphorus is not significantly leached.

Flooding and partial drowning of tobacco ("partial" means it recovers from wilting after after several days) may benefit from a supplement of fertilizer, but stationary water does not necessarily leach nutrients. An application of 15 or so pounds each of nitrogen and potassium per acre somewhat improved the yield of partially drowned tobacco.

Nitrogen: A number of studies have demonstrated that the chemical source of the nitrogen makes little difference in the quality and yield of tobacco. Nitrogen is often not reported on a soil analysis, since it is highly variable, and not particularly useful. Just assume a "standard" application rate for tobacco or for tomatoes. In general nitrogen is applied at a rate of 50 to 80 pounds per acre, or about 1.15 to 1.8 pounds *of nitrogen* per 1000 square feet. (So, with 10:10:10 fertilizer, 1000 square feet would receive 11.5 to 18 pounds of that fertilizer.)

The span of standard nitrogen rate recommended is in relation to topsoil depth. Use 50 pounds per acre for a topsoil depth of 5 inches, and the 80 pound rate for topsoils with a depth of 20 or more inches. Interpolate in between.

Phosphorus is needed for healthy root growth and blooming. **Potassium** is needed for healthy root growth and strong development of the tobacco stalk. Your soil test will guide you in deciding if a balanced fertilizer is what you need.

Most fertilizers also contain many other elements and trace elements. If a soil test indicates a deficiency of any of these, then you may need to purchase them separately. If your soil test suggests that you not apply dolomitic lime (used to make the soil less acidic), then pay attention to the calcium analysis and recommendation, as well as that for magnesium.

A nutrient diagnostic key is available on-line from NCSU:

https://diagnosis.ces.ncsu.edu/tobacco/

A 10:10:10 vegetable fertilizer from Southern States. The label states specifically that it is low in chlorine. The lower left corner even presents a somewhat meaningful application rate for this formulation (40 pounds per 8000 square feet), which comes to a meager 5 pounds per 1000 square feet—less than half of the "low" general recommendation for tobacco.

Appendix 6.
Experimental Crossing

Tobacco is self-fertile, and is insect pollinated—by flies, moths, bumblebees—and may also be pollinated by hummingbirds. Cross-pollination has been documented to occur from other varieties of *Nicotiana tabacum* over a distance as far away as 1/2 mile. It is generally not wind pollinated. So bagging the blossom head with insect barrier assures the production of seed of a pure strain.

Nicotiana tabacum is unlikely to be pollinated by other species of *Nicotiana*, though intentional attempts to pollinate *N. tabacum* with the pollen of *N. rustica* have a success rate in the range of 1%. So home-growers of *N. tabacum* have little to be concerned about, with regard to exposure to other *Nicotiana* species. By contrast, using *N. tabacum* pollen to intentionally pollinate *N. rustica* is successful in more than 30 to 70% of the attempts.

But new varieties of tobacco have been produced for over a hundred years by intentional crossing of one *N. tabacum* with a different variety of *N. tabacum*. (Today, many newly introduced varieties—usually with a desired disease resistance—are created using genetic engineering, rather than by cross-pollination methods.)

If you wish to intentionally cross two tobacco varieties, expect a project of 5 to 7 years (5 to 7 generations), planting hundreds of individual offspring each year, tracking them carefully, curing and finishing samples of each, and testing them for their smoking qualities. It's worth the time to read-up on basic genetics (which is not discussed here), before making such a substantial commitment of time and effort.

The basic process of intentional crossing

To begin, you will need to grow the two varieties you intend to cross. You should plan to cross a dozen or more of the plants in both "directions". That is, multiple instances of the cross should be made, and should be performed using the pollen (male) of variety 1 to pollinate the pistil (female) of variety 2, AND the pollen (male) of variety 2 to pollinate the pistil (female) of variety 1. The stem of each individual blossom that is pollinated requires a durable identification tag, so that the resulting seed pods can be properly identified.

The tagged seed pods will need to be collected at maturity. Many instances of the seeds of *each* pod must be planted the following year. So, a year after the initial cross, you will finally see what the plants *look like*—their phenotypes. Attributes that are not visible will require testing to clarify. This first generation is an F1 hybrid, and will not produce predictable offspring. You have to plant many seeds of each F1 generation (for each direction of the initial cross), collect the seeds they produce (now the F2 generation), and plant those the following year. A typical, relatively stable result can usually be produced by F5, F6 or F7.

Each year, for the new generation, your selection criteria (broad leaves or darker color or whatever you are striving for) will determine which plants of that generation should have its seed collected and propagated for the following generation. When the desired attributes are stable over two generations, requiring little selection, then you are done.

2-1/2" Tyvek tag labeled with a Sharpie
Little Dutch X Mt. Pima
Host plant   Pollen source

The host blossom (female side of the cross).

How to do the cross

You need to observe the bud heads of your two varieties, so that you can obtain mature pollen (male) from one, at the same time

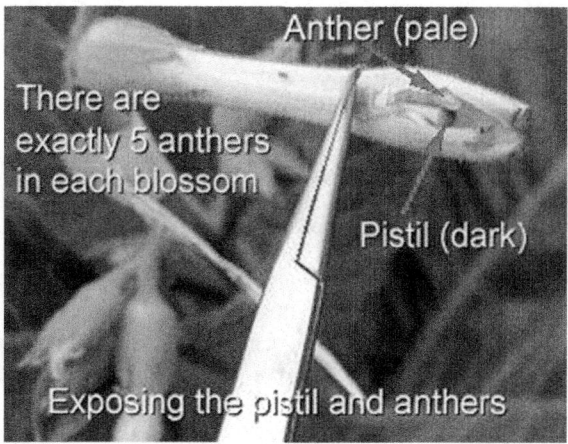

that an immature, *almost open* blossom (of the intended female) of the other variety is available.

Open the immature blossom, with scissors, and remove its immature anthers. There are 5 anthers per blossom, each with a bulbous end, and a single, central, dark green pistil. With clean instruments, remove several *mature* anthers from the male contributor to the cross, place them into the blossom from which the 5 anthers have been removed, then seal the blossom, and tag its stem.

An unsuccessful cross will result in a tagged stem with no seed pod that develops. A successful cross will produce a normal appearing seed pod, which will need to be harvested and saved along with its tag.

Infertile.

A fertile, successful cross.

I use Tyvek, cut from a Tyvek mailing envelope, to create durable tags, and mark them with a fine-point Sharpie. With a little scissors work, it can be sculpted into a tag that will lock itself around a stem. Only the female side needs to be tagged. The pollen donor does not need tagging or following (other than being noted on the tag).

A cross of Indonesian Kasturi with Dutch Amersfoort. [Anton Eise de Vries]

Any varieties of **N. tabacum** will readily cross with one another.

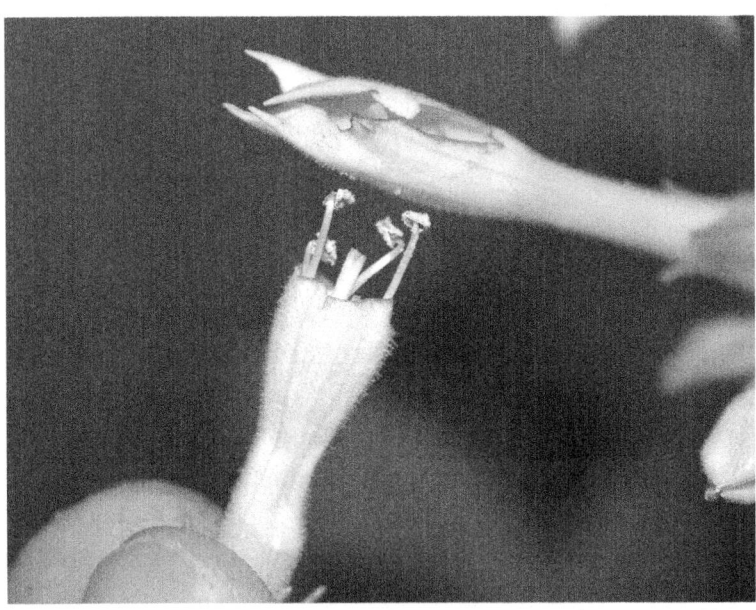

Crossing Samporis, from East Java, with Connecticut Broadleaf. [Anton Eise de Vries]

Appendix 7.
Resources

Open-Source Literature on Tobacco Growing

The various web links presented below were current as of the fall of 2019. Web servers and their link structures are constantly changing. My apologies for any broken links.

ARS-GRIN

The **Agricultural Research Service-Germplasm Resources Information Network** (ARS-GRIN) maintains an on-line, searchable database of all plant, animal and microbe species for which germplasm is held in the United States seed bank repositories.

https://npgsweb.ars-grin.gov/gringlobal/search.aspx

"[The GRIN] web server provides germplasm information about plants, animals, microbes and invertebrates. This program is within the U.S. Department of Agriculture's Agricultural Research Service." With regard to tobacco accessions, the federal government no longer funds the project. It is currently maintained by private grant funding at North Carolina State University (NCSU), but is nonetheless listed within the GRIN database. The tobacco seed repository at NCSU is, for apparently political reasons, no longer listed with contact information in the main GRIN list of contacts and repositories.

Searches for tobacco varieties from the above page will require that you use the search terms, *"Nicotiana tabacum"* or *"Nicotiana rustica"*.

To search for a specific tobacco variety by PI, TI or TC number (see below), as well as some variety names, add those terms to the search terms list.

This will return a list of tobacco accessions meeting those search criteria. Clicking on each item in the list will lead to a detail page for a particular variety, and may reveal a name, the country of origin and the accession date. For older accessions, there may be meaningful information available (including otherwise unmentioned varietal names) by following the "View original Plant Inventory data (PDF format)" link, though not all varieties have such entries. Some of these "original" entries for tobacco date back to nearly 100 years, and may serve as a rich source of ancillary information. If the detail page contains a link to "Observations," usually near the bottom of the page, then you can inspect a varying set of physical, chemical and classification data for that specific variety.

The accession date for a specific variety may be the actual date of its original collection (e.g. Machu Picchu, Peru, 1936), or may simply be the date—sometimes decades later—when the resource was formally transferred to the tobacco seed bank. *One clue in sorting out the actual accession date, should you be looking for older varieties, is that TI numbers were assigned chronologically by the original collection date. [Thanks to Jessica Nifong, curator of the Nicotiana germplasm bank at North Carolina State University, for this valuable clue.]*

- PI: Plant Introduction. This includes all plant species.
- TI: Tobacco Introduction. Exclusively tobacco.
- TC: Tobacco Cultivar. Exclusively tobacco.

IPM Images

The link below leads to an excellent collection of photographs of various tobacco abnormalities, including pests, chemical and environmental factors. If you have a mystery tobacco abnormality, scanning though these images may help in identifying the problem, or at least narrowing the possibilities for further searches of other resources.

IPM Images is a joint project of the Center for Invasive Species and Ecosystem Health, Colorado State University, USDA National Institute of Food and Agriculture, Southern Plant Diagnostic Network. The University of Georgia – Warnell School of Forestry and Natural Resources and College of Agricultural and Environmental Sciences.

http://www.ipmimages.org/browse/Areasubs.cfm?area=62

Tobacco Information from Cooperative Extension Services

Due to the current political climate, many state university extension services have eliminated or hidden their previously expansive web pages on the subject of tobacco growing. With some, if you navigate to the main page for the extension service, then search "tobacco", available pages and publications might be found.

North Carolina State University:
http://tobacco.ces.ncsu.edu/

University of Tennessee Knoxville:
http://tobaccoinfo.utk.edu/InformationResources.htm

University of Kentucky Burley Extension Service:
https://burleytobaccoextension.ca.uky.edu/

Cooperation Centre for Scientific Research Relative to Tobacco (CORESTA) links: https://www.coresta.org/

Virginia Tech Virginia Agricultural Experiment Station: https://www.arec.vaes.vt.edu/search.html?q=tobacco

Clemson Cooperative Extension:
https://www.clemson.edu/extension/agronomy/

Free Books About Tobacco
Many books on tobacco history and tobacco production were written over the past 140 years. Of these, many are not under copyright protection, and are available for free download.

One outstanding source is:
https://archive.org/

Search for "tobacco". This search unfortunately results in a flood of health related publications, mingled among the literature. That single search term will display over a thousand results. You may find browsing through these to be interesting.

Several years ago, one of archive.org's content servers was destroyed. Many scanned manuscripts were lost. Some have since been replaced.

For a more direct list of worthwhile publications, knowing the titles or authors' names will simplify your search. The following is a list I recommend. There are, of course, many other gems.

Curing and Fermentation of Cigar Leaf by Oscar Loew (1899)

Principles and Practical Methods of Curing Tobacco by W.W. Garner (1909)

Report on the Culture and Curing of Tobacco in the United States by J.B. Killebrew (1884)

Tobacco, Its History, Varieties, Culture... by R.R. Billings (1875)

Tobacco Leaf, Its Culture and Cure, Marketing and... by J.B. Killebrew and H. Myrick (1898)

Buffalo Bird Woman's Garden

For a wonderful accounting of Native American gardening, including the planting of wild tobacco, *Nicotiana quadrivalvis*, you may enjoy reading this delightful, cultural anthropology study:

Agriculture of the Hidatsa Indians: an Indian interpretation, by G. Livingstone (1917)

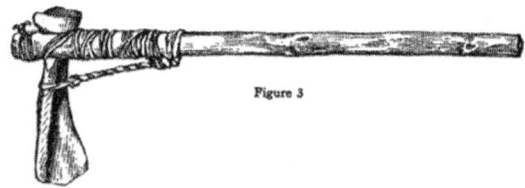

Figure 3

Hoe made from the scapula of a deer.

It is available in text form, with some illustrations, at: https://digital.library.upenn.edu/women/buffalo/garden/garden.html

—END—

Printed in Great Britain
by Amazon

23366055R00207